BEAR TRAP

BEAR TRAP

THE FALL OF BEAR STEARNS AND THE PANIC OF 2008

BILL BAMBER and
ANDREW SPENCER
Foreword by Fernando Diz

Brick Tower Press
New York

Brick Tower Press
1230 Park Avenue
New York, NY 10128
Tel: 212-427-7139 • Fax: 212-860-8852
bricktower@aol.com • www.BrickTowerPress.com

The Brick Tower Press colophon is a registered trademark
of J. T. Colby & Company, Inc.

Library of Congress Cataloging-in-Publication Data

By Bill Bamber and Andrew Spencer.
Bear Trap

ISBN-10: 1-883283-63-9 • ISBN-13: 978188283636
LCC#2008929923

First Edition September 2008
Includes index.

Cover design and typesetting by The Great American Art Company

10 9 8 7 6 5 4 3 2 1

Contents

Acknowledgments

Writing a book is, by its very nature, a collaborative effort. And when a book has two authors, the fact that it is a collaborative effort is doubly true. We are both indebted to John Colby of Brick Tower Press for putting this project together and making it a reality, and to Alan Morell of the Creative Management Group Agency for bringing the different players together. We're also indebted to Betsy Colby for all of her help, photographic and otherwise. Aydin Caginalp reviewed the final manuscript with his lawyer's glasses. We're very grateful to Jeanne Kramer at NBN for all of her encouragement, support and related efforts. Mike Stromberg did the typesetting. Thanks also to Fernando Diz for writing the foreword, and to Ellen Beck for introducing us to Fernando. Whew!

But wait, there's more.

From Bill:

I would like to acknowledge first and foremost my former colleagues at Bear Stearns, an amazing group of people with whom I have experienced so much. This is your story. Special thanks to all my friends for their encouragement and support of me and this book. To Holly Bamber, Jason Prole, Dagmar Smek, Heather Stewart and Claire DiLorenzo, and the Rubino Brothers for their feedback on drafts. And Leigh, for your love and amazing spirit. No matter how wild the terrain you are always game for the adventure.

From Andrew:

I, too, would like to thank the former Bear Stearns employees for unwittingly allowing me into their world; I wish you all the best of luck in your future endeavors. Special gratitude to Bill Bamber for entrusting me with this opportunity and for his endless vaults of knowledge and patience, both of which helped me to understand the secret language of investment banking, no matter how many times he had to explain it. David Edwards of Heron Capital Management and George and Arnold of the Family Spencer all provided advice, feedback and direction. Lucretia Voigt of Mitchell's Book Corner in Nantucket, Massachusetts, offered invaluable feedback on drafts. Many thanks to Mom and Dad, of course, for everything. Arnold Willcox once tried to teach me about the stock market; with any luck, his spirit shines through here; maybe a little of his wisdom does, too. And Jill, I never could have gotten through this—and none of it would have been worth doing—if it weren't for you.

Foreword

The experts think it could have been the end of the U.S. financial system. So much so that the U.S. Treasury and the Federal Reserve felt compelled to intervene and prevent the real possibility of a financial debacle the effects of which, to this day, nobody can estimate with any certainty. The fall of Bear Stearns will be studied for years to come and, to be sure, we shall learn that things could have been done differently. But the path leading to Bear's fall is not unlike the path followed in other spectacular falls. Bill Bamber and Andrew Spencer put you in the front seat and let you watch the events as they unfold from the perspective of those whose livelihoods were at stake.

But what started the downward spiral that led to the eventual demise of Bear Stearns? A good old-fashioned rumor that Bear Stearns was having liquidity problems. Reader beware: The power of rumors should never be underestimated. Gustave Le Bon, a studious researcher of the popular mind, knew how powerful rumors could be back in the nineteenth century. He had clearly identified the ingredients necessary to imbue the mind of a crowd with certain suggestions or beliefs. For a rumor to have the devastating effect it had on Bear Stearns, several conditions needed to be in place. First, the public needed to be preconditioned by certain events or circumstances. There is no doubt that the public had been preparing for a catastrophe to happen somewhere in the financial system; the highly publicized troubles of two of Bear Stearns' hedge funds, large writedowns at many financial firms and the subprime mortgage market dislocations were just a few of those preconditioning events or circumstances. However, the preconditioning only paves the way for a rumor to start.

The next ingredient of an effective rumor is affirmation. As Le Bon states: "Affirmation pure and simple, kept free of all reasoning and all proof, is one of the surest means for making an idea enter the mind of the crowd. The more concise an affirmation is, i.e. 'Bear is insolvent' or 'Goldman will not do business with Bear,' the more weight it carries." Affirmation, however, has no real influence unless it is constantly repeated, and this leads us to the third ingredient for an effective rumor: Repetition. Quoting Le Bon: "The thing affirmed comes by repetition to fix itself in the mind in such a way that it is accepted in the end as a demonstrated truth." What better than a media machine operating in overdrive to provide such repetition? After all, rumors make good media stories, especially if the rumor validates what the public has already been conditioned for.

Anybody that watches the financial press on a daily basis understands how effective it is in giving a rumor the repetition it needs to become what is perceived to be the truth. But repetition is no longer confined to the realms of television, radio, or the printed press. Today, you only need to go to Google Finance, type a ticker symbol and look at the news for the ticker to see the same story presented countless times from different sources. When a rumor has been effectively repeated and there is unanimity in its repetition, it is transformed into current opinion, and contagion follows. The opinions and beliefs of crowds are propagated by contagion, but never by reasoning. One only needs to visit the blogosphere or the countless numbers of social Internet sites to realize how fast a rumor can spread. At this point, the rumor is no longer a rumor and it can no longer be stopped. People complaining that a rumor does not die do not realize that it has reached the contagion stage and that it will not die because it is now the truth. Bamber and Spencer's account of the events leading Bear to a financial crisis reads remarkably like a case study of Le Bon's predictions. It is fascinating to see how even Bear insiders like Bill Bamber can become hypnotized by the power of rumors and how the media seems to play a pivotal role in accelerating the downward spiral by repeating it relentlessly.

But can rumor, and rumor alone, lead a company to its financial demise? The answer to this question was precisely put by famous investor Martin J. Whitman in a recent letter to the shareholders of his Third Avenue Value Fund: "One of the important lessons from the Bear Stearns debacle . . . is to avoid owning common stocks of companies where the businesses need to have relatively continuous access to capital markets in order to survive as going concerns. It is also important to avoid common stocks of companies where the customer base can be lost because of a rumor campaign and where [the investor] would suffer losses were there to be a run-off of the business."

FOREWORD

The rumors about Bear's liquidity problems created a self-fulfilling prophecy convincing principal customers that Bear was not creditworthy and that it was easy and cost free to transfer accounts from Bear Stearns to their competitors. Rumors-turned-truth ended up creating an all too real run on the bank. This run on the bank could have been either prevented or reversed had Bear had access to capital when it needed it the most. But surprisingly, Bear had lost such access. A few hypotheses are put forth by the authors to explain such loss, one of which hinges on the fact that Bear had always been a sort of a maverick firm, not getting along by going along. Another points to the fact that it was highly unlikely that a key piece of the U.S. financial system was going to be let go into foreign hands. Whatever the reason for the lack of access, it became apparent that Bear could not be let go like Drexel Burhnam Lambert Group, Inc. was in 1990.

From this point on, the plot thickens. By now the U.S. Treasury Department and the Federal Reserve Bank of New York must intervene, and the fate of the company is no longer being decided by its management, shareholders or employees, but rather by the Treasury and the Fed. Why? Regulators do not want to be blamed for the effects that a Bear Stearns collapse will have on the U.S. financial system. The issue now is how to prevent Bear's financial fall, and the authors provide a lot of insight into what the decision makers may have been thinking in the process of structuring a deal. On the evening of Sunday, March 16, the announcement hits the press: JP Morgan buys Bear Stearns for $2 a share with the help of a $30 billion guarantee from the Fed, backed by Bear's less liquid assets. Bear employees who own thirty percent of their company watch as their stakes are reduced to almost nothing and they begin to fear for their jobs.

More puzzling to them and the public at large is the simultaneous announcement that the Federal Reserve of New York had created a lending facility to help primary dealers (like Bear) provide financing in securitization markets. The facility would be in place for at least six months, could be extended if conditions warranted, and credit extended could be collateralized by a broad range of investment-grade debt securities. Why was this facility not made available to Bear to prevent its fall in the first place? Why was Bear given to JPMorgan at a fire sale price? Why JPMorgan and not some other bidder? Bamber and Spencer go to great lengths to explain why events turned out the way they did. In the end, they conclude that Bear was offered up as the sacrifice needed to show the world in general and Wall Street in particular that there is no such size as "too big to fail." Moral hazard is what they call it; the risk that if you bail out the perpetrators of bad behavior, others will take notice, behave badly and expect to be bailed out when their time comes. This seems to have been the overriding guiding principle for offering Bear as a sacrifice, and in so doing, ensuring that it would not happen again.

—Fernando Diz

Fernando Diz is The M.J. Whitman Associate Professor of Finance in the Syracuse University Martin J. Whitman School of Management. He has also been Visiting Associate Professor of Finance at the Johnson Graduate School of Management at Cornell University, teaching Derivatives and Financial Engineering courses. Professor Diz is also the founder and President of M&E Financial Markets Research, LLC. He specializes in value and distress investing, and the use of derivative securities in investment and speculative portfolios.

His research has appeared in many academic journals as well as in industry publications such as *Managed Account Reports (MAR), Barclay Managed Futures Report, Energy in the News, Metals in the News, Futures Magazine,* and others. Professor Diz consults with the Independent Consultant to UBS under the SEC Global Settlement and has presented and discussed research at academic forums as well as industry forums such as the American Stock Exchange (AMEX) Derivatives Colloquium, the Managed Funds Association's Forum for Managed Futures, and the Chicago Board of Trade Research Seminars.

Companies that Prof. Diz has consulted with include New York State Electric and Gas, El Paso Power Services, Citizens Power, Connectiv, Agway Energy, Niagara Mohawk Power Corporation, Barclay Trading Group, Caixa Catalunya and MEFF. Professor Diz received his doctorate from Cornell University.

Prologue

"What is past is prologue."
—WILLIAM SHAKESPEARE

In the prologue to *Romeo and Juliet,* William Shakespeare uses a grand total of fourteen lines of text to tell the audience exactly what is going to happen in the play. We learn that there are two households in Verona that are engaged in a familial feud. From these families will emerge two lovers who are described as "star-cross'd." We also learn that they will die as a result of their love that springs from this feud. We get all of this before the action of the play even starts. So what's the point of sitting through (or reading through, as the case may be) the entire play? We know the whole story already.

As a way of answering that question, I will refer to a news item from the turn of the twentieth century. The year was 1906, and vacationers at a resort community discovered an overturned boat on the shores of Big Moose Lake in upstate New York. Those who found the boat also found the body of Grace Brown, a 20-year old working-class woman who had been rumored to be romantically linked to Chester Gillette, a young man who worked in his uncle's skirt factory, the same skirt factory where Ms. Brown was employed. Gillette's stories about what had happened on the lake varied and he was eventually taken into police custody and charged with the murder. It was revealed that Ms. Brown had informed Gillette that she was pregnant with his child; meanwhile, Gillette had taken up with a more aristocratic group of friends, and Grace was not a part of that future. The murder trial captivated headlines and dominated news stories. Gillette was found guilty, sentenced to die and was executed in the electric chair in March, 1908. Gillette's diary and several letters were published a century after his death, proving yet again the ferocity of the public's interest in the macabre.

While the event itself was quite the scandal in the early twentieth century, the hoopla eventually died down and the public's attention turned elsewhere. There were the Olympic Games in London that year, as well as the start of the revolution in the Ottoman Empire led by the Young Turks. Henry Ford produced his first Model-T and the Chicago Cubs won their second (and, as of this writing, their last) World Series title. With so much going on, it's easy to see how a single execution could have fallen from the public microscope. But one man, a writer by the name of Theodore Dreiser, was fascinated by the Gillette case. He saved newspaper clippings from the case. He read everything there was to read on it. He purportedly thought about the case obsessively. And then, in 1925—nearly twenty years after the original crime—Dreiser put his thoughts on paper. Lots of paper. Over 900 pages, in fact. 900 pages to talk about a case that was not only twenty years old, but one that had already been dissected and decided.

Why? Why would somebody spend so much time and effort writing about something that had already happened? And what's more, why would anybody plunk down their hard-earned money to buy this book and then spend the better part of a month actually reading all 900-plus pages? After all, we all know how it's going to end. Chester Gillette—Dreiser changed his name to Clyde Griffiths in the novel—is going to fall in love with two women, get one pregnant and then try to kill her. And in the end, he's going to be found guilty of murder and sent to the chair. That is the very, very long story short.

We read these sorts of stories not for the suspense that one gets from reading murder mysteries. Rather, in the case of Dreiser's *An American Tragedy,* we read it for the insight into the human condition that the author affords us. We read it because Dreiser—accusations of long-windedness aside—is a master at divining what it is that makes a man do what he does. Case in point, for a young man in the prime of his life who seems to have it all to suddenly commit murder, there must be something, some force greater than himself, driving him. And it's that force that Dreiser illuminates so well. As the author himself once said of the human condition, "All of us are more or less pawns. We're moved about like chess pieces by circumstances over which we have no control."

So just like we read Shakespeare's story, even though we know how it's going to end, we read Dreiser's, so that we can see how we get from point

PROLOGUE

A to point Z. It's those steps in the middle that are what make the story so interesting. It's the discussion of those circumstances over which we mere mortals have no control that we read, and it's from that discussion that we come away better informed.

The story you are about to read here is pretty straightforward. Bear Stearns, a New York-based investment bank, went bankrupt. It's that simple. A firm that had existed on Wall Street for over 80 years ceased to be. But that story has been in the news since the firm started its downward spiral; there's nothing new in the report that Bear Stearns is no longer in business. But how did it happen? What went so drastically wrong with the system that the fifth largest investment bank in the United States went bankrupt in the space of a week? That's the question that begs to be answered. Dreiser had it right. Circumstances over which we have no control. That's what brought down the Bear of Wall Street.

In the months following the collapse, there was a host of different articles that appeared in various publications. The *Wall Street Journal* ran a three-part story that summed up the basic facts of what happened and when it happened. *Barbarians at the Gate* co-author Bryan Burrough penned his version of the story for *Vanity Fair* in August of 2008, offering a little more insight than the *Journal,* and much of his analysis sounds a lot like what you're going to read here. And people asked me, as we were finishing up this project, if this was going to be the only book on the subject. I assured them it would not be, but I also assured them that there was more than enough room in the world for many books on the collapse of Bear Stearns. You don't just wipe away 85 years of history without a couple of words to say about it. Nope, there's enough room on the shelves for a few Bear Stearns books.

Because this is a first-hand account of what happened inside the office at 383 Madison Avenue, it's a personal story. And like all personal stories, it's got its own accusations and moments of finger-pointing. One such accusation is that the Secretary of the Treasury actually wanted to see Bear go down. Of course, short of being a mind-reader, it's impossible for me to say for certainty that those were his explicit intentions. I suggest a case for it; it's up to you to decide if I'm right. But consider the fact that the federal discount window—which had long been closed to investment banks—was opened to those financial institutions only *after* Bear had collapsed. Quite soon after Bear had collapsed, actually. I realize that, from my vantage point, suggesting something like that can sound a lot like sour grapes. After all, it's a dog-eat-dog world on Wall Street. Or, in this case, a dog-eat-bear world.

But consider the fact that in early July 2008, the Federal Reserve made public the estimated value of Bear Stearns' assets. The number they came up with was $28.9 billion. That's a lot of collateral, when you sit and think about it. It's a pretty amazing figure, too, considering the fact that Bear was also declared completely insolvent. But what's more interesting is the fact that, if Bear had been given access to the Federal discount window, we could have borrowed money against that $28.9 billion. Money to keep us afloat, to keep us in business. To keep the wolves at bay so that Bear could live to fight another day. But the discount window wasn't available to investment banks. Not until after we were declared finished. You can draw your own inferences. But please don't jump to any conclusions. Read the whole story—you already know how it's going to end—and make an informed decision about what really happened to Bear.

Yes, it's old news that Bear Stearns is dead. So old is the news, in fact, that in an earlier paragraph, it took me just ten words—just one sentence—to tell you nearly everything relevant that happens in this story. But there's much, much more to it than just those ten words. There's a whole story within the story. There are circumstances beyond anyone's control that drove this story to its climax, circumstances that, truth be told, still exist on Wall Street today. With any luck, those circumstances be held at bay by investors and traders. After all, those who don't learn from history are condemned to repeat it.

And after reading the following story, if that thought doesn't scare the hell out of you, then you aren't paying attention.

Introduction

"How do you document real life when real life
is getting more like fiction each day?"

—*RENT*

Y*ou just can't make this shit up.*

I have no idea who deserves the credit for first coining that phrase, and I have to plead an equal level of ignorance when asked to identify the number of times it has been invoked over the course of human history to describe a given situation. But I do know, without the slightest shade of any sort of doubt, that there has never been a more appropriate description for a situation like the one I lived through beginning on Monday, March 10, 2008. So appropriate did I find the phrase, in fact, that it was the last thing I said to a co-worker, a friend who, because of the time he'd spent on a Navy attack sub, had acquired the nickname of Captain Nemo on the trading floor. And so perfect a summation of our situation was it that the phrase became something of a battle cry for the two of us as the days went by, a sort of inside joke that made the pain of our demise more bearable. And it started on Monday, March 10, 2008, the day that, in my mind, came to be known as the beginning of the end.

The day began innocently enough. I awoke, as was my custom, at five o'clock in the morning. I did the obligatory check of emails that had come in overnight on my Blackberry—mostly a flurry of questions and concerns related to the overseas markets interspersed with a few offers to increase my manhood—and went for a morning run around my neighborhood and through Central Park. I showered, watched the early market reports on CNBC and got dressed. I was able to grab a quick espresso and bid good-bye to my family, and then I was out the door and on my way to the office on Madison Avenue. The only thing remarkable about the morning's routine was the sheer lack of anything remarkable associated with it.

I usually opted for a taxi in the mornings, preferring the flexibility of hailing a cab to the rigid schedules required by New York car services. And what's more, I worked at Bear Stearns, the company whose former CEO was notorious for the circulation of memos reminding us to save paper clips whenever we received documents from sources outside our office. It was, to his mind, a cost-cutting measure. So you could say I was baptized at the church of saving money, and the ten dollar cab ride was easier to rationalize, financially, than a car service. And I also managed to convince myself that it was a luxury when compared to the subway, so it made me feel pretty good all-around to take a cab. I made it to the office in about fifteen minutes, and I was at my place on the trading floor by seven-fifteen, ready for whatever the day might throw at me. Or so I thought.

What I loved most about my job was that it was always changing, never predictable, and I never knew what to expect during the course of any given day. Whereas a salesman knew he was going to be selling all day and a teacher knew he was going to be teaching all day, there was no discernible routine for me; my "typical" day was anything but typical. My specialty was structured equities, which means that I spent the day creating securities that have what you might call interesting payoff profiles. That's Wall Street talk for "making rich people richer." And despite the mundane sounding nature of that job description, there was a very fluid nature to its dynamic, and I was constantly investigating new strategies and angles from which to approach issues. And yes, that means I was constantly trying to find ways to make the aforementioned rich people even richer. But today, Monday, March 10, 2008, was going to challenge both my views of what qualified as "anything but typical," as well as my feelings towards that descriptor.

For those who have never actually been in the environment of the New York financial world, it often comes as a surprise that a trader's "office" is actually a long desk on the trading floor, an open space that he might share with up to four hundred other human souls. It's a far cry from what one might expect of the environs of that segment of humanity Tom Wolfe labeled "the Masters of the Universe." At the table on the floor where I spent the better part of my waking life—one of four trading floors in the Bear Stearns New York headquarters—I was one of many crammed into a space designed for half our number. Each individual desk served as the work area for twelve people, six to a side. It's something like a very crowded, very loud video game arcade, with video monitors and people everywhere. Or perhaps NASA Mission Control on a bad day. To those of us who work in these dwellings, it's known as simply "The Desk." It is the central nervous system of an investment bank, and often serves as the place where we eat every meal of the day.

There is no such thing as privacy in this world. The phone bank at my place was linked in to forty separate phone lines, and my coworkers could just as easily eavesdrop on any of my calls as I could on theirs. Successes and failures become public knowledge instantaneously in an environment such as this one. And rumors. Rumors run rampant in a place like this, like chicken pox in an elementary school. There's no place for them to hide, and there's no place to hide from them. As soon as I took my place at my spot on the trading floor, the rumor fire started, first as a spark, and soon grew into a full-on blaze.

My place within this technological sardine can faced directly into four separate computer monitors, each with a specific and equally vital purpose for my daily activities. And while financial information related to specific markets flashed across the various displays, it was my Bloomberg that was to become the object of increasingly intense focus as the day went on.

The Bloomberg machine, just the "Bloomberg" in market parlance, is as vital a piece of equipment for a trader at an investment bank as a hammer is for a contractor. It provides the user with, among other features, an amazing array of information about important news relating to specific companies and financial markets. On this morning, the specific company in question was Bear Stearns, the specific financial market was our own and the important news was bad.

Words like "liquidity" were popping up on the Bloomberg, and those reports that were using the word were referencing a discernible lack of capital in the coffers of the company that had served as my employer for the last six years. But I didn't put a whole lot of faith in these rumors, because that's all they were. Rumors. Viscous rumors. Bear Stearns had always had the reputation of being a maverick in the world of investment banking. This was, no doubt, just another attempt by some jealous rival to bring us down. Investment bankers could be downright petty when they wanted to be.

Yes, we'd gotten stung the summer before, when the subprime mortgage crisis made financial headlines and two of the firm's hedge funds had collapsed. But we'd recovered. Our Chief Financial Officer told us—hell, he told the whole world—that we were doing fine as recently as February: "Our capital position is strong," Sam Molinaro had told our investors in a conference call whose transcript had been strategically circulated to every major news outlet in the country. He said that our balance sheet showed financial improvement and that we'd cut our risk level across the board. Nowhere in any of those reports was there anything about liquidity, insolvency or bankruptcy. And while perhaps I was being naively fed—and equally naively eating—the party line being offered by the hands of a bunch of spooked corporate executives, there was nothing that I could see from my vantage point that gave any credence to these rumors. So I went about my day, trying to block out the distractions.

But those rumors kept coming and those distractions became harder and harder to ignore. The higher-ups within the company made it a policy not to comment on rumors because they were of the strict belief that commenting on rumors did nothing but give substance to them. And rumors about investors panicking and withdrawing money in massive amounts due to a lack of money within the firm wasn't one you wanted to give any kind of credence to. The rumors basically feed themselves, the conventional wisdom dictates, and once someone within the company has uttered the words, suddenly the rumors gain traction and begin to grow.

But after hours of cable television talking heads announcing to their viewers that Bear Stearns was on the verge of financial collapse, our executives broke with tradition and issued a statement. "There is absolutely no truth to the liquidity problems that circulated today in the market," the release said at the close of trading Monday. And the Bear Stearns treasury department backed up the rhetoric with numbers. We were showing $17 billion in cash-on-hand. That's billion with a b. To top that off, the firm's balance sheets showed $11.1 billion in tangible equity capital and $395 billion in assets. In the world of investment banking, that's sitting right on top of the mythical catbird seat. In other words, liquidity problems within the safe confines of the Bear Stearns universe were the punch line for jokes about other firms.

Of course, none of us were privy to the fact that the firm had been turned down for a $2 billion loan the Friday before. Declined. There's no nice way to say it, sir, but your credit card was refused. And I know that a couple of billion dollars is not the sort of loan you typically walk into a bank and ask for. But in the world of *über*-high finance, this was an every-day thing that should have been an open-and-shut deal. A $2 billion loan is pocket change for these people, the kind of money you give the homeless guy on the street so your girlfriend thinks you're a humanitarian. We were Bear Stearns, for God's sake, the fifth largest investment bank in the country. Asking for and subsequently being approved for a loan of that amount is commonplace in the circles that people like us lived and associated within. It ceased being so commonplace, however, when we were denied the loan.

But none of us on our trading floor knew anything about it on that Monday.

So instead of worrying about things like non-approved loans for our company, we slogged through the day in our blissful ignorance, deflecting these nasty rumors about our beloved firm's balance sheets and credit worthiness. I did notice that I was spending more time than usual calming the nerves of jittery counterparties and investors who were calling with their concerns in regards to these unfounded stories, but all in all, the rumors weren't causing too much damage. It never ceased to amaze me that well-educated people who trusted us with millions of dollars each were so easily influenced by the mere suggestion of trouble. One little pebble slips from the mountaintop, and suddenly all of Park Avenue is a-twitter with nerves about an impending avalanche. Fortunately for all of us, though, the news of the day took a sudden detour, knocking the Bear Stearns problems off the top of the news networks' radars.

Our salvation came in the form of a 22-year old Madonna, of sorts, in a story broken by the New York Times.

Her name was Ashley Alexandra Dupre, also known as Kristen. She was a call girl for the Emperor's Club VIP escort service in New York City. In and of itself, the existence of an attractive twenty-something plying her trade as a member of the world's oldest profession serving the white collar executives of Manhattan wasn't necessarily front-page worthy. She lived modestly in a walkup in the Flatiron District and counted among her career aspirations that of becoming a singer. Again, nothing Earth-shattering. But when the authorities busted the prostitution ring and made public the client list, "Client 9" turned out to be none other than the Governor of New York, Eliot Spitzer. Spitzer's five-grand-an-hour dalliances overtook Bear Stearns' financial problems as the scandal *du heure*. Apparently sex sells more papers than financial ruin. While I felt like I should have been mortified by the fact that the general American reading public was more concerned about yet another politician getting caught with his hand in the cookie jar than with the equivalent of all-out financial Armageddon on Wall Street, I was relieved that we were, at least temporarily, less newsworthy. God bless America.

People have asked me if I saw it coming. If I knew, somewhere in my inner-most soul of souls, that these rumors had not only substance, but arms, legs, feet and hands. That these rumors were much more than fantastic stories designed to bring down the Bear of Wall Street. And every time I'm asked, I answer the same. I didn't know. I had no idea that the firm that had lured me away from another investment bank with the promise of a higher salary and more lucrative bonus structures in 2002 was on the verge of financial ruin in 2008. Perhaps it was some sort of deep-seated need to believe that the rumors weren't true, some sort of inherent survival mechanism honed over millennia of DNA mutations within the genetic history of humanity. If these rumors were true and Bear Stearns was about to be declared financially insolvent, the ramifications were potentially disastrous. If Bear Stearns went down, the rest of Wall Street was suddenly very, very vulnerable. And the results of that meltdown would be more disastrous than any financial panic in the history of the United States or the world at large. And to accept that possibility as reality was more than my brain could withstand at the moment. So I chose not to believe.

But Ashley saved us. Or at least distracted the world long enough for the rumors to be dispelled for another day. And there were other days. Lots of them. And as each of those days passed, more rumors surfaced. And as more rumors surfaced, some began to stick. It was like throwing spaghetti against the refrigerator. You keep throwing it long enough, eventually something sticks. And the more things began to stick, the bleaker the future looked for Bear Stearns. Our stock price plunged from over $80 a share to just over $2 a share in the course of a week. I personally lost several million dollars of my net worth. In the midst of my Bear stock losing approximately 97 percent of its value, it suddenly became harder and harder for my self-preservation disbelief operation to function properly. But despite my own catastrophic losses, I considered myself lucky to have only lost the amount I did. There were thousands more just like me, and many of them had been far more invested in Bear stock than I, and thus lost even more. And it all started for us on Monday, March 10, 2008.

INTRODUCTION

But this story, like all stories, has a beginning and an end, and Monday, March 10, 2008, was neither. It just happened to be the day that the horrific news of the all-too-real possibility of impending worldwide financial ruin was supplanted in the minds of Americans by the story of a twenty-two year-old hooker from the Jersey Shore who'd decided to make her fortune in the Big Apple, in part, by screwing the governor.

Like I said. You just can't make this shit up.

BEAR TRAP

CHAPTER ONE

Of Bulls and Bears

"Beware the Ides of March."
—*JULIUS CAESAR*, I.II

On March 19, 1831, a gentleman by the name of Edward Smith entered the City Bank on Wall Street. Even in the early 19th century, a man entering a financial institution in Lower Manhattan was a pretty common occurrence. In Mr. Smith's case, however, his mode and time of entry were less than common. Using a duplicate set of keys he had obtained, Mr. Smith entered the bank that Saturday after the bank had closed for business. He helped himself to approximately $245,000 from the bank's vault, a sum that was more than many people at the time could ever hope to make over the course of a lifetime. Mr. Smith was soon apprehended, tried and convicted. He spent five years as a guest of the State of New York at the newly constructed penal facility at Sing Sing. It would become the first in a long and sordid history of crimes in the area, though many of those crimes go unpunished daily. Arturo DiModica, however, was not so fortunate as the average snake oil salesman found on Wall Street today. Much like Mr. Smith, he got caught.

A few blocks south of the original City Bank site, one finds Bowling Green Park, the oldest existing public park in Manhattan, where there sits a 7,000 pound bronze statue of a charging bull. The story of its arrival in that location, much like the story of Edward Smith's sudden influx of personal wealth, came about as the result of an illegal act. Arturo DiModica cast the statue himself at his own expense and deposited it outside the New York Stock Exchange in 1987 following the market crash in October of that year. He felt that the bull—the metaphor financiers had chosen long before as the symbol of increasing stock prices—best symbolized the American people's "strength and power," according to reports. On December 15, 1987, DiModica left the statue outside the Neo-Classical building at 18 Broad Street that housed the floor of the New York Stock Exchange. It was, he said, a Christmas gift to the residents of New York City.

Because this act, regardless of how generous the artist's motives, had been in no way sanctioned by any authority figure in the city, the statue was immediately impounded by the New York City Police Department. The people of New York, however, were not to be denied. In an act that perhaps proved that they were much the like the metaphorical bull, residents from all over the city petitioned the New York City Department of Parks and Recreation to save their gift. The authorities finally conceded, and the statue was relocated to Bowling Green Park, two blocks south of its original resting spot outside the Stock Exchange.

The bull statue, despite its relatively young age in terms of the chronology of the Stock Exchange, has become one of the most often visited tourist attractions in the Financial District, and it has also become one of the most photographed objects in the entire city. However, noticeably absent from Bowling Green Park, or anywhere else in the city for that matter, is a statue of the bull's financial nemesis, the bear. While I cannot confirm whether or not bulls and bears are actually inclined to attack one another when meeting in the wild, the two were historically pitted against one another in staged fights as a form of entertainment. And much like those fights put on for the enjoyment and betting pleasure of spectators, in the realm of the American investor, the two animals are mortal enemies, locked in a perpetual struggle to seize control of the action within the financial sector.

Owning a share of stock in a publicly traded company is equivalent to owning a piece—albeit a miniscule one—of that company. The stock's price is determined in much the same way that every other tangible, sellable asset's price is determined, namely by what a buyer is willing to pay for it. In the most basic sense of the equation, if two people want to buy and one person wants to sell, the stock's price will go up, as the two potential buyers will have to outbid one another in order to attract the seller. If, however, two people want to sell and only one wants to buy, the stock's price will go down, as the two sellers will have to undercut one another on the price in order to get the sale.

An example of this buyer-seller relationship serving as a dynamic in the determination of price is illustrated by frontiersmen who served as the liaisons between buyers and sellers in the bearskin market. These earliest of commodities traders would sell skins that they had not yet received, and thus were also some of the earliest commodities speculators. It was the hope of these traders that the price they would have to pay for individual skins would be less than what they were selling them for. In other words, they were hoping for an overabundance of sellers of bearskins and a lack of buyers, a combination resulting in lower prices for the skins and higher margins for the traders. These traders were known locally as "bears," and thus a market that worked in their favor financially speaking became known as a "bear market."

In today's financial world, a bear market is, at its core, simply a situation in time when there are more people looking to sell than there are people looking to buy. And because a stock's price is controlled by exactly those two dynamics, a bear market is characterized by pessimism in the larger investing community brought on by lower stock prices. Lower stock prices tend to scare sellers and attract buyers, which lowers prices further, thus creating a nasty little cycle. And though there is no hard-and-fast definition of what qualifies as a bear market, it's best thought of as a period of at least two or three months during which prices decline significantly. In other words, the typical investor does not like a bear market.

Thus, it seems odd today to consider that one of the original New York equity trading houses took as part of its name the symbol of falling stock prices and investor worry. It was, quite frankly, nothing more than an unfortunate biological fact, this seemingly odd choice of names for an investment firm. It was simply a case of a son taking his father's name. Joseph Bear partnered with Robert Stearns and Harold Mayer to form the company in 1923. The company was founded with the sum of $500,000. The post World War I economy had created a situation whereby the average man of average intelligence could do quite well for himself financially by investing. Initially the trio operated out of a one-room office space at 100 Broadway one of the stops along the same route New York City's famous tickertape parades follow in the stretch of real estate that is known today as the Canyon of Heroes.

Ten years following the firm's inception, the market for government securities was burgeoning, and the fledgling investment firm now known as Bear Stearns pounced on the opportunities present in the market. The firm's founders envisioned a brokerage service; but investor money was pouring into institutional bonds. Thus, more from a necessity than a desire, the firm established its first institutional bond department, which was the precursor to the fixed-income division that would come later. The stock market was booming, bonds were all the rage, investors were making a killing in the market, and their brokers were more than happy to take their commissions. Everywhere in America at the time, it was a period of too much in all aspects of life—too much fun, too much happiness, too much optimism. In short, it couldn't last. And it didn't.

The crash came, as we all learned in history class, in October of 1929. This was the Big One, like the legendary earthquake that seismologists predict will one day forever change the landscape of the west coast of the United States. On October 24, 1929—Black Thursday, they called it— the market crashed, with the then unheard of volume of 12.9 million shares trading hands. The following Monday, the Dow Jones Industrial Average lost 13% of its value. And from there, the panic was on. The market bottomed out and the Great Depression set in. It was the start of a long, painful bear market. Bear Stearns, despite the economic situation of the time, continued to prosper. The firm did not lay off a single man during the time and, in fact, continued to pay bonuses to its employees throughout, bucking the trend of the rest of corporate America. Quite remarkable, considering the circumstances. The seeds were sewn for what was to be Bear's remarkable reputation as an industry loner who didn't play by the conventional rules.

An important development of the time, though, was the passage of the Glass-Steagall Act established in 1933. Glass-Steagall was passed in response to what many legislators saw as too heavy an involvement by commercial banking interests in the stock market. The problem arose when the stock market crashed. With so much of their investors' money tied up in stocks, banks were in a precarious position immediately before the crash, and in an impossibly staggering position immediately after. Two important effects of the passage of Glass-Steagall were the creation of investment banking as a separate entity unto itself and the creation of the Federal Deposit Insurance Company, which insured bank customers' deposits with the full faith and credit of the United States government.

At about the same time, President Franklin Delano Roosevelt and his New Deal were poised to solve the country's economic problems. Much of the New Deal relied on the creation and sale of bonds, much like the ones the federal government issued to fund the Civil War. Bonds are instruments by which companies could borrow money from individual investors. So whereas owning a share of stock in a company is the same as owning a piece of the company itself, owning a bond is simply owning a piece of the company's debt, a debt that the company must repay in full with interest. And while the reward isn't, on average, through the roof for the average investor, it's tough to find a safer bet than a bond with a good credit rating. Bear Stearns, like many other financial institutions at the time, realized that there was a great deal of money to be made in the selling of these bonds, and because the demand for bank loans had sunk to basement levels, large banks had a great deal of cash-on-hand. The Bear Stearns team put two-and-two together and created an institutional bond trading department within the firm. The bank declared itself an investment bank, per the regulations stipulated by Glass-Steagall, and they were off and running. The Bear grew from the ashes of the worst bear in history, like the phoenix rising from the ashes.

From there, the firm expanded, first into Chicago, then throughout the

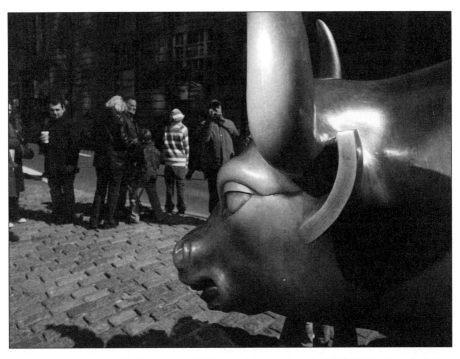

NEW YORK—MARCH 17: Tourists visit Wall Street's Bull on March 17, 2008 in New York City. Stocks are volatile on Wall Street following news of JP Morgan Chase acquisition of Bear, Stearns & Co, for $2 a share, with help of $30 billion in financing of Bear, Stearns assets from the U.S. Federal Reserve. (Photo by Michael Nagle/Getty Images)

rest of the United States, and eventually into Europe and the Far East. The company's history, almost from the beginning, had been intrinsically linked to risk-taking. In 1975, for example, the city of New York was, for all intents and purposes, bankrupt. So Bear Stearns invested heavily, pumping $10 million into the city's coffers. The firm made out like a bandit, but only after nearly losing everything. That hell-for-leather attitude gave Bear Stearns the aura of being savvy, the reputation of an investment bank that marched to its own beat, always working alone and independent of other banks, willing to do things differently from other financial institutions, so long as the price was right. And the greater the risk, the higher the price.

Soon the attitude at the uppermost levels of the executive tree became one of instant gratification and immediate rewards. The whole idea of long-term planning and conservative investing wasn't a philosophy embraced by men like Cy Lewis and Ace Greenberg, two of the earliest chairmen of Bear. By 1980, Bear was known as the biggest takeover artist on Wall Street, and its reputation as a loner in the world of finance continued to solidify. The firm's public persona was morphing from that of street thug to underworld kingpin. Case in point, in 1982, Bear waged a proxy battle against Global Natural Resources. The basic idea in any proxy battle is that the entity waging the battle, be it an individual or a corporation, wants to take over the target company. In this case, Bear was waging the battle against GNR in hopes of doing precisely that. The goal from the perspective of the entity waging the battle is to garner control of the proxy votes of shareholders and thereby vote their own agenda. And while this isn't an unheard of tactic in the backroom dealing world of high finance, Global Natural Resources was a client of Bear Stearns. The firm was taking over its own client. Needless to say, this did nothing to alter sentiments about the firm's maverick sensibilities.

And lest anyone find themselves misinformed about the lengths to which Bear would go to make the almighty dollar, consider yet another blemish on the Bear Stearns road to Eagle Scout status. In 1986, the US Justice Department and the Securities and Exchange Commission were forced to file suit against several Bear clients implicated in a stock parking scheme (Ross, et al. v Bolton, et al). Clients were allowed to buy stock under Bear Stearns' name, thus allowing shareholders to vote through Bear Stearns without divulging their own names. The long and the short of the deal is that Bear was facilitating corporate takeovers by allowing clients to shield their identities in a quasi-legal—and subsequently deemed explicitly *illegal*—setup.

Then, in 1985, Bear made the decision to go public. The goal was to put the firm in a position to be able to raise higher levels of capital so as to allow them to finance larger and more lucrative trades. Hand-in-hand with the IPO went the creation of Bear Stearns Companies, Inc., the holding company that came to include the full-service offerings of the ever-expanding firm. A host of new divisions within the firm were created and folded into the all-encompassing umbrella that was Bear Stearns Companies, including the fledgling mortgage bond trading division. And it was that little division that handled the underwriting and sale of mortgage bonds to savvy investors that would become the linchpin in the greatest financial disaster of the twenty-first century.

The concept of the buying and selling of mortgage bonds is a relatively new one in the world of financial markets when you consider the fact that the New York Stock Exchange officially formed in 1792 with the Buttonwood Agreement. The bonds really first came into existence in the late 1970's when a Salomon Brothers bond trader by the name of Robert Dall, who began to look at the debts in what was a completely revolutionary way. Dall's theory relied on the concept that any debt could be sold as a bond; it was just a matter of structuring it so as to make it financially worthwhile for all parties involved. A single home mortgage wasn't worth the effort; if John Doe had a mortgage on his $300,000 home in Scarsdale with a 6% annual rate, it didn't generate enough interest, in any sense of the word, to raise any eyebrows on the trading floor. But, Dall reasoned, if you could take thousands of home mortgages from across the country and lump them together, suddenly you were talking about numbers that got the interest of serious investors and traders alike. Suddenly John Doe's Scarsdale starter home was worth more to bond traders than it was to Mr. Doe himself.

The thing about mortgages, though, is that no two are alike. While the aforementioned Mr. Doe in upstate New York might be an up-and-coming young accountant, there are plenty of other would-be homeowners who might not have the financial wherewithal to afford that $300,000 mortgage. Due to a host of factors—be it location, be it lack of opportunity, be it flat-out bad luck—they can't pay that much. And what's more, these same people have had a few financial setbacks in the past. Maybe they made some less-than-intelligent decisions about credit cards or car purchases or whatever else, and now they don't have the sparkling credit history of the CPA doing the taxes for the plastic surgeons in Westchester County. But they want their piece of the American Dream, too, and there are financiers out there who think they deserve it. Of course in order to get the loan, they're going to have to pay extra for it, but that's the bank's reward for taking the added risk.

Those deemed high-risk loans were labeled as subprime mortgages. From an outsider's perspective, it might seem like a bad idea to loan money to someone with a history of not paying it back. Fair enough. But the thing you've got to remember about a mortgage is that it is backed by immediately available collateral, the property itself. It's what we call a collateralized asset. So if you default on your mortgage, the bond holder can take the house. And the added bonus is that the property, if real estate prices are doing what they should, is worth more than you originally paid for it. So the bank wins no matter what. We call this an asset-backed security, or an ABS. No matter what you call it, it almost sounds too good to be true. And, as luck would have it, it turned out to be exactly that.

Loans are classified by their default risks into different classes, what investment bankers call tranches, which is French for "slice." Each tranche has its own repayment schedule attached to it. The better the credit rating, the higher the tranche; the higher the tranche, the sooner the repayment. As a way of offsetting the later payment—and therefore the higher default risk—of lower-level tranches, they are sold with higher return rates. So what this all boils down to is the fact that for mortgage lenders, there was all of a sudden an incentive for them to write as many loans as they could, no matter the risk level. After the paperwork was signed, the lender could then sell the mortgage to an investment bank, and the default risk was no longer his problem. The bond trader would sell it to an investor, so he wasn't too worried, either. And if the investor lost money, well, *c'est la vie.* Investors should consider the risks involved before plopping their money down. Caveat emptor.

This lust for mortgage bonds coincided with one of the greatest housing market booms in history. The Fed had lowered interest rates following the attacks of September 11 in the hopes of slowing the economic downturn that had resulted. By lowering the federal funds rate, the hope was to increase the amount of money individuals would borrow and, in turn, spend. So beginning in 2002, lenders started playing very fast and very loose with their own lending restrictions. Things like proof of income as a way of actually paying back the loan lost importance. After all, the President of the United States was telling us that spending was our patriotic duty. So we spent. And when we couldn't find any more money to spend, we borrowed. Repayment wasn't a problem; by the time the loan came due, the economy would be growing again and we'd all be fat and happy. No problem.

This mentality of buy-now-and-hope-to-be-able-to-pay-later fit with a marketplace where investment banks were geared to parse questionable mortgage assets into securities for institutional investors. The Bear's mortgage bond division sprouted, grew and prospered right along with the country's housing boom. And just like in 1929, there was too much of a good thing. It couldn't last. And this time, the results might take more than a new deal. This crash might just call for blood. Bear blood at that.

▲ ▲ ▲

So the stage was set for God only knew what in the financial market. All it needed now, from my perspective, was my presence on the scene. So into this seamlessly blended pool of historical risk-taking, financial genius and maverick sensibilities I dove. I fit the description perfectly for the willing Bear Stearns employee, namely I fit the PSD model. I was *poor* and *smart* (P and S), with an incomprehensibly strong *desire* to be rich (D). But I didn't just fall out of the sky and land in this exact position one day as a fully-formed human being. Just like Bear Stearns, I, too, have a history.

I was born in a small town just west of Toronto, Canada. The semi-rural nature of the place bred and fostered within me a deep yearning for an international life, a desire further fueled by a jet-setting aunt who travelled the world and occasionally bequeathed me with gifts acquired during her travels. One such gift made me the envy of everyone I knew. My aunt brought me a Walkman in the days when the portable tape players were still unheard of in North America. She'd purchased it during a trip to Japan, and it was another couple of years before this technological marvel made its way to Canada. My Walkman and I were the talk of the town. That experience, and many similar ones, only served to intensify my desires to get out and see the world. That was where the excitement was. Little did I know that I was already nurturing my inner investment banker.

I was the first in my immediate family to go to college, so when it came time to decide on a course of study, I had no useful guide on whom to rely. However, with my strong yearnings to see the world, I gravitated towards diplomatic work. I applied to and was accepted at a university known for its excellent diplomatic corps training program. However, after a year in the program, I decided that I was, quite possibly, the least diplomatically inclined member of my class and I left the program. I searched the school's course offerings for something that appealed to me and could potentially satisfy my longing for international excitement. I settled on economics and history.

So much for excitement.

I still hadn't truly settled on a career path in 1987, the summer before my final year in college. I had accepted a seasonal position on the floor of the Stock Exchange, an experience that would make an indelible impression on my collegiate mind. The excitement and organized chaos of the floor was electrifying. This was a far cry from lengthy economics lectures in stifling hot lecture halls. This was action. After graduating from col-

NEW YORK—MARCH 24: A man walks out of Bear Stearns headquarters March 24, 2008 in New York City. A new agreement will give Bear Stearns shareholders ten dollars per share, five times the payout outlined in a JPMorgan Chase & Co. buyout deal last week. *(Photo by Chris Hondros/Getty Images)*

lege, I returned to the floor of the Exchange and stayed for several years. The atmosphere was still as exciting to me on my last day of work as it had been on my first, but my inner traveler was breaking out. I had to see the world.

But before I could expect to land a decent job in any kind of international investment firm, I knew I would need a graduate degree, so I returned to school and earned an MBA, graduating in 1994. From there, I went to work for one of Canada's premier investment banks. I started off as a bond salesman, then moved into the derivatives division. I found that working with derivatives—securities with prices that are directly dependent upon other underlying assets—to be incredibly challenging and rewarding. I worked on a variety of asset classes within my division and was exposed to some incredibly interesting work. I was eventually transferred to the bank's New York headquarters. Despite the excitement and vibrancy of work in the "city that never sleeps," I heard the Siren song of emerging markets; I longed for adventure elsewhere. I scanned the globe for a new challenge, and I found it in the then-emerging market of South Africa. I relocated to Johannesburg and continued my work with derivatives for the next few years, and in the process helped to create the world's first emerging market Exchange-Traded Fund (ETF). An ETF is a fund that has positions that include stocks, bonds and other assets, and which typically tracks a market index like the Dow Jones Industrial Average or the Standard & Poor 500.

We stayed in Johannesburg until my wife became pregnant with our first child. The time was right, we decided, to return to New York City. And though I was leaving the excitement I'd always associated with international work for the comparatively pedestrian New York City, I felt that New York was the center of the investment banking world, and I needed to be there.

Once back in the city, I stuck to what I knew. I accepted a job with a major investment bank, doing much the same derivatives-based work I'd been doing for the last ten years. I settled into my old routine in a new setting and figured I'd do the same thing every other professional in his mid-thirties did. Namely, I'd work for the company for the next thirty-or-so years, watch my kids grow up and get married themselves, and then I'd finally retire. Then I'd spend summers in the Hamptons and winters in Palm Beach, growing old with my wife by my side. Both houses would naturally be big enough to accommodate a bevy of grandkids coming to visit on school holidays. I'd play a lot of golf and smoke a few cigars. Drink a little single malt. Maybe start a new hobby. Fly-tying had always struck me as an artistic outlet that allowed one's creativity to thrive while still maintaining a masculine façade.

Please. I was in derivatives. I don't play golf and I don't drink Scotch. And what's more, that whole scenario lost any sort of basis in anything resembling my version of reality at the working-for-the-company-for-the-next-thirty-years part. You can't tie us down to an office; for that matter, you can't tie us down to a specific country. I wanted to be a global nomad, and I had found the perfect adventure.

Investment banking is a world of vast paradoxes. Our lives are living, breathing contradictions. As traders, we're expected to make the best deals. For the company, that is. We're supposed to buy something for as little as possible and turn around and sell the same thing for as much as we can possibly get for it. Somebody is selling something because they think it's going to decrease in value, whereas somebody else is buying it because they think it's going to increase in value. Part of our job as traders is to convince both of them that they're simultaneously right. And suddenly the title of trader takes on a whole new meaning, at least auditorially.

In turn, we expect to be rewarded for our efforts, serving as we do in the role of eloquent sophists working to bring the firm wealth and glory no matter the cost to our clients. Or to our souls. But as investment bankers, our professional lives are something of a double-edged sword: we have both the fortune and the burden of working for investment bankers just like ourselves, only more experienced. The people paying our salaries and bonuses are trying to buy us and our services for as little as they can in the form of those salaries and bonuses, all the while selling us and those same services for as much as they possibly can in the form of the sales figures that we generate annually. In a hideously ironic twist of semantics, the sellers become the sold.

After being back in New York for just over a year, a new version of the Siren song began to play in my ear. This time, though, it wasn't calling me to some exotic foreign port of call. Rather, I was getting itchy to move from the large firm I was currently working for. It was nothing personal against that particular firm, it just wasn't a culture that I particularly subscribed to. Opportunity presented itself when my phone rang one day with a call from someone at Bear Stearns. Everything I knew about the firm came from what I'd read, and what I'd read made me think it would fit better with my outlook on life. I had a few interviews—one memorable one that focused on the relative wisdom of marriage and the finer points of skiing—with different people at the firm, and they eventually made me an offer. I, like the firm offering me that job, am a bit of an anomaly in the world of investment banking. And for that reason, I felt instinctively drawn to Bear; I really did want to work there. Although I would be making more money at Bear, that wasn't the force that drove me to take the job. I took it because I felt like it would present me with a better opportunity and more adventure. The whole atmosphere at Bear seemed more exciting. Little did I know how much more exciting that atmosphere would become over the course of the next six years.

In essence, by taking the job, I had implicitly gone over to the Bear Stearns way of thinking. I had subscribed to the firm's philosophy of living for the moment. I had accepted a higher salary at a firm that, if I'd taken the time to consider it, wasn't necessarily looking out for my best interest. I walked into it with my eyes wide open, like a kid in a candy store, but still not really seeing anything. I absorbed the atmosphere, I relished in the newfound status afforded me as a Bear trader. I was simultaneously respected and hated, simply because of the company I chose to work for.

And what's more, it was March. A time of rebirth. Of new beginnings. I was a newly-appointed Managing Director for one of the nation's most formidable investment banks. This was my dream shot.

According to literary scholars, a tragic hero is someone who has some sort of titanic downfall as a result of his own actions, which are usually guided by the hero's hubris and pride. One such character from the annals of history is Julius Caesar, who, in Shakespeare's version of the story, was warned to be wary of the Ides of March by his personal soothsayer. I am not a person who is easily frightened by the prospect of potential risk, and perhaps that is why I didn't listen to the voice in the back of my head that was questioning my decision to leave the safety and security of a more conservative firm to go to the much riskier and more aggressive Bear Stearns camp. Anybody in my position would have done the same, given the money and prestige that accompanied the offer. It was certainly less risky than robbing a bank, and the financial gains I stood to make far eclipsed the take of Edward Smith or any other bank robber you'd care to mention. And besides, I'd taken much more dangerous risks with my professional career, and they'd all worked out fine.

BEAR TRAP

I should have listened to that soothsayer voice in the back of my head, the one telling me the house in Palm Beach wasn't such a bad retirement gig. Ever since that first bank robbery in 1831, March has historically not been the kindest of months on Wall Street. But I pushed ahead, daring the fates to do their worst. I reported for my first day of work at the offices of Bear Stearns at 383 Madison Avenue one day in March, 2002. Six years later, I would discover that March wasn't any kinder in 2008 than it had been in 1831.

CHAPTER TWO

Hedge Your Bets

*"There will be many disasters in the hedge fund industry
coming both from incompetence and dishonesty . . .
It is all going to come to a bad end."*

—JIM ROGERS

According to an *Associated Press* report from April 16, 2008, John Paulson was the highest paid hedge fund manager in the history of the industry. His income for fiscal year 2007 topped out at $3.7 billion. A management consultant pointed out that Paulson's hourly wage alone eclipsed the median annual income for the average American family. When used in terms of an individual's income, the numbers that top fund managers like Paulson bring in are staggering, even by investment banker standards.

The funds themselves have been around since 1949, when Alfred Winslow Jones "invented" the idea of investing in such a way as to hedge against potential losses in the principal markets. The funds themselves are veiled in secrecy, relying on legal regulations stemming from the Investment Company Act of 1940 that dictate that a fund may be exempt from direct regulation if it is open only to a limited number of accredited investors. So the hedge fund manager gets to pick and choose the kids he wants to play with after school, and they all have to meet his specific criteria for membership in his club. The translation there is that if you have to ask about investment minimums, you can't afford it. And what's more, you probably shouldn't even try. Because they aren't subject to regulation, hedge funds are allowed to keep private a significant portion of their daily operations, including how, exactly, they can offer return averages in the triple digits for their investors. The basic concept, though, is that hedge fund managers, in direct contrast to their more conservative counterparts overseeing mutual funds and the like, actually seek out risk. They relish it. Live for it. Eat it for breakfast. Risk is what drives these people.

You want to manage a hedge fund? If your palms get a little damp and your pulse gets above 75 beats per minute when your fund is losing $500 million before ten o'clock in the morning, it's not for you. These are members of a special race of humankind who basically offer nothing but contemptuous glares down long noses for those of us who are so brazen as to call ourselves risk takers when we're only sticking a pinky-toe into the risk pool. They look at a deficit of half a billion dollars as not only a starting point. By God, it's a dare. And these boys don't back away from a dare, no matter who's throwing it down. It's an all-or-nothing sort of game, hedge fund management is, and those who accept the challenge of managing these massive funds thumb their noses at Wall Street Rule #1, which says that if you're playing with money on the Street, you need to cover your own ass. Hedgies could care less about covering their asses; there's nowhere near as much money to made in safety as there is in all-out risk.

So how do these people make their daily bread-and-butter? While there are a host of ways an investor can hedge in the market, some of the most popular methods include such strategies as short selling, betting on derivatives like futures or swaps, and leverage. Like I said, risk is their drug of choice, and they do what they can to risk as much as they can. However, these guys aren't dumb. Quite the opposite, in fact. They're other-worldly smart when it comes to analyzing financial markets and data. They take risks you or I might not be comfortable taking, but the risks they take also offer tremendous up-side potential. Things like interest rate swaps, for example, where investors in different countries swap interest rates with one another in order to capitalize on various lower rates in either fixed- or floating-interest rates. Or buying and selling basket correlation risk, which is betting on whether or not an event (such as a default on a loan) within a specific credit sector will affect another sector. Then there are some funds that specialize in short-selling assets such as stocks, which is the quite delicate art of selling a stock that you technically don't own by assuming you'll be able to buy it back for less than you actually sold it for; in essence, the short seller "borrows" the stock from someone else with the goal of buying it back at a later date, and at what he hopes will be a lower price. It's the old adage of buy low, sell high, only with a slight modification. In short-selling, you borrow low, sell high, then buy back low.

Much of hedge fund management involves a lot of the same techniques that drive the average guy in line at the betting window at Churchill Downs on the first Saturday of May. You analyze the data, you read the reports. When your turn comes at the window, you place your bet with as much conviction as you can muster. Then you hit your knees and you pray like hell. If the fates are with you and your analysis of the data was right and you read the conditions properly, you win. If not, well, you don't. The same basic underlying principals—and much of the same terminology— guide hedge fund managers. They are, for all intents and purposes, betting on specific outcomes. But their bets differ from those of the average Big Board investor or the average horse track chalk player. Whereas the everyday investor is at the mercy of stock or bond prices going up or down and the guy playing the trifecta at the Kentucky Derby is reliant on the 4:1 to show, a good hedger wins no matter what. And John Paulson, he of the annual salary rivaling the GNP of most countries, is a prime example of a very, very good hedgie.

Real estate is traditionally a good investment. Just ask Donald Trump. For the most part, when you buy a home, its value increases. It's the way of the financial world. Stock prices fluctuate. Bond prices can take a dip here and there. Gold, oil, pork bellies, whatever, they're all commodities with sometimes drastic price changes, both up and down. But real estate has generally been a rock. In an average market when financial forces operate as we expect them to, home prices are constantly going up. While some speculators—often speculators who are trying to sell you a house— will throw out the statistic of a home's value doubling every ten years, I'm not going to say that's true, per se. But suffice it to say that real estate is a pretty stable, safe investment that will result in monetary gain for the owner. Almost always.

Pay attention to that word "almost," because it's a six-letter word that means "potential disaster" in investing terms. Real estate can also be a fickle mistress. Trump can speak to that reality, too. But usually real estate slumps mostly hit developers, like the Donald, and spare average homeowners like John Doe, the accountant in Scarsdale with the good credit and the starter home that he's hoping will increase in value enough over the years for him to upgrade to a larger house. Mr. Doe's investment is, by pretty much all conceivable conventional wisdom, safe from some sort of catastrophic decline in value. Almost always.

Our friend Mr. Paulson, though, didn't see things that way. He, like other good hedge fund managers, puts zero stock in the conventional wisdom so many of us rely on to help us get through the day. He blows his nose on the rag that is "almost always." Paulson bet a vast sum of money that housing prices across the country would plummet. Paulson further hitched his financial wagon to a bear market in real estate by betting that, in addition to housing prices going down, mortgage bonds would default in astronomically high numbers. When you add in the element of leverage—borrowing money to increase the amount he was betting—you can understand the risk Paulson was taking. Not only was he betting his own money and the money of his investors, he was also borrowing even more money on top of that to augment his already mammoth bets.

So here we have a man who, by all accounts, should be locked up in the financial world's version of a room with padded walls. At the very least, he shouldn't be allowed to play with money, and certainly not with other people's money. He's the kind of guy who took Harvard to cover the spread against Yale in 1968 and placed the bet with a minute left in the game, just because he had, you know, a gut feeling. Conventional investing wisdom, not to mention just plain old common sense, says that everything he was doing at the time was wrong. The story ends, though, with Paulson laughing all the way to the bank. Nostradamus himself could not have predicted the future with any more perfect clarity than John Paulson did.

By the middle of 2006, Paulson was looking like the true financial genius that he is. New home sales began to stall out on their climb to unheard of heights. Interest rates were creeping up. Words like "inflation" and "recession"—with the accompanying visions of gas stations flying red flags to indicate there was no room at the inn—began to appear in news reports. And most importantly, reset dates for the first of an incalculable number of adjustable-rate mortgages began to come calling.

Adjustable-rate mortgages, or ARMs, were first available in the mid-1980s and became very much in vogue in 2005 and 2006. They were the natural result of so many mortgages being sold to investment bankers. In a sense, it was a bull market within the mortgage business. The investment banks were buying the bonds faster than the mortgage lenders could actually put the loans together. As then-Federal Reserve Chairman Alan Greenspan said in February of 2004, "American consumers might benefit if lenders provided greater mortgage product alternatives to the traditional fixed-rate mortgage." In other words, Greenspan was suggesting that adjustable-rate mortgages would save the average borrower. He said exactly that, too: "Many homeowners might have saved tens of thousands of dollars had they held adjustable-rate mortgages rather than fixed-rate mortgages during the past decade." So you've got Greenspan telling Americans they should be getting ARMs, plus there's a vacuum created by the overabundance of people seeking mortgages.

That vacuum in the industry, coupled with Greenspan's endorsement of them, led mortgage brokers to create new products, one of which was the ARM. ARMs offered would-be borrowers a teaser interest rate that was comparatively low. But as any six-year-old can tell you, when the clock strikes midnight, Cinderella better be back home where she belongs, or else her secret will be out. And in the case of ARMs, the fine print in the contract is the secret that will pop out and let you have it.

And sure enough, after a few years, the metaphorical clock struck midnight on those adjustable rates and the teasers turned not into pumpkins, but rather massive ballooning financial obligations. And those obligations quickly became too much for average homeowners with average incomes to carry. Default rates began to rise. And then they began to skyrocket. Suddenly the house itself, what is known as the collateralized debt, which was the safety net for the mortgage bonds that investors had so greedily snatched up was worth less than the debt itself. And owning a worthless piece of paper that is backed by what is now an equally worthless piece of collateral is a very bad situation to find yourself in as an investor.

So while many Americans were losing their homes to foreclosure, many investors were losing their shirts to the mortgage bond market. And John Paulson was raking in the money on both fronts. But Paulson wasn't the only hedge fund manager with interest in the real estate market. It was no secret to anybody on Wall Street that the mortgage bond market was ripe for picking. The mortgage bond tree was bearing fruit, and there's nothing like the lure of easy money to bring investors out of the woodwork. Bear Stearns managed two hedge funds that had a lot riding on the mortgage bond market, too.

Unfortunately for Bear, though, we bet the wrong horse in this race.

▲ ▲ ▲

A year before Paulson was making headlines for his masterful clairvoyance in regards to the housing market, I'd been involved in the creation of a note for our investors that was a bearish play on housing via the equity market. While Paulson was shorting the actual mortgages themselves, we were offering notes that offered tremendous potential for would-be investors. Just as the stock market has indices—the S&P 500 or the Dow Jones Industrial Average, for example—the housing market has its own index, the Philadelphia Stock Exchange Home Builders Index, known simply as the HGX Index. The HGX is an index tracking the stock of homebuilders throughout the country, so a drop in the HGX signifies that homebuilders' stocks are dropping, which is indicative of a drop in the housing market at large. Through our note, if the HGX fell, our investors would make huge returns. We offered the first version of the note in July, 2005, when the index value was sitting very near 300 points. By the time Bear was breathing its last, the index had lost over half its value. I had done my research and analyzed the markets and developed my theories. In the end, I had guessed right.

But I wasn't in charge of the Bear Stearns hedge funds.

It was June, 2007, when the first inkling of a hedge fund crisis began to appear in the offices of Bear Stearns. Our asset management unit had evolved via Bear's involvement in the bond and structured credit markets. It was an area that, as a firm, Bear knew quite well. It made natural sense for Bear to offer asset management products that capitalized on the firm's expertise, products like hedge funds. Asset management, by its very nature, offers firms a very attractive revenue stream. Hedge funds and the like generate management fees—"2 and 20" in broker lingo, a reference to the industry standard of a management fee that totals 2% of the fund's net asset value, plus a performance fee of 20% of gross returns. So let's say that our hedge fund made $1,000,000 in returns on investments over the course of a year, and that $1,000,000 brought the total value of the fund up to $10,000,000 at the end of that year. In the 2-and-20 system, the fund manager will take home 20% of the $1,000,000 (the gross returns) and 2% of the $10,000,000 (the net asset value). The manager is looking at $400,000 for his take-home pay this year. Those fees are a very nice addition to the more traditional transaction-generated revenues that tend to make up the revenue base of a typical investment bank.

In basic terms, the Bear hedge fund investment strategy was designed to take advantage of the high interest rates afforded by structured credit products, some of which involved subprime mortgage bonds. The first step was the purchase of collateralized debt obligations (CDO). A CDO is simply a debt obligation—meaning a debt that a debtor is obliged to pay back—that is backed by collateral worth at least the amount of the loan. In the case of a mortgage, one of the most common CDOs, the property itself is the collateral for the debt. Because of the historic rise in the value of real estate, mortgage bonds are often thought to be as close to a fail-safe investment as one is likely to find. Our fund managers had opted for the AAA- and AA-rated tranches of various CDOs and other structures that had subprime mortgages. Basically they were hedging their bets on the subprime mortgage bonds by making sure that they were in the first group of bond holders to get paid once the notes came due. It was a way of balancing the risk, even though we all pretty much felt like the risk was minimal as it was. Keep in mind that these managers weren't bearish on the housing market the way my notes were. They were just banking on people with less-than-superior credit to put their homes ahead of other expenses and make sure that the mortgage got paid in full to avoid foreclosure.

The rating agencies that were assigning the credit ratings were using past default rates—rates that reflected actual due diligence on the part of those writing the mortgages—as one of the determining factors in rating these CDOs. Because the default rates historically were low, the CDOs were given higher credit ratings. However, it was a classic example of comparing apples to oranges. The new mortgages, the ones that were actually backing these CDOs that the managers were acquiring, had been written in the housing boom when everybody was buying houses. Mortgage lenders couldn't write loans fast enough to satisfy the need. And as a result, credit checks were less than adequate. And in the end, did it really matter if people could afford the house? If they defaulted, the bank got the real estate which, historically, had been the best investment around. So these bonds were rated based on the historical figures, with the expectation that, worst case scenario, the banks could repossess the house in the event of default and sell it for a profit.

So our hedgies were gathering up these CDOs that were built on the shakiest of foundations and pinning their financial hopes to them. Once the manager had acquired the CDOs, he'd use the resulting credit balance in leverage to buy more CDOs based on the value of the bonds he'd already purchased. In other words, managers were extended lines of credit based on the value of the CDOs, and they in turn used this line of credit to purchase more CDOs, which they in turn used to by even more. And so on. It's important to understand that from the fund manager's perspective, this was a way to increase the potential return. Every single bond pays an interest rate on top of the actual principal, so every new bond adds to the potential return for the investor. So in this case, our hedge fund managers were counting on a very low default rate in the bonds. Again, they were putting a lot of trust—in hindsight, too much trust—not only in the homeowners, but also in the entire system of ratings and valuation methodologies of these classes of assets.

This acquisition of more bonds that came with a higher rate of potential default through leverage was a relatively risky move in and of itself. Managers were basically robbing Peter to pay Paul; they were cash advancing a credit card with a lower interest rate in order to pay off another card with a higher interest rate. The main problem there is that the net result of the transaction is that the debt amount remains the same. If you cash advance $100 to pay off another card that you owe $100 on, you're still on the hook for $100, just to a different lender. If, however, you're thinking that you're going to make $200 by paying off the higher rate bearing card, the transfer makes sense, because you'll come out ahead in the end.

The same thing applied to the acquisition of CDOs through leverage. The managers were betting that the returns were going to be stable. The were willing to buy up CDOs earning more interest than what they were able to borrow against, thus generating more money on the return than they were paying in interest. For example, a fund manager might buy up senior tranche CDOs—meaning those with the lowest risk factor and AAA-credit ratings—that earn LIBOR + 100 bps. In turn, they borrow against the investor's cash and pay roughly LIBOR-flat. The manager picks up about 100bps per year and, if you lever that up 10 to 12 times, you end up with a return of 10-12% without subjecting yourself to a lot of financial risk. This is among the holiest of grails involved in running a fund. You find a double-digit return with low volatility, and you've cracked the code.

LIBOR is yet another acronym in the overcrowded slang dictionary of the world of high finance. It stands for London interbank offered rate. It is the interest rate that one bank will charge another when loaning money. The rate is fixed daily by the British Bankers' Association, and is basically a distillation of the interbank deposit rates for all of the most creditworthy banks around the globe. LIBOR is also one of the gold standards by which short-term interest rates are determined throughout the world. And the better your institution's credit rating, the closer to LIBOR you can borrow money. So let's say your credit worthiness suggests you've got to pay an additional 20 basis points above LIBOR to borrow money short-term. That would look like LIBOR + 20 bps when you're using that pesky investment banker language. The higher that basis points value is, the lesser your credit rating. And basis points are 1/100th of a percentage point, so LIBOR + 20 bps is the same as saying LIBOR + 0.20% , or .002. Let's you borrow $100 at LIBOR + 20 bps, and we'll assume you've got the rate locked-in and that the LIBOR rate stays constant. Over the course of a year, you would pay $2.70 in interest on that $100.

As recently as June, 2008, however, there grew some grumblings from certain sources when the LIBOR rate didn't seem to reflect the volatility we were seeing in the market. People began claiming that British banks were only quoting their lowest rates, the rates reserved for their best customers. If this was, in fact, what was going on, then borrowers were getting a huge rate break, whereas depositors were getting the raw end of the deal. In response, the BBA issued a statement saying they would be changing the stringency with which they investigated the LIBOR reports. BBA Chief Executive Angela Knight said of the changes, "These changes will further strengthen [LIBOR] and the confidence of its many users."

What this potential scandal points to is the fact that our economy—the world's economy, for that matter—relies heavily on individuals' willingness to play by the rules. Our markets are, to a great extent, self-policing, which means that the markets and the economy they drive are very, very fragile. And if people choose to violate the good-faith rules set down by the larger community, the ramifications can be disastrous.

But our hedge fund managers were, ostensibly, playing by the rules. At least as far as we knew at the time. And what's more, these managers aren't dumb. They recognize the fact that the use of leverage to purchase new bonds increases the risk profile of the fund as a whole. So, even though they were acquiring AAA tranches of CDOs with some subprime mortgages, the overall risk inherent in the fund was growing. If a higher-than-expected rate of default started to show itself, the domino effect would kick in, and the leveraged bonds would suddenly become major weights, and the funds would have no way of preventing or stopping the free-fall that would inevitably start. So, just to be on the safe side, the managers opted to buy credit default swaps to insure their bonds against a drop in the credit market, generally relying on the figures provided by one of the representative indices to go short.

A credit default swap, what we call a CDS, is, in the simplest terms, an insurance policy that acts as a way of transferring the risk of default on a fixed-income security, like a bond, to another party. The seller of the swap is like the insurance agent who is guaranteeing the credit worthiness of whatever it is that the buyer is trying to insure. In this case, our hedge fund managers were trying to insure the credit of the mortgage bonds they held. The simplest way to think of CDS is to look at them as just another sort of sales transaction. You've got a buyer and a seller. The buyer—in this case, the Bear hedge funds—seeks protection against a default on debt. The seller of the protection offers to pay the notional (or face) value of the contract in the event that the aforementioned default does, in fact, come to fruition during the term of the swap, the benchmark tenor of which is usually five years. This insurance policy doesn't come free for the purchaser. The cost is LIBOR plus a spread of basis points. When you're talking about CDS, the seller of the protection will be charging LIBOR + X bps, where X is the variable dependent on what your specific institution's credit rating is. When our hedge funds were seeking the protection, they were getting somewhere in the neighborhood of LIBOR + 30 bps. And to put that in perspective, in our last days on life support, Bear was getting LIBOR + 1000 bps.

So everything was in place. The bonds had been acquired, both through actual money and leveraged transactions. Those bonds had been insured with credit default swaps. The table was set, grace had been said, and now it was time to eat until we were full. This setup was what we called positive carry, which was just our way of saying that we were expecting a positive rate of return. Saying things like "positive carry" sounded so much more professional than guys in $5000 dollar suits running around the trading floor screaming, "CHA-CHING! CHA-CHING!"

Basically this strategy was fool-proof. Almost. Our managers had set up a fund that contained quite a bit of calculated risk, but they'd hedged it out so that it seemed like there was no way it could fail. Real estate generates steady and predictable returns, so this should have been easy. It was an example of what is called an absolute return strategy, because it was idiot-proof. But as the old saying goes, make something idiot-proof, and the world invents a better idiot. In this case, though, it was more that the world created a better financial disaster. Just pay attention to that pesky "almost" again.

The trick of any gamble is that it relies on things happening in a statistically predictable way. Counting cards in a Vegas casino isn't a guaranteed way to win. However, if done correctly, it can substantially increase the counter's odds at beating the house, simply because it removes the statistical advantage the house maintains over the average bettor and transfers it to the person counting the cards. He knows the statistical probability of a specific card's coming up next, at least within a certain range. If, however, the house suddenly interjects a new variable at some point during the process—for example, five new decks randomly inserted halfway through the card shoe—all bets are off in terms of the predictability of what the next card will be. Hedge funds are just like blackjack in that they rely on statistical probabilities to offset the massive amounts of risk they make themselves prone to.

Hedge fund managers have a faith rivaling any religious convert, but their faith is in the market itself rather than a spiritual entity. Managers believe to the deepest reaches of their souls that the market will behave the way it is supposed to. After all, this isn't some petulant child we're talking about here. This is the financial world. Numbers. Math. Statistics. These things are governed by laws beyond human control and they operate independently of human emotions. Whereas you might have arguments with a child about doing the right thing, you could always count on the market to do what it was supposed to do, what you expected it to do. And it always did what it was supposed to do.

Except for those times when it didn't.

The subprime mortgage crisis started to really cause problems for investors in early 2007. The combination of ARMs affected by rising interest rates and the downturn in the economy precipitated a spike in the number of Americans who were defaulting on their mortgages. That scenario was coupled with the fact that the bottom had basically dropped out of the housing market that had been going up-up-and-up on what so many investors seemed to think was a never-ending climb. In other words, the hedge fund managers of Bear Stearns were looking down the triple-barrel of a big gun that was aimed directly at their financial futures.

The *Titanic* and its tragic maiden voyage is a very apt metaphor for the Bear hedge fund collapse, because so much of what led to the sinking of the world's most luxurious ocean liner came into play at Bear, too. Consider the self-assurance of the ship's designers. The ship was designed to carry and launch up to 48 lifeboats of varying sizes, which was enough to safely transport the entire population of the ship if the need arose. Estimates on the total number of passengers on board at the time vary, but 2207 is the usually agreed-upon number. However, due to a desire to retain open deck space and save a few dollars in the process, the designers cut the number of lifeboats to 20, which was enough for just over half the ticketed passengers. And when you really thought about it, it's not like they were anything more than decorative. If the ship acted the way it was supposed to, there would be no need for any lifeboats.

The Bear managers were guilty of the same level of self-assured hubris, and the same blind faith in the unknown potential behavior of the financial markets. As the prices for mortgage bonds began to fall like a stone dropped from the top of the Tower of Pisa, it suddenly dawned on our managers that they didn't have the requisite insurance through CDS to cover the losses they were about to be facing. It's important to remember, too, that a lot of the bonds that these guys were counting on had been leveraged. So, even though that higher-rate credit card had been paid with cash advanced on the lower-rate card, the lower-rate card bill was coming in the mail, and there was no money to pay it with. The iceberg was looming, and the managers were faced with the same hideous pair of options that faced the captain of the doomed *Titanic:* do or die. Barrel one of that big gun was locked, loaded and fired, scoring the first of three direct hits.

According to many studies about the *Titanic,* if the captain had simply ordered that the ship drive directly into the offending iceberg, several things would have happened. The ship would have sustained immense amounts of damage. The crew would have been summarily blamed, and no doubt many of them, including the captain, would have lost their jobs. The White Star Line would have, temporarily, been a laughing stock in the world of seagoing transportation, due to their inability to hire a captain who could avoid massive blocks of ice floating around in front of him.

But the ship would have remained afloat.

By trying to avoid the iceberg, the captain was acting much like a hedge fund manager. Both despise looking like they made stupid decisions, so they will do anything within their power to avoid it. The captain of the *Titanic* chose to avoid the iceberg, and as a result, ripped open a lengthy gash down the side of the ship. That opened up the airtight floatation chambers within the ship's hull, and the rest is an all too well known tragedy.

The same thing is true for the Bear Stearns hedge fund managers. Rather than cut their losses, they chose to keep chugging ahead, full-steam. They were losing money hand-over-fist, but they kept up the façade that everything was going strongly. But numbers—those little symbols with their comforting assurances of predictable behavior—don't lie. And while that is usually to the benefit of managers, such was not the case in this instance. The Bear hedge funds were posting massive losses, and the creditors who had financed the leveraged positions in mortgage bonds were feeling less confidence in the market than perhaps the fund managers were. They wanted new collateral to offset the losses sustained by the existing collateral, the real estate backing the mortgage bond CDOs.

The huge number of defaults within the mortgage industry, and especially within the higher-risk subprime mortgages that the Bear hedgers had so liberally surrounded themselves with, created a precipitous drop in the price of mortgage-backed securities. So our boys on Madison Avenue were left holding the tab after everyone else had left the dinner table, and it was a pretty hefty tab, at that. At this point, though, the managers could have cut and run. They could have taken it on the chin, gotten yelled at by upper management for making stupid bets, and gone on with their lives. But they didn't. They went down with the ship.

For an individual investor with a brokerage account, he has the ability to withdraw money against a line of credit based on the value of his portfolio at any given moment. This is called buying on margin. The investor can use his margin account for whatever he so desires. If he wants to buy a house, so be it. More stock, we're here for you. A Bentley, is there any other car? The only catch is that it's like a credit card. Your credit line is based on the value of the portfolio, which is itself a fluid number. If the value of your investment goes up, so, too, does your credit line. But if the value goes down, you might be getting a little phone call from your broker suggesting you offer up a cash infusion in order to bring your balance back to within your limits. This is what is known in the industry as a margin call, and it is typically met with either a cash transfer from the investor's bank or the sale of assets within the portfolio to pay down the balance. Things get a little sticky, though, when the value of your portfolio is such that your assets have declined in value so substantially and so quickly that you can't sell enough to cover the outstanding balance. In those cases, we're all keeping our fingers crossed that your bank account is flush with zeros to the left of the decimal point.

In June of 2007, the Bear hedge funds weren't in the enviable position of an overabundance of cash-on-hand to cover what were basically margin calls that were coming in from the creditors seeking additional collateral for the leveraged buys. The only solution that they could find was to start selling bonds to pay the creditors. But the reason the creditors wanted collateral in the first place was because those bonds were losing value. The firm had to extend a $1.6 billion loan to the funds in an effort to save them from what was rapidly becoming an increasingly dangerous downward spiral.

But the Bear wasn't dead just yet. The cigars upstairs figured their hot-shot progeny would find a way out of this, so they did what any responsible parent would do, and they forked over the money. But the managers were still selling bonds like there was no tomorrow. And remembering the concept of what now seems to be the incredibly sardonically-named bear market—irony, thou art a cruel jester—when there are more sellers than buyers, the price goes down. So as the Bear guys are desperately selling their bonds, potential buyers are in the position of being able to determine the price, and they're driving a hard bargain. So these bonds, which are supposed to be bringing in sufficient money to cover the margin calls, are losing value with every passing moment. In other words, the *Titanic* lifeboats are going off half-full, leaving passengers on the deck to die.

The rest of the Wall Street hedge fund gang rose up *en masse* and literally conspired against Bear. It was almost a game for these guys. See how much they could screw with a dying animal before it finally gave up the ghost. The hedge fund community, saints that they are, worked as a unit to drive subprime mortgage bond prices even lower, which was the equivalent of unplugging the respirator. The lead from the third barrel exited the muzzle and planted itself firmly and fatally in the heart of the Bear hedge funds.

On July 17, a letter was sent to the unfortunate people who counted themselves as investors in two of Bear's hedge funds, the Bear Stearns High-Grade Structured Credit Fund and the Bear Stearns High-Grade Structured Credit Enhanced Leverage Fund. These were high net worth individuals, many of whom were covered by Private Client Services (PCS) at Bear Stearns; the average PCS client had a net worth of at least $10 million. While I myself was not privy to the content of those letters, I knew from the start that they weren't any kind of courtesy update from the asset management division. Nope. This was bad news. Thin envelope at college acceptance time bad news. The reports were worse than grim. The Structured Credit Fund had lost 90% of its value, which came to a figure somewhere in the neighborhood of $900 million. The Structured Credit Enhanced Leverage Fund had fared slightly better, losing only $600 million. The caveat of the latter, though, was that the fund had only started with $600 million. The Enhanced Leverage Fund was now effectively worthless. Completely liquidated.

The two hedge funds, in a matter of several weeks, had lost approximately $1.6 billion of investor capital. On July 31, both funds filed for Chapter 15 bankruptcy.

The managers of these two funds, just like the guy sifting through the non-winning tickets at the track and the captain of the *Titanic,* are prime targets for second-guessing. You can look at the horse race bettor and chastise him for wasting money on such long odds. They call those kinds of bets a tax on people who failed statistics. And the captain of the *Titanic,* despite the urgency of the situation, should have instinctively thought first and foremost to save the lives of his passengers, human beings who had put their safety and well-being in his hands. And the hedge fund managers should have been more careful, especially given that they were playing with other people's money. Other people who, like the passengers on the *Titanic,* thought their futures were safe in the hands of these experts. It was a trust that, while not necessarily violated by the managers, certainly wasn't at the forefront of their thinking as they racked up a mountain of debt upon debt in the hopes of a big payday on the other side.

Of course hindsight is 20/20, so it's easy enough for me to sit in the relative safety and comfort of a time removed from those days and say who should have done what when. But the reality is that the managers allowed themselves to be blinded by the potential returns. Perhaps they were too wedded to their strategy. Whatever the reason, they were unable to see the perfect storm forming in front of them. It is impossible for me to say, as only they can tell exactly what they were thinking regarding the decisions they made. We do know that that there were several senior people within Bear who were trying to sound warning bells regarding the fund's strategy. These people were terrified that the fund's strategy could lead to a complete meltdown of our asset management unit and, potentially, Bear as a whole. There were a lot of super-smart people at Bear—among them my own boss—who were sounding their warnings. If only things had taken a different course and the funds had reduced their leverage profiles, they might have survived with just some serious wounds. And just maybe, by extension, Bear itself could have been saved.

A little research into the subprime mortgage market might have shown these guys that they were walking on precariously thin ice. The subprime market had spread itself so thin that there was absolutely no room for error. The risks that were being taken by mortgage lenders in giving money to people who couldn't possibly be expected to sustain the payments over a period of time were being passed on in exponential form to investors.

Macroeconomic theory, that Godforsakenly boring course those of us in the field of economics and business all had to suffer through in undergrad, tells us that the economy as a whole is a product of the pieces that make it up. So when mortgage lenders are overextending themselves and the people to whom they are lending the money are overextending themselves, the numbers don't work. The levels of output and consumption at the time were not in any way levels that the economy could maintain. The US economy had been showing signs of slowing to the point that it wasn't just Wall Street insiders who were talking about it. Hell, *USA Today* picked up on it more than once. So one would expect Ivy League MBAs who are managing billions of dollars to be clued into at least the same intelligence as the publication they ridiculed as "McNews." And as would become apparent many months later, they might have known far more than they were letting on to their investors, if the Federal Bureau of Investigation was to be believed.

Obviously the managers guessed wrong, and that's not totally their fault. But they can be faulted for not providing for a worst-case scenario like the one that happened to befall them. Sort of the "save something for a rainy day" philosophy. Any good stock broker will tell his clients to maintain a cash reserve as a hedge against a market correction or major downturn. But these guys didn't take that advice. Because they didn't have the cash-on-hand to cover their debt obligations, they were forced to unload their positions in a bad market, which is a direct violation of the buy low, sell high mantra. They'd bought low, but were selling even lower. And they were doing it because they had to. No investor wants to be forced into selling; it's just not a good position to find yourself in. You want to buy on your own terms and sell on your own terms, not because some third party is forcing you to do so. If they'd just maintained a cash balance to cover their leveraged positions, it would have been like the *Titanic* ramming the iceberg head-on. They might not have had the stellar return numbers to show their investors and they might have been forced to settle for a slightly lower bonus, albeit one that would have still been the envy of most human beings. But their ship would have stayed afloat. They wouldn't have brought it all down with them.

HEDGE YOUR BETS

After all was said and done, though, what it really boiled down to was the fact that Bear fund managers hadn't made their clients a lot of money. Hedge funds collapse with a great deal of regularity, and it rarely makes the news when a smaller fund ceases operations. There was a period of time in the late 90's when the failure rate for hedge funds was over 14% annually. The biggest crime our managers committed was that they weren't John Paulson. They just guessed wrong. If they'd happened to have guessed right and made their clients hundreds of millions of dollars instead of losing it, we'd be having an entirely different conversation right now. But they didn't. They guessed wrong, and they guessed wrong in a big way. Such is the world of investing. The difference between a genius and a fool on Wall Street is that the genius does the wrong thing and makes a fortune as a result.

Yes, I've said that John Paulson is a financial genius, and as evidence I've pointed to his decision to go contrary to conventional wisdom and bet against a rise in the value of real estate. And yes, I've faulted our own managers for failing to do the same thing, which might seem like something of a contradiction. But the true fault lies in their failure to practice the very name of the sector in which they work, namely that of hedging. They didn't hedge their bets sufficiently. They were so dead sure of themselves that they couldn't fathom the possibility of a drop in the market. For the average guy on the street, that's acceptable, perhaps. But when you're running a hedge fund for a major investment bank, you have to cover all your bases. Paulson is a genius, no doubt about it. But Paulson also covers his own ass when it comes down to it. The Bear managers left themselves wide open by relying so heavily on one potential outcome. So it's not so much that I'm faulting our managers for not being genius-level investors like John Paulson, but rather I'm faulting them for making bush league mistakes.

For example, as coincidence would have it, I was part of a team from equity derivatives that pitched an idea to these funds. The idea was what we call a CCO, or a collateralized commodity obligation. Basically a mortgage bond, but tied to commodities instead of real estate. The pay-off for the note was tied to the bet that commodities in general—oil, gold, wheat, anything that is bought and sold, basically—would not drop massively in value. The AAA-rated tranche for the trade was paying at LIBOR + 200 bps, which is, by investment standards, an insanely good return. As the market for those can't-miss CDOs went south, the demand for commodities skyrocketed. The commodities play made an absolute mint. And this wasn't some sort of blind luck, mind you. We worked with some of our colleagues at an Australian bank to develop the CCO and then worked with our head institutional salesman and our head of equity derivative strategy to pitch it to appropriate clients. for two of the Bear Stearns Asset Management division funds, or BSAM for short, as it was an uncorrelated asset class, but one which used the same tranching, or rating, technology that the managers were familiar with. In the end, though, they stuck to their mortgage bonds and rode them all the way into the abyss.

After the collapse, Bear was sued by a group of the shareholders who had all suffered losses of staggeringly huge sums of money. Looking at it from my perspective today, again using the luxury of perfect hindsight, those lawsuits were the tip of the iceberg. I just didn't realize then that this time, I was on the ship headed right for that iceberg. And there weren't enough lifeboats for all of us. This coming tragedy would involve complete destruction, just like the hedge fund collapse. It would involve lawsuits, too. But this one wouldn't offer up the convenient sacrificial lambs, even in hindsight, that the hedge fund collapse did. As soon as the destruction was confirmed, there was no captain to be found that could be blamed for the destruction, no single decision to point to as the cause of the meltdown. The ship that was Bear Stearns was on a collision course, and it was about to be every man, woman and child for themselves.

CHAPTER THREE

Shoot to Kill

"I'm just a patsy."
—LEE HARVEY OSWALD

I have found, over the years, that assassination is an interesting topic of study. I don't mean that in the sense that it's a subject I enjoy studying in order to perfect my own techniques. Rather, it is a subject that is rife with scandals and mysteries, the sort of stuff that Hollywood blockbusters are made of. Conspiracy theories. Undercover foreign agents. Murder. All that good stuff. But there's more to assassination than just killing somebody. Take, for example, John Hinckley. By all accounts, everyone said he was a nice kid growing up. Perhaps a little bit of a loner, but then people always say that about guys that go off and try to kill the president. It's sort of a fallback position: "You know, he always did seem like something of a loner, now that I think about it." And that inevitably leads to labels like "social outcast" or "misfit." My personal favorite is the "he never really fit in" one. Who ever really *did* fit in as a junior high student? But what has actually happened in those brief moments, those little sound bites from the concerned neighbors who used to peep through the opening in the Venetian blinds, is a juxtaposition of the actual event and the actors. It's a role-reversal of sorts. The assassin himself has become the target of assassins.

Character assassination seems to follow any kind of crime—assassination is a convenient one, given the similar nature of their relationship—like a dog chasing a stick. It's just behind it, maybe out of sight for the moment, but you can bet it's on the way. And you can be absolutely sure that, given enough time, the dog is going to catch up to the stick, just like the character assassination is going to catch up to the assassin himself. On Wall Street, character assassination has been elevated to an art form, and investment bankers are some of its most skilled practitioners.

The days and months after the collapse of the two hedge funds were akin to being hit with the same club twice from two different directions; kind of like getting assassinated by some crazed lunatic on the first day, then being told it was actually you, the victim of the assassin's bullet, who was the crazy one, and what's more, you deserved it. It's a bitch of a couple of days, basically. In regards to the hedge funds, hindsight started rearing its ugly head again after the smoke had cleared, and everybody began pointing fingers. And though none of the fingers were pointed at any specific person by most of us, we were all very careful to make sure our fingers were pointed exactly 180-degrees away from wherever we were standing at a given moment. Woe be it to the poor son-of-a-bitch who happened to be sitting across the room. All of this finger-pointing, though, only really started after the cable news economics "experts" had dissected the situation and offered their quasi-informed opinions on it. There's nothing quite like the safety net of looking at a teleprompter and reading story lines written by someone else to help develop an inner sense of being the local authority on a subject about which, if they'd been asked to speak on it two weeks prior, all of these resident founts of knowledge would have responded with a blank stare and a line about Britney Spears' latest driving difficulties.

According to a Business Wire article, before that letter of July 17 in which the fund managers fell on their collective swords, Rich Marin, the CEO of BSAM, had said publicly, "We are working with counterparties to stabilize the situation by stabilizing the funds' leverage and improving the liquidity. Our goal is to achieve the best possible results for the funds' investors under the circumstances, and our efforts and our discussions with counterparties are ongoing." And yes, in case you're tracking that sentence, Marin basically used a lot of polysyllabic words to say exactly nothing. As I've said, I was familiar with at least one internal "counterparty" who had tried to save the drowning funds, and those offers of assistance were rebuffed. So who these anonymous "counterparties" were, I have no idea. And as for achieving "the best possible result for the funds' investors," I think the results speak for themselves.

That said, I can't fault Rich for trying to convince everyone that he was going to solve the problem. I don't think he had reviewed all the available information, in all honesty, because I don't think he had any idea how serious the problems really were. Truth be told, few of us within the firm knew how serious those problems really were. Sure, we knew the funds weren't knocking the cover off the metaphorical ball, but we all had our own jobs to do, so we didn't really have time to focus on the ups and downs of hedge funds. But there's more than just a lack of time; in the legal sense, we actually weren't allowed to know what was going on.

Within the safe confines of investment banks, where things like cultural sensitivities and political correctness go to die, there are invisible divisions known as Chinese Walls. A Chinese Wall, while not necessarily visible, is an all-too-real division between the different departments within a financial institution like an investment bank. The theory behind a Chinese Wall is that it will prevent discussions that could lead to instances of insider trading. Because an investment bank is such a multi-faceted company, we've got clients with interests that could affect decisions made by other clients. So if somebody on one floor knows something about Client X that could make Client Y a lot of money but it's not information that is yet public knowledge, that somebody can't go give the information to the guy one floor up who's managing Client Y's account because of the Chinese Wall. It would be a violation of the conflict of interest laws.

Chinese Walls have an interesting history, especially within the context of the demise of our beloved Bear Stearns in 2008. The Walls were the result of a 2002 investigation into the dealings of then squeaky-clean Merrill Lynch. It seems that the boys on the Merrill floor were trading information across the water cooler, information that was actually confidential information about clients. The problem with that exchange is that it created a massive conflict of interest within the investment community, and that led to investment advisers offering public and, oftentimes, not-so-truthful assessments of stocks of companies that the bank did business with. So after a pretty lengthy investigation by the New York State Attorney General's office, Merrill got slapped with a $100 million fine. The firm had to reform its practices as a way of protecting information about clients within its own walls. And they got pretty well publicly humiliated. You might even go so far as to say they were the victims of character assassination.

So once the findings of the investigation were made public, we all breathed a collective sigh of relief and figured we'd best clean up our own acts. The Attorney General's office, though, wasn't going to trust the investment banking community to police itself. We'd already proven—or at least, Merrill had already proven, the rest of us had covered it up better—that we weren't necessarily to be trusted, and the exchange of this information was actually illegal in the first place, because the Glass-Steagall act had created a clear and definite distinction between investment banks and brokerage firms. Clearly this whole mess required some sort of higher-level regulation so as to ensure it wouldn't happen again. At least that was the perspective of the folks in then-AG Eliot Spitzer's office. So the concept of the Chinese Wall came into existence, or at least the enforcement thereof. Again, this whole set of actions had been illegal since the 1930's and the inception of Glass-Steagall.

The name of the metaphorical division—the Chinese Wall—is taken not, as is commonly thought, from the Great Wall of China, but rather from the free-standing screens that create moveable, temporary walls, and which are common in Asian homes. The Chinese moniker, though, is strictly the work of a Wall Street sense of humor, such as it is.

The real joke, though, at least from my vantage point, is that the guy who prosecuted Merrill was an up-and-coming lawyer in the AG's office. He was quoted as saying, "This was a shocking betrayal of trust by one of Wall Street's most trusted names. The case must be a catalyst for reform throughout the entire industry." Political hyperbole at its finest. Especially when you consider the fact that it's not like the guys at Merrill had done something morally reprehensible. It's not as if they were being publicly drawn and quartered for cheating on their wives. Like Eliot Spitzer, for example, when he was outed as an adulterer on that fateful Monday six years later. The same Eliot Spitzer who was working for the New York State Attorney General's office in 2002. The same Eliot Spitzer who, at the time, had successfully wrenched a $100 million dollar settlement out of the bank account of Merrill Lynch in the interest of rectifying "a shocking betrayal of trust."

Discussions of the moral failings of Wall Street and its investigators aside, with the Chinese Walls in place at Bear Stearns, most of us were unable to talk shop with the guys in BSAM insofar as specific investments were concerned. The fixed-income area was especially sensitive in relation to the BSAM offices. The explanation for why that was the case is relatively simple. The hedge funds' investments were geared mainly towards bond strategies; pair that with the element of anxiety that pervaded every action we took after Spitzer's investigation, and you can understand why we were so scared about how easily any involvement with the BSAM guys could be seen as a conflict of interest. If our hedge funds had bought Bear-created CDOs, we'd be double-dipping on our fees, due to the fact that we'd be banking a management fee for the purchase plus a seller's fee for the sale of the bond.

Because of the delicate nature of that relationship between fixed-income and BSAM—not to mention the fear of God that Spitzer had instilled in each and every one of us—we didn't lend them any money in the form of leveraged notes. So because we didn't lend them any money to fund their leveraged positions, there was no credit oversight at the investment bank level; in other words, there wasn't what we'd call a credit-intensive relationship between fixed-income and BSAM. All of the funds' leveraged income was from other Wall Street banks, so the credit issues weren't our problem. In other words, they didn't owe us any money, so we did not have a way to see inside to determine what was happening. I realize it sounds a little weird, but such is life with Chinese Walls. Governmental-imposed regulations often don't take into account the concept that every department is linked, almost like they're a married couple. And as any marriage is only as good as the quality of its communication between partners, the lack of communication between fixed-income and BSAM can really be looked at as one of the root causes for the market problems that hit Wall Street on the heels of the hedge funds' collapse.

Because our credit department was in the dark regarding the positions at BSAM, that meant that they also weren't too hip to sending teams of credit guys in to oversee the goings-on with them. The thing that we over on the trading floor side of the building found really odd was that according to our operations guys, there was just one person over there looking at the credit and leverage aspects of those funds. One person overseeing one of the most sensitive areas in terms of risk potential that could affect a billion-and-a-half dollars levered up to $20 billion. What's more, Bear had a great risk-management product called Bear Measure-risk. BSAM used this tool in most of its funds to assess various risk measures. I heard from a source close to that group that there were only two funds in BSAM that were not using this tool. Both of them, coincidentally enough, had only one person analyzing their credit and leverage aspects. And yes, coincidentally enough, the two funds that were allegedly not using Bear Measure-risk also happened to be the two funds that collapsed. So there were a lot of pieces in place that led to the meltdown. Because of the lack of risk oversight, the funds were primed for a major disaster, like the one they had, if the values of their respective assets dropped, which they did.

So you've got billions of dollars tied up in a single department stretched across a pair of investment funds, funds that specialize in high-risk and leverage. And that's only a single part of the rest of the department, which was responsible for approximately $20 billion just in those two funds. One person, $20 billion. I don't like those odds, no matter who it is that's overseeing it. $20 billion dollars at stake, yet despite that mammoth number, they put one person in charge of overseeing the whole credit side of that operation, simply because there wasn't a whole lot of Bear Stearns' own money tied up in those funds. That's one person who may or may not even understand all of the elements of the investments and the risk they're undertaking, yet is in charge of making sure the funds don't overextend themselves. For a firm that prided itself on risk management, Bear really fell down hard when it came to BSAM. I think, though, it was more a byproduct of over-arching regulations that had limited our interaction with one another as a firm, the Chinese Walls that basically forbade us from engaging in what amounted to a day-to-day business relationship with Bear Stearns Asset Management.

BROOKLYN, NY—JUNE 19: Matthew Tannin walks out of a Brooklyn courthouse after posting bail June, 19, 2008 in the Brooklyn borough of New York City. Former Bear Stearns hedge fund managers Ralph Cioffi and Matthew Tannin were arrested early this morning at their homes in New Jersey and Manhattan and have been indicted for conspiracy to commit securities fraud and mail fraud and could face up to 20 years in prison. *(Photo by Spencer Platt/Getty Images)*

SHOOT TO KILL

Immediately after the collapse, which had occurred despite Rich Marin's assurances of the firm's desire to make everything A-OK, the accusations started flying. There was a regularly-scheduled meeting of the firm's Senior Managing Directors on June 23, and at that meeting Rich assured us that everything would be fine. Nothing to worry about, all is well. Rich had everything under control and he would make it all just hunky-dory. Somehow, though, Rich had managed to find enough time to attend a screening of "Mr. Brooks," a movie about a well-respected businessman who has an alter-ego that is a homicidal maniac who manifests himself as a serial killer.

The metaphorical parallels between the movie and his own life were apparently lost on Mr. Marin, as he advised against seeing the film. On his blog, that is. Just when it seemed that this whole situation couldn't get any more ridiculous, we all learned that our esteemed colleague, in addition to being a financier extraordinaire, was also an amateur movie critic. Rich not only watched the movie over the weekend while the hedge funds that his own department was immediately responsible for were disappearing, he took the time to give his personal recommendations on his Internet blog. What is truly amazing to many of us is that he somehow managed to find the time to write about movies and talk about life as a wheeler-dealer on Wall Street, all in the midst of, to quote an entry from June 23, "trying to defend Sparta against the Persian hordes of Wall Street." At least we couldn't accuse him of not being eloquent. But I must say that, in Rich's defense, a number of colleagues posited the idea that he must have gone to some midnight screening of the movie, because he was around the office during all hours of the day and much of the night, trying desperately to fix the situation.

Immediately after the story had broken in the *New York Times,* Marin changed his personal site to a password-protected fortress to which only those invited few were allowed to enter. But the damage had been done. Five days after telling us how he was going to sprinkle fairy dust on the whole hedge fund quagmire and make everything all better, he was removed from his position as head of BSAM and reassigned as an advisor. Certainly not the best outcome one in his position could have hoped for. I can only imagine that the feeling of being reassigned like that is like getting on a train to the Gulag. And what scared us was the fact that we were all in danger of riding that train into oblivion, and the fight to stay off it was going to get increasingly more difficult.

BEAR TRAP

Long story short, the mood in those days was pessimistic at best. If you couldn't laugh at things like high-ranking execs getting caught writing personal blogs during the single most important emergency we'd been through in recent history, you were in trouble. But when it suddenly occurred to you that this was your firm, your job, your life, at which you were laughing, you found that sanity-saving laughter to be an odd reaction, regardless of the level of comfort it might seem to provide. I had the good fortune to have planned a vacation to surf in western France long before any of this had surfaced; it was nice to be able to count myself among those with what appeared to be good luck at a time like this. In an effort to purge myself of all the negativity and angst that had accompanied the previous months at the office, I unloaded my concerns on my wife while we crossed the Atlantic at 40,000 feet. I told her how glad I was that we were escaping the mess at 47th and Madison. I confided to her that I was afraid that heads were going to roll. Heads, I feared, that would belong to Warren Spector and Jimmy Cayne.

She disagreed with me, though, as she felt like both Warren and Jimmy were too important to be let go over something like this. They were Bear institutions. And what's more, if they were vulnerable to being fired, then no one would be safe—not that you are ever truly "safe" at an investment bank. After all, that's part of the edge, what keeps you focused. Having been an investment banker herself, she knew the score. A drop in returns meant a loss of income, and a loss of income meant the need for blood. And in a firm the size of Bear Stearns, patsies were easier to find than investment advice. But I figured that if it all went down and heads started rolling—heads that might include my own—I'd just stay in France and surf a while longer. There are, after all, worse places in the world to be stranded.

Warren Spector was the Chief Operating Officer of Bear, and he was widely regarded as the heir-apparent to the exulted throne of Chief Executive Officer, assuming that Jimmy Cayne ever decided stepped down. Warren always reminded me of Clark Kent, with his Buddy Holly-esque black framed glasses and dark hair that had probably looked pretty much the same in his fifties as it had in his second grade yearbook picture, with just a little more grey slipped in to add a level of distinguished maturity. And while he was, technically, reporting to Cayne, we all knew that Warren was both the brains and the brawn that conceived of and executed everything related to trading at Bear. He'd pretty much built the structured mortgage bond division. And we, the rank-and-file Senior Managing Directors on down, supported Warren in everything he did. I couldn't really see the firm going forward without Warren at least in the upper echelon of leadership roles, if not the absolute lead role. In my mind, Warren was—and still is—brilliant, talented and charismatic. In short, he's a rock star in the world of high finance.

And despite the fact that I think I knew it was going to happen on some deeper, subconscious level, it nevertheless came as a pretty sudden shock to my system, not to mention my vacation-induced inner peace, when I got a text message from a colleague in New York. Warren had been sacked. Hand over your ID, Mr. Spector, and this large gentleman in the security officer's uniform will escort you from the building. Rule number one on Wall Street: It doesn't matter where the fault lies, as long as you can deflect the blame to someone else. Make sure those fingers point away from you. Many of us in the trenches felt that Jimmy Cayne had sent Warren to the top of the volcano and thrown him in as a way of appeasing the angry financial gods who were calling for a blood sacrifice.

I was blown away by not only the suddenness of Warren's departure, but also by the larger fact that he was gone at all. Somehow, in the midst of trying to wrap my own mind around the fact that Warren wouldn't be running the show in future years, I felt the need to connect with someone who could relate, someone who could understand what it meant to have Warren Spector so suddenly gone from our lives. I phoned a colleague who was vacationing in the same area as I, and we spoke for quite a while about the situation in New York. We were both in shock, despite the fact that we had, underneath it all, both suspected it. It was the bad news you know is coming, but that still knocks your legs out from under you once it shows up and suddenly becomes your new reality. I told him about my wife's thoughts on the plane, and admitted that I'd allowed myself to believe her. But now I had come crashing back down to reality.

We were in full agreement that the blood-letting was not yet finished at Bear Stearns, not by a long shot, but we also both figured that we were safe for the time being, at least in terms of our own job security, as we were in the structured equities department, where we were having a great year riding on the back of the all the volatility in the various markets. Your greatest fear as a derivatives guy is that one day stability will break out. It was a comforting thought, if not necessarily one backed up with a lot of conviction on our parts. Most of all, though, we were very sure that the wrong person had been let go. Warren Spector had been a patsy for the Bear Stearns higher-ups who needed a fall-guy. But the villagers anxious to appease the violent temper of the avenging gods had sacrificed the wrong guy. And though the gods might have been quieted for the moment, they weren't about to allow the sins of the many to be paid for with the blood of a relative innocent. More sacrifices would be called for. And soon.

In retrospect, Warren was luckier than any of us could have realistically hoped to be. In his never faltering desire to find the silver lining in a cloud, he exercised his option to cash in his previously non-vested stock options. As he was no longer employed by the company, vesting of previously restricted stock ceased to be an issue. So he cashed in his options, 229, 855 shares, according to the *Wall Street Journal*. He sold them at a price approaching $100 a share. So as a result of his being fired, Warren was the beneficiary of a cash windfall to the tune of $22.9 million. If he'd stayed on at Bear and ridden out the storm, his shares would have been worth approximately $500,000 after all was said and done. The lesson to be learned here is that a gift may take many forms. It might even show up on your desk as a pink slip.

Meanwhile, with the reassignment of Rich Marin and the subsequent vacuum within the leadership role of the BSAM, Jeffery Lane was lured away from his vice chairmanship at Lehman Brothers Holdings to lead the now severely ailing department. His pedigree sounded impressive enough, what with his having been on Wall Street for forty years and having served as the CEO of Neuberger Berman, a pretty successful mutual fund company. So you can't blame the guy for wanting to make a positive impression during his first days on the job. And you can't blame him for his unbridled optimism. He assured investors and Bear employees alike, "We'll dig our way out and emerge stronger. None of us in this industry can get away unscathed forever. The great ones overcome the problems and move forward."

It remained to be seen if Bear Stearns was still one of "the great ones."

The realities associated with investing—and by that, I mean any sort of investing, but in the case of hedge funds, it's especially true—you're taking a risk. And you're willingly accepting that risk when you put your money down. I've never seen an investor complain that his investment made him too much money. So it boggles my mind to consider the seemingly benign ignorance so many people employ when they start investing.

They think that because they're turning their money over to some high-minded manager, that their money is safe. Oftentimes they don't research the fund as well as they should before sending in their money, and equally often they don't monitor the fund as closely as they should after they've invested.

As flawed as the strategies were that these two funds were employing—again, I'm relying on hindsight to say that—investors should have been paying more attention to where their millions were going. Regardless of the strategy, there was what we call an arb, as in arbitrage, here. What that means is that there was a system whereby the managers were purchasing and selling the same commodity in order to take advantage of price differences in different markets. The funds themselves were valued at about $1.6 billion in cash from investors. But they made investments that totaled in the $20 billion range.

Now, if they take that amount and lever it up ten or twelve times and then fund the margin loans at close to LIBOR, they're basically printing money for their investors. In this strategy, they're pulling in double-digit returns. It was, to use the mortgages themselves as a parallel, like buying a house. You buy a house for $200,000, but you only pay $40,000 up front. You finance the rest. Same thing here. In the case of the Bear funds, a hedge fund manager would buy highly-rated credit structures such as CDOs for about 100bps above LIBOR. Think of that as their mortgage on the "house" that is the CDO in question. The thing to realize there, though, is that the interest rate they were paying was 1% (100 bps) lower than the investments themselves were yielding.

As I've said, risk goes hand-in-hand with hedge funds, but what these investment managers ran the risk of, though, is the fact that if the equity they had invested in the underlying assets went south—even by just a few points—they were going to be in serious financial trouble. And if that equity went south by more than just a few points, like it ended up doing, then you're talking about complete and total losses. It's a pretty basic investment strategy, at its core. It's not rocket science, but despite its relatively simplistic nature, it can make you a lot of money. But it can also bite you square in the ass if you're not careful.

Go back to our $200,000 home. You've got your $40,000 worth of equity built in from your down payment. In today's housing market, let's say the value of your home has depreciated below $160,000. Suddenly your $40,000 equity has been wiped out. But fortunately for the home owner, there's no margin call on his mortgage. In other words, the bank isn't calling and requiring our homeowner to put $40,000 more into some escrow account to compensate for the drop in value. Investment funds, however, aren't so lucky. They're subject to margin calls, and when the value of their assets drops too low, those margins have to be made up with cash. And when those mortgage securities became so devalued, the managers were effectively dead in their tracks. But none of their investors, that I know of, called them on it. They trusted the managers, just like so many other investors do. The message here is that you should always keep an eye on your investments, no matter how large they might be or where the manager went to B-school.

As it turned out, on June 19, 2008, Matthew Tannin and Ralph Cioffi, the managers of the two ill-fated hedge funds, were taken into federal custody by agents from the FBI. While it is not a federal crime to make a stupid investment decision—or to suggest others make equally stupid investment decisions and then charge them a great deal of money for doing so—it is a crime to lie to your investors. According to reports, Cioffi allegedly transferred out $2 million of his own stake in the funds, all the while assuring investors that everything was going to be fine. All the while they were trading emails with one another, emails that said things like, "The subprime market looks pretty damn ugly," and, "I think we should close the funds now." It was the first pair of criminal charges brought against investors as a result of the meltdown in the subprime mortgage market, though speculators who predicted these sorts of things felt that it wouldn't be the last. And despite media reports to the contrary, the arrests were not the result of Bear's collapse. Rather, they were simply the result of two men lying to investors in regards to their hedge funds. It was, for me, another very sad footnote in the story of the demise of the firm I had loved.

▲ ▲ ▲

I returned to the office after my vacation in early August, reenergized by my time away, but still nervous about what the future held in store for me. Back in New York, the mood around the Bear Stearns office was akin to a funerary wake. My colleagues felt beleaguered after having been in the news day after day; it was, unfortunately, something they'd grow more accustomed to in the months ahead. We all walked around in a sort of daze, waiting for our fairy godmother to float down from the ceiling and fix all this, this mess, this financial wreck that had been wrought on us. Maybe she had some new-and-improved fairy dust that Rich Marin had been unable to get his hands on. It had truly gotten to the point where we were praying for some sort of divine intervention, some kind of *deus ex machina* to save us from ourselves. Whatever joy there once had been in the simple act of reading the day's newspapers had been stripped away by the act of reading the news itself. Bear was a joke in the press. More than that, Bear was an object of abject criticism by economic pundits who felt that our financial disaster was a by-product of our own making and was symptomatic of larger problems within the firm. Basically the sentiment expressed by so many economists seemed to be that we got exactly what we deserved.

As Bear employees, we were the objects of sidelong glances, discreet finger pointing, and contemptuous snickers when we went out for coffee or drinks after work. Despite the size of the Financial District—the FiDi is home to about 300,000 professionals on the average workday—everyone knows what firm you're with, basically because we all know somebody at all the other firms. And when you're seen in the company of some of the people we know from those other firms, you're associated with that firm. It's the corporate America version of six degrees of separation. And as a result, an area of 300,000 people within a city of 10 million residents becomes oppressively small when things are going poorly in your corner of the world.

And it wasn't just in social settings that we were getting crucified. The rest of the business world was treating us like some sort of population of infected and contagious lab rats, refusing to even acknowledge our existence on the financial front. We were the lepers of Wall Street, the ones who had hedge funds overseen by an investor-cum-film connoisseur and a COO who had been fired because he happened to find himself in the wrong place at the wrong time when the firm had needed a patsy.

But most of all, we had the stink of failure attached to us. On Wall Street, being a part of a financial meltdown of this magnitude is like getting sprayed point-blank by an angry skunk, and there's no amount of tomato juice on the planet to take that smell away. And even when you get rid of it, there's still the memory of it. And we're all familiar with the powerful role that smells play in memory recall. You just can't escape it. And once you've been sprayed by that skunk up close, you never forget what it smells like. But what's more, nobody who comes in contact with you ever forgets what it smells like, either. And Bear had gotten sprayed.

Badly. We were covered in the stench of failure, and nobody in the Financial District was going to forget it. There were not enough degrees of separation in the world to remove us from who we were.

But then, just like Warren's own pink slip had been a gift of sorts, Bear got itself an equally unlikely gift, namely the credit crisis that gripped Wall Street, the inevitable result of the same failure in mortgage-backed securities that had doomed our hedge funds and put us in this position in the first place.

The subprime mortgage avalanche that had killed our hedge funds caused banks to write down their own loans. In effect, that meant that the loans were notched as bad debts in the banks' ledgers, debts that would never be repaid. So the balance sheets reflected those write-downs as unrealized losses, meaning a reduction of the value of the position. By the autumn of 2007, an ironic season for a market fall, somewhere north of $200 billion dollars worth of loans had been written down by banks across the country. This brought on an industry-wide refusal by other lenders to give money quite as freely as they'd been doing in the past. Suddenly, most all investment banks were on equal footing because now everyone's business was staggering to a halt. Misery loves company, and there was plenty of misery to go around. Bear was no longer the leper of the Financial District. Or, if we were, at least we weren't the only leper on Wall Street. Water had sought its own level, and this particular flood of misery had made us all equals in the face of this credit collapse.

For the briefest of moments, we reveled in our newfound status as Wall Street equals in the halls of Bear Stearns. No longer were we targets of critical jokes. No more were we dodging phone calls from reporters anxious to further smear Bear blood across the front pages of the business section. We were able to hide in plain sight, the purloined letters of investment banking. We were used to this; it was the other guys who were suddenly feeling the heat for the first time.

And then the sun came up one morning, and Bear Stearns once again found itself on the front page of the *Wall Street Journal*.

It was November 1, 2007, a Thursday. I'd heard the stories before I actually read the paper that morning, but I still plopped down my buck-fifty at the newsstand on the corner just to see it for myself. And there he was. It was the same kind of pencil sketch the *Journal* has made part of its trademark, but the likeness was eerie and the face that was looking at me was unmistakable. It was our own CEO, James "Jimmy" Cayne. The oval glasses perched atop the prominent nose. The grey hair just formal enough to be professional, but yet seemingly mussed up enough to lend an air of hip credibility that told you he was in touch with society and the modern-day factors that influence the market. While the sketch artist had been kind in his rendering of the man, this was very much Jimmy Cayne looking back at me.

It was a well-known fact around the office that Jimmy is an excellent bridge player. And when I say excellent, I mean he's very good. Very, very good, in fact. World-class good. He's won the North American championships many times over, and he represented the United States at the Bermuda Bowl world championships in 1995. In fact, there are a lot of Bear employees who play bridge; it's one of the things that makes our corporate culture that much more unique. I myself am far from an expert at the game, but I have managed to teach myself to play by myself on the computer; those of us on the trading floor were generally too busy to play against real human beings. In essence, the strategy of the game hinges on a player's ability to correctly analyze his own hand to determine an optimum balance between the number of hands he expects to win and how many of each suit he expects to win. The suits of the cards themselves are ranked as major and minor strains, and thus add a level of complexity to the bidding.

In the bidding stage of the hand, players participate in a mind game of sorts, whereby they must determine the strength of their own hands, but also the relative strength or weakness of their opponents' hands. If a player bids too high and is unable to meet the minimum standards of his contract, he loses points. If he bids too low and meets his own contract with ease, he won't garner as many points as he could have had he bid a more appropriate, higher number. He has to guess exactly right, repeatedly, in order to be a player of the highest caliber. In other words, the exact qualities that go into making a world-class bridge player are the same ones that go into making a world-class investment banker.

And Jimmy had it all. The ability to read an opponent. The ability to objectively analyze his own strengths and weaknesses. The ability to correctly ascertain the ideal bids. He knew how to exploit others' weaknesses—and their strengths, for that matter—as a way to further his own gain. He knew when to take his losses and live to fight another day. And most importantly, once the fight was over and it was time to go home, Jimmy was able to remove himself from the battlefield, be it at the card table or on the trading floor. But the *Wall Street Journal* was taking issue not so much with his abilities as a card player as they were the timing of his bridge playing.

According to the article, Jimmy Cayne spent 10 of 21 working days during the month of July, 2007, out of the office. On many of those days in question, hc was in Nashville, Tennessee, at a bridge tournament. And he was apparently playing cards, completely engrossed in his game despite the crisis that he was well aware of which was playing out at his home office. People in the financial arena questioned whether a 73-year old was capable of really focusing on so many things—bridge tournaments, golf engagements, running a Fortune 500 corporation. He was compared to his counterparts at other firms, counterparts who had cancelled planned trips to beach houses or family time with kids while the summer's financial roller-coaster was having its ups and downs. And the comparisons were not flattering to Jimmy. But he remained stoic in the face of controversy. He didn't back down from his critics. He was good at his job, he was good at bridge, and he could manage the two of them easily enough. Or at least that's how his side of the story read.

At this point, there began to grow a groundswell of opinions being thrown around the office and trading floors. When I first read the *Wall Street Journal* article, I really felt it was a hatchet job. I said to my boss that it struck me as the first signs of the "Foxification" of the venerable paper that was being acquired by Rupert Murdoch. People around the office, though, began to openly voice their grumblings about the guy in the CEO's office. We felt like his time to go out on top had long passed him by, and now the best he could hope for would be to get out before his reputation was completely trashed. And now this. Our internal spin-doctors could have explained his lapse in judgment. They could have talked away the fact that our CEO had been playing cards while the rest of the world was wondering what his company was going to do in order to stem the tide of money flowing out the door. I mean, by this time, we had enough experience in explaining away problems that something as minor as a CEO playing in a bridge tournament was child's play. After all, the funds were dissolved, the lawsuits were pending, and it was all pretty much yesterday's news, regardless of when the *Journal* had chosen to run the story.

It was the drug use that was going to be a tough thing to explain away.

According to the story on the front page of the *Wall Street Journal* on Thursday, November 1, 2007, Jimmy Cayne, CEO of Bear Stearns, was more than an above-average golfer and a world-class bridge player. He was also a dope smoker. Apparently Jimmy's ability to leave the fighting on the battlefield when the day was done was facilitated, at least on occasion, by a liberal dose of self-medication with delta-9-tetrahydrocannabinol, otherwise known as THC, the active ingredient in marijuana. Alan Schwartz, who was to replace Jimmy as CEO soon after the story's publication, offered up an ironic comment about Jimmy's professional performance that would become quite the joke in Wall Street locker rooms: "Anyone who thinks Jimmy Cayne isn't fired up every day and ready to get to work hasn't been living in my world." Fired up indeed.

Despite the tabloid-nature of the story, the credibility of the *Journal* gave credence to the stories of Jimmy smoking weed after bridge games. Citing a specific incident at a DoubleTree Hotel men's room in Memphis with a female bridge player in which multiple witnesses reported seeing him "smoking a joint," Jimmy uttered a complete denial that the event had taken place. Asked in a more general context if he ever smoked pot on a regular basis, Jimmy replied that he would only respond to specific allegations. Hedging his bets to the very end. Personally, I did not care what he did or did not do in his free time, nor did I care with whom he did it. Not only was it none of my concern, the fact of the matter was that Jimmy had presided over what were arguable the most successful years in Bear's history. The firm was, in many ways, what Jimmy Cayne had made it into; he had shaped Bear Stearns in his own image. So it was hard for me to criticize him. But this was not the kind of additional hit our reputation needed to take right now.

The response to this latest assault within the Bear offices were, predictably enough, generally negative. Those private grumblings about Jimmy's being past his prime became conversations, and many of us found that we were in full agreement with one another in our feelings that it was time for Mr. Cayne to step down from his perch. Jimmy was no longer an asset to the company, despite his history with the firm and the strength of his financial brain. Jimmy had become an albatross chained to the necks of every Bear employee, from the lowest mailroom clerk all the way up to the office of Alan Schwartz. He had shot the bird for no reason, and now we were all being forced to deal with the ramifications of upsetting the cruel hand of fate. The mood in the office had changed; there had been a noticeable, palpable shift in people's feelings towards Jimmy Cayne and his longevity at the firm.

BEAR TRAP

2007 did not end well for most of the investment banks on Wall Street, with the possible exception of Goldman Sachs. Bear Stearns was not spared. The fixed-income engine at Bear had seized up with the credit crisis. The stock was down. There were frowns everywhere you looked in the office. The equity derivatives area had experienced a pretty good year, and I myself had experienced my best year to date. But at the macro level, in the big picture scheme of things, the firm had survived a horrible year, a year which had included the hedge fund debacle. And in the spirit of pay-for-performance that defines investment banking bonus structures, our top four officers—Jimmy Cayne, Ace Greenberg, Alan Schwartz and Sam Molinaro—all decided to forego their bonuses for 2007. They got nothing outside of their salaries, which is hard to argue with. Jimmy would be allowed to finish the year as CEO; but come January, he would be reassigned to the position non-executive chairman.

It was after the firm had dissolved and those of us still left in the office were awaiting our fates at the hands of our new owners, JPMorgan. Because our days now consisted of leisurely activities like eating breakfast in the 12th floor dining room instead of eating like traders at our desks, many of us at the Senior Managing Director level had a lot of time to talk. And with the collapse of the company, our talk oftentimes turned to subjects that we considered to be, at least in part, some of the direct causes of that collapse. Jimmy was one such subject.

One conversation we had about Jimmy involved an illness he was rumored to have had, an illness that had presented in the fall of 2007, and had been serious enough to warrant real concern from his family and friends. The word "fatal" had been mentioned in context of this rumored illness.

"You know, he could have died," one diner remarked.

"That's terrible," another replied. "If he had died, the firm might have survived."

CHAPTER FOUR

Truth Is What You Make It

"Rumor is not always wrong."
—PUBLIUS CORNELIUS TACITUS

On November 17, 1988, Neil Simon, one of Broadway's most prolific and best-loved playwrights, debuted *Rumors,* a story of four different couples who arrive at a dinner party to celebrate the anniversary of friends, only to find the friends themselves absent from the event. The would-be host is suffering the after-affects arising from a gunshot to the earlobe, and his wife, the would-be hostess, is missing. The ensuing action follows the innuendo and, at times, quite funny stories that the couples come up with in order to explain the situation. The final story, which is the version eventually told to the police by one of the party-goers, involves Hispanic servants with knives, a gun accidentally going off, and the hostess being inadvertently locked in the cellar after falling down the stairs and losing consciousness. This particularly ludicrous version of the story is concocted by a character who later admits that he was making it up as he went along, riffing like a good Jazz musician on a trumpet. The punch line, however comes at the end of the play, when there is a knock from inside the locked cellar door, and the voice of the missing wife calls out for help. In other words, the suggestion is that the ridiculously impossible explanation for the couples' situation is actually factual.

Oftentimes art and life imitate one another, and Simon's own play could have been based on the week beginning Monday, March 10, 2008. That was the day that rumors began to spread, eventually elevating themselves to the level of fact. In the end, those rumors became our new reality.

And though relating a tale from the end and working your way backwards is often considered bad form in storytelling, I do feel like it's oftentimes useful to look at a story such as this as if it were a map. A script, if you will. If we can look at where we ended up, it helps to explain, at least in part, how we got there in the first place starting from where we did. So, looking into the future, I see that on April 3, 2008, after the meltdown was complete and Bear was no longer alive in any recognizable form, Alan Schwartz was asked to testify before a Congressional subcommittee investigating the heretofore inconceivable scenario of a major investment bank going completely belly-up, especially in so short a span of time. He spoke intelligently and passionately about things like the subprime crisis and the ensuing credit crunch that had wracked Wall Street for several months. He went on to suggest that Bear had plenty of disposable capital to cover its leveraged equities, and that there were no liquidity issues within the firm. Yes, the subprime crisis had hit Bear hard, due in no small part to the fact that Bear was well-known as one of the most leveraged firms on the Street. Yes, the firm itself was now dead, its existence now folded into the arms of JPMorgan Chase. But no, distinguished gentlemen of the committee, it wasn't due to any fault of anyone at Bear that the firm withered away in a matter of days.

You want to know who to blame? You want to point a finger at the source of this destruction, distinguished gentlemen? If you ask Alan Schwartz—as well as many of us who worked for him—it's the members of the media who were among the culprits. In the world of twenty-four hour news networks airing stories seven days a week, the rumors were perpetuated and all of this false information and kept getting repeated by those news networks until they'd destroyed the firm. Simple as that? Not exactly, but it's a pretty good start.

Even though numbers are facts unwavering in the harsh light of reality, Schwartz basically said what so many of us felt. Rumors, he said, had caused the destruction of Bear Stearns. The firm had fallen victim to "the unprecedented speed at which rumors and speculation travel and echo through the modern financial media environment. The rumors and speculation became a self-fulfilling prophecy." And while it is easy to brush Schwartz to the side as something of a sympathetic parent trying to make excuses for his child's poor performance in the championship game that led to the team's loss, there is some truth to what he said. If we'd known on Monday what we knew just days later, I assure you that Bear executives would have taken on the rumors and publicly screamed bloody murder. This is not to say that the firm would have been salvaged, because I don't think that we could have stopped the momentum of this runaway freight train. Because we kept our silence, the rumors took on a life of their own, and once people started believing them, there was nothing we could do to stop the destruction. So the rumors were not wrong, simply because they claimed to be true. *Cogito ergo sum.* I think, therefore I am. The rumors, because of the very fact that they had been uttered, became truths. But those truths were nothing more than stupid, inconsequential rumors on that Monday morning.

In the months after "Bridge Gate," as some were referring to the publication of the story regarding Jimmy Cayne's card-playing and illicit drug use in the *Journal,* Alan Schwartz had risen to the position of CEO after Cayne's "retirement" from the position. Jimmy, adamant to the end, though, stayed on at Bear, in the position of non-executive chairman. That's the sort of thing they give you when you aren't the big winner on a game show; it's a "lovely parting gift" for the also-ran contestant. We were still reeling, to a degree, from the fallout from the hedge funds' collapse and the other black eyes we'd sustained through the course of the beginning of the year, but all signs within the firm pointed towards a full recovery.

Smiling portrait of Bear, Stearns & Co. CEO Alan Greenberg. *(Photo by Kimberly Butler/Time Life Pictures/Getty Images)*

Yes, the Friday before we'd been denied a loan, but none of us knew about it. And what's more, the firm had come up with it somehow, I don't know how, so the point was moot anyway. We had no liquidity crisis. Yes, we were leveraged to our eyeballs, but that's what you do in investment banking. Nothing ventured, nothing gained. You take risks and you get paid very well for doing so. According to our accountants, we had $11.1 billion in tangible equity. That's money in the bank, so to speak. Some economic critics, if you can call that a genre of professional journalism, pointed to the fact that we also had $395 billion in leveraged assets, which meant we had something like $35.50 leveraged for every dollar we actually had in our account. But again, this is Wall Street we're talking about. Leverage is part of the game. Worst case scenario, we had $17 billion in cash reserves. Regardless of what anyone might have thought, this was not the beginning of the hedge fund collapse of a few months before. We'd learned our lessons and our collective asses were covered well.

And what's more, we had our reputation.

On Wall Street, like on the playground when you're a kid, reputation is everything. You've got to fight to earn it, but once you earn it, it's yours to keep. We'd been around for 85 years and we we'd been through our battles. We'd gotten beaten up, we'd grown tough, and we'd survived. We weren't the biggest kid on the block, but we weren't getting kicked around by the playground bully, either. And we sure as hell were certainly big enough to take on the young punks that might try to challenge us. In the last year alone, we'd survived the hedge fund crises, plus the shake-up of our executive tree that had included the ousting of the man we all thought would one day assume control of the firm. This whole issue related to our bread-and-butter, which was bonds, and we knew what we were doing when it came to selling debts. We had earned the right to be where we were, and we'd earned the respect that we had from other banks. At least we thought we had respect.

The guys on the trading floor are a lot like millions of other Americans in many ways, not the least of which is how we get our news. We watch CNBC, too. We're full-fledged news junkies. We live and die by who said what to whom at what time. And what's more, we're into vocal inflection like you can't even believe. Guys will sit in front of a TV trying to analyze what the Fed chairman meant by "hello." Was that a tone of anger laced with bitterness, or was it optimism mixed with caution? The more literary amongst us sometimes resorted to their mental thesauruses in order to pick just the right word. Odd as it might sound, it's that sort of information that can determine where on the table you put your chips before they call for all bets in. So between the cable news channels and the Bloomberg machines, everybody on the trading floor was ingesting news like oxygen.

The liquidity rumors were everywhere. And the more these rumors popped up, the more phone calls I fielded from nervous counterparties. And the more phone calls I dealt with, the more I came to the sick realization that it was possible that these rumors were gradually becoming self-fulfilling. Cable news reports were spending increasing amounts of time speaking about the liquidity rumors, and that meant every television in America was suddenly a potential outlet for providing traction to these stories. It wouldn't be long, I knew, before these same rumors were all over the Internet. And then there would be no finger big enough to stick in the dike to plug the leaks. We'd be staring at an oncoming tsunami when that happened.

Alan Greenberg—"Ace" as he is widely known—went on CNBC himself to state on the record that the liquidity rumors were "totally ridiculous." Anybody who knew Ace would have put their own financial lives as well as those of their children in his hands without question. Ace was the heart and soul of Bear Stearns. He was the rasion d'être for a lot of us. So when Ace said they were ridiculous, I put my faith in the intelligence of our investors to trust our spiritual leader, assuring myself that these people were surely intelligent enough to see through this smoke screen that was coming from God only knew where. And why. That question continued to pick at me, even as I reassured myself it was nothing. Why would someone want to start this rumor about Bear? This was what my grandfather used to call "dirty pool." On Wall Street, you win by whatever means necessary, but we're not the cannibals that our reputations might suggest. You don't start telling lies about your competition when those lies could result in the complete dissolution of a firm.

But publicly-spoken words are odd things. They're far more powerful than anyone realizes. Pearl Strachan Hurd, a 1930's British politician, once likened the power of words to destroy to that of an atomic bomb, as she urged users to exercise caution with both. I think there is no arena on Earth where this axiom is proven more true than in the world of high finance. And no matter how big we might have thought ourselves or how strong our reputation, we couldn't fight against words.

Regardless of the source or the reasoning, the stories were spreading. At one point, I likened it to a snowball rolling down a hill, something out of a Charlie Brown cartoon. The snowball rolls down the hill, getting bigger, and eventually slams into one of the kids. All you see is feet and hands sticking out, as the snowball keeps on rolling down. Of course, the kid gets out of the snowball and brushes himself off, while those little squiggly lines above his head show us that he's dizzy from his trip. But he's fine in the end. In a way, that image helped me to keep everything in perspective during this frustrating insanity, because what it all boiled down to was that these were rumors, nothing more, something a child might find amusing if he could understand the situation. And while traders live and die by financial rumors—Did you hear that OPEC is going to cut production in half? And the guy who announced it had this tone that was a mix of euphoria and exasperation—when those rumors start to take over the day's business and affect your firm's daily existence, it's time to figure out how to stop them from propagating.

WASHINGTON, DC—April 03: James Dimon, chairman and CEO of JPMorgan Chase, and Alan Schwartz, president and CEO of Bear Stearns, defer to each other before responding to a question during the Senate Banking hearing on Bear Stearns and recent turmoil in the financial markets and efforts to address it. (Photo by Scott J. Ferrell/Congressional Quarterly/Getty Images)

TRUTH IS WHAT YOU MAKE IT

But there was nothing on anyone's radar screen to indicate that there was a problem. The level of frustration was unbelievable. If someone, anyone, could have just named something, anything, that could have caused this whole mess, I'd have accepted it. I would have accepted it because I could have refuted it. I could have come out swinging and fought against the untruths. But there was not a single person I could find who was able to even offer a made-up reason for what was happening. So we were trying to explain away things that technically didn't exist. And how did we know they didn't exist? Because they didn't. The circular logic wore on me as the day progressed.

I'm a firm believer in giving our clients accurate news, be it good, bad, or indifferent. Much like investment banks on Wall Street, investment bankers on Wall Street are also no better than the perception that people have of them, and I'd worked hard to establish my own reputation as someone who was always upfront and honest with our clients. So this growing wave of phone calls coming in asking about the latest liquidity crisis updates were unnerving, because I wanted to be sure I was fulfilling my self-imposed duty to my clients. In my mind, if I were providing information that was false, even without realizing it was false, I was betraying the trust put in me by the firm's clients. And I had to make sure, just to quiet that wee-little voice in the back of my head that said there might be some truth to these things. So I made my own inter-office calls to various departments. Finance assured me there was no basis to the rumors. Legal backed up their story. Every division I called said the same thing: Nobody had any idea what was going on or where these rumors were coming from. Questions shouted across the trading floor were met with confused looks, shaking of heads, shrugging of shoulders, and upturning of palms. Nobody had a clue, which is not like the trading floor, where the collective knowledge base usually covers every conceivable piece of public information. There was no fact to support any of these rumors, yet they kept coming. And that just intensified the confusion and frustration within the building, especially there on the trading floor. The whole ball of string was unraveling, and there was no way to stop it. But what was more unnerving was the fact that there was no discernible reason in the first place for the unraveling to be taking place. We were fighting an invisible enemy. In a way, it reminded me of my response to a friend in Johannesburg right after the initial attacks of September 11th. I told him, "We are at war. With whom, we do not know."

BEAR TRAP

Thank God for Ashley.

The *New York Times* that morning had carried the story of then-Governor Eliot Spitzer, "Client 9," and his *liasons dangereuses* with high-dollar call girl Ashley Dupre, whom he knew as Kristen. "Spitzer Is Linked to Prostitution Ring," announced the headlines. The writer led with Spitzer's investigation of Wall Street wrong-doings prior to his ascension to the governor's mansion in Albany. "I have acted in a way that violates my obligation to my family and violates my or any sense of right or wrong," declared the governor. A story that, while yellow journalism at its finest, was at least based in fact was there for everyone to read. And the fact that it was in the *Times* made it "real" journalism. But despite the facts—facts like Spitzer had been caught in a wiretap, facts like he was plopping down five grand an hour for this girl, facts like he was married with children, facts like he'd campaigned on the idea of cleaning up New York's morally-bankrupt areas—the rumor of a potential Bear Stearns liquidity issue, a rumor with no apparent basis in fact whatsoever, was deemed more newsworthy on cable networks that had grown too accustomed to sex scandals in the political arena. But an apology, complete with his attractive wife in tow, was another matter altogether.

By the middle of that Monday, Governor Spitzer had decided that it might be worth his while, not to mention his political future, to concede defeat in this little tête-à-tête and admit that he'd done the deed. Come clean and swear you'll never do it again. Americans love an apology from a fallen angel almost as much as they love the fall in the first place. So there was our beloved governor, live and in color on national television. The screen shot on one of the news networks' website showed Spitzer with a less-than-flattering expression on his face, his lips turned in as if he was in the initial stages of trying to completely ingest himself, and thereby hide from the army of reporters and cameras and microphones in front of him. His wife stood by his side, ripping a page from Hillary Clinton's playbook as the supportive spouse. But her expression belied the façade of forgiveness she might by trying to project. No, her face was that of a woman scorned. More than that. This was a woman who was pissed off, a woman who knew she would win every argument in her marriage from now until hell froze over and thawed out again.

And just to add insult to injury, the Bloomberg report included the fact that in 2004, Spitzer, then acting in the role of Attorney General, had gone after and successfully prosecuted what he called "a massive prostitution ring that operated in New York City, Long Island, Westchester and New Jersey." So this man who had risen to the top by playing the part of Messiah here to save New York from the vile ills of society that had plagued it for lo, these many years had apparently not only failed to prosecute at least one major prostitution ring in the city, he'd assisted in financing the operations in his own little way. At least there were no reports of illegal insider trading based on the activities of those houses of ill repute. At the close of business on Monday, the Bloomberg had returned Spitzer to his rightful place atop the day's news headlines. The Bear Stearns problems had been relegated to third place on the list of importance, which many of us took as a good sign. If the Bloomberg agency was putting less importance on our story, maybe the rumors would subside everywhere and we could all get back to work.

It's worth saying again. You just can't make this shit up.

But a little detective work showed that, despite the lower ranking we'd been given in the day's top news headlines, the Bloomberg agency was, in their own little way, already lining up the nails for our coffin, using the words of another hedge fund manager, Eric Sprott. Sprott Asset Management handled about $7 billion at the time, and its manager was predicting with eerie foresight Bear's future. Sprott saw the price of gold going as high as $2000 an ounce, which may have been somewhat optimistic on his part. But he also saw on the horizon "the collapse of a North American bank" as a very real possibility resulting from the global credit crunch brought on by the subprime mortgage collapse. He didn't specifically refer to Bear, but he clearly had some names in mind: "We're in a systemic financial meltdown. There are probably 10 companies that are broke that are still trading—banks and financial institutions," he was quoted as saying. He was shorting financial stocks, and making it public knowledge that he was doing so. I don't have any idea what premonition led him to say this; perhaps he was trying to facilitate the Bear collapse as a way of hedging his own bets. Whatever his reasons, though, the news was there on the screen, available for reading by anyone who cared to get that far into the article.

The fact that a hedge fund was shorting financials in general and, by implication, Bear stock specifically, wasn't any great shakes on the trading floor. Shorting a stock, as a reminder, is when an investor temporarily "borrows" shares at one price then sells them with the hopes of buying the same stock later at a lower price. When a major fund is shorting your stock, you look at it like a Mafia killing. It's nothing personal. It's just business. But what had happened to us on this Monday wasn't business. Somehow, a rumor about our liquid assets had started. A truly vicious rumor that had somehow blossomed like a wildfire out of control almost immediately, and ended up taking on a life of its own, growing and morphing and growing still more. No, this wasn't business. This was murder, for all intents and purposes, and any good Mafia Don knows that murder just for the sake of murder is wrong. It ceases to be business and becomes personal, and that's not the Mafia way. But I still couldn't point to the murderer, which made the whole situation very, very difficult to wrap my mind around.

The traffic heading uptown that Monday was heavier than usual, and the cab ride lasted for what seemed like an eternity. Uncomfortable situations tend to have a mystical way of slowing the passage of time, leaving you with far more time than you wanted or needed to contemplate the situation at hand. And an overabundance of time to think about a situation, when paired with the mind of a Wall Street trader, is a dangerous combination. We're trained from the outset to be analysts, first and foremost. In fact, a lot of us started out in the job of analysts during our nascent careers at various investment banks dotting the city.

Mind you, "analyst" as the term is used in investment banking parlance is as big a misnomer as you're going to find in the English language as a whole; *analyste commercial* is an equally large misnomer in French investment banking circles. While the translation of the word into this world of investment banking is nuanced by the specifics of the environment, "paid slave" comes pretty damn close. These poor kids—and that's what they are, barely out of college most of them—work 80 or 90 hours a week. They sleep at their desks when they're able to find enough time to actually shut their eyes for longer than a quicker-than-average blink. They spend their time at Bear or Morgan Stanley or Goldman Sachs or wherever else crunching numbers and doing research. They aren't allowed to have original thoughts or opinions, because those are luxuries reserved for people above them. And they're sure as hell not allowed to offer any kind of analysis, at least not to anybody that matters, because to do so would require that they have both original thoughts and opinions based on those thoughts. But they're analysts, by God. And as such, they get sucked into the business. Once in the inner sanctum, they're chewed up for a couple of years then spit out into the world of top-flight MBA programs, with promises of brighter futures that don't include words like "analyst" upon their return to the firm after they've gone and gotten the requisite education in the hallowed halls of Harvard or Yale or Stanford or, worst case scenario, Penn or Columbia or Dartmouth.

So with a career path that begins as an analyst, no matter how far from the truth that descriptor is, it's pretty well ingrained into your brain that you're supposed to analyze things. And you find that you're pretty good at it, too, especially when you've got time on your hands. Like when you're sitting in the backseat of a cab driven by a man with an unpronounceable

WASHINGTON, DC—April 03: James Dimon, chairman and CEO of JPMorgan Chase, during the Senate Banking hearing on Bear Stearns and recent turmoil in the financial markets and efforts to address it. The Fed in March engineered the acquisition of Bear Stearns by JPMorgan Chase & Co. at a bargain price of roughly $2 a share and averted a rapid unraveling of Bear's financial commitments to other major banks. *(Photo by Scott J. Ferrell/Congressional Quarterly/Getty Images)*

name who smells like incense and lamb gyros. Mimicking a scared turtle, you retreat into yourself to get away from the sights, the sounds, the smells. And in that sacred space, it's just you and your thoughts. And if you're a former analyst, that's a bad place to be alone. But that's precisely where I found myself on Monday evening as we wound our way through the crowded streets of midtown Manhattan.

The in-cab television in the back seat, thankfully, wasn't yet cued up with the rumors about Bear; they weren't even talking about Governor Spitzer. The tourist-friendly video loop featured benign stories about what was hot on Broadway—Patty LuPone was returning to the Great White Way in *Gypsy* at the end of the month—and something about an apartment in Chelsea for a million-six. Tourists love to hear about New York rents, something that has always escaped my understanding. It's like they're staring at the Lucite sides of a toy-store ant farm to see how the little worker ants actually live. They point and they gasp when they see how much we residents of the colony actually fork over for our domiciles. *Can you believe it's that expensive, Marge? Over a million dollars, and that's all you get! I couldn't live like that!* And that's in Chelsea, for God's sake. They didn't share with the visitors the Upper East Side prices, as nobody wants to see that kind of financial abuse.

Because I was not interested in the goings-on with the theatrical set nor with the unholy prices of real estate south of Hell's Kitchen, I muted the volume and sank back into the cracked vinyl seat. The driver had begun a conversation seemingly with himself, though after a moment's investigation I saw that he had a mobile phone earpiece wedged against the side of his head like some sort of atomic cockroach emitting a blue pulsating light. Calling on my superior Wall Street training, I tuned him out and focused solely on my analysis. If a hedge fund the size of Sprott's was potentially shorting Bear stock, there was something afoot. At least it made sense that there was, but how was anybody keeping this big of a deal a secret? Maybe that was the rub, actually. Maybe it wasn't a secret. Maybe these rumors were actually the truth. But if that was the case, then why did nobody within the firm know what the hell was going on? Or were they just not telling us, the traders, the whole story. And what's more, was there somebody there on the grassy knoll? The conspiracy theories were running laps around the inside of my skull.

Trying to make sense out of this whole mangled situation was enough to induce a migraine in my already overtaxed head. I knew I had to let it go, or I was going to lose my mind. I closed my eyes and let the world pass me by unseen. I was deathly afraid that these rumors, much like Neil Simon's comedy, would develop staying power. But then I laughed silently, my own private joke. We're Bear Stearns. We're smart people. This is going to be one of those things we all laugh about over glasses of wine some weekend. Neil Simon's play was a fictional story, just like the stories being told about Bear. What made the play such a success with audiences was that it was so outlandish, so far-fetched that it could never happen. The curtain fell, the lights came up, and the audience gave a standing ovation for the actors. The rumors had all been neatly tied-up and contained; the story had ended. And as soon as the sun came up tomorrow, this story created by baseless rumors about Bear Stearns would end, too. And just like that, I was home.

At the close of trading on Monday, Bear's stock price, which had closed on Friday, March 7, at a price of $70.08 per share, had dropped almost eight dollars to $62.30. This drop was a sign of what was to come, but I didn't realize it just yet.

CHAPTER FIVE

Circular Reasoning

"There was only one catch and that was Catch-22, which specified that a concern for one's own safety in the face of dangers that were real and immediate was the process of a rational mind. Orr was crazy and could be grounded. All he had to was ask; as soon as he did, he would no longer be crazy and would have to fly more missions. Orr would be crazy to fly more missions and sane if he didn't, but if he was sane he had to fly them. If he flew them he was crazy and didn't have to; but if he didn't want to he was sane and had to."

—CATCH-22

When Joseph Heller penned *Catch-22* in 1961, he probably had no idea that his little satirical take on the military was going to so firmly imbed itself as part of the American lexicon so quickly. In the novel, pilots are forced to fly bombing missions which are growing increasingly dangerous. If a pilot wants to be excused from combat duty on the grounds that he is insane, all he has to do is ask for the discharge. However, only a sane man would want to save his own life by asking for a discharge on the grounds that he is insane; on the other hand, a legitimately insane man would happily continue to fly those missions, as he wouldn't be afraid of dying. So by going through the proper steps and asking to be relieved from duty, the man is only proving that he is perfectly sane, and thus he must continue to fly the missions. Of course, anyone who actually wants to continue flying them is welcome to do so, regardless of level of sanity. That was the catch; since the novel's release, catch-22 has become part of standard American English, and means "any illogical or paradoxical problem." I remember the first time I read the novel. I was driven to near insanity myself by the convoluted linguistic structures Heller employed to create the protagonists' situations. But while it seemed confusing at first glance, the whole concept was actually brilliant in its simplicity. And it was also horrifyingly frustrating when you found yourself living through it, as I increasingly found myself in those days during the second week of March, 2008.

The front page of the *New York Times* on that Tuesday, March 11, was dominated by stories relating to Governor Spitzer's infidelities, thank God. As a way of balancing out the multiple angles from which the editorial board was examining Spitzer's sex life, the front page was also pocked with a couple of human interest pieces. Stephen Schwarzman, CEO of the Blackstone Group, had donated $100 million to the New York Public Library on Fifth Avenue. A roadside bomb in Iraq had taken the lives of five more American soldiers. Take the good with the bad. Yin and yang. Balance is the key to harmony, especially on the front page of the nation's most widely-read daily newspaper.

And there was a piece on that part of Wall Street that specializes in buying out troubled companies. "Buyout Industry Staggers Under Weight of Debt," the headline declared. In what would have been, in any other setting, a too-good-to-be-true shocking twist, the Blackstone Group—they of the $100 million donation elsewhere on page 1—were featured as one of the biggest losers on Wall Street as a result of the subprime mortgage crisis. But after the events of Monday, there was not a news story in the history of man that could have shocked me. Buried there in the heart of that same article was a mention of the Carlyle Group, described as "a highly leveraged firm," and their fight against insolvency. It was, for the guys at Carlyle, literally the fight for their very lives.

And if you weren't looking for it, you probably would have skimmed over it. But if you were a Bear employee and you knew your day was going to be a constant barrage of requests for information about the financial state of your firm—or if you were one of the investors who would be the source of those infinite requests—the words were huge and bold, like a pull-out quote in a four-color glossy: "Carlyle's troubles, along with rumors that Bear Stearns might be running short of cash, helped drive stocks lower. Bear Stearns denied the rumors." There it was, in black and white on the front page of the goddamn *New York Times*. Yes, it was couched with things like "might be" and "denied." But it was there and anybody that cared to pay attention wasn't going to see the side dishes. They were going to see the main course: "short of cash."

CIRCULAR REASONING

When I got to my seat on the trading floor, we were picking up right where we'd left off the day before; the rumor mill was still generating stories about Bear, and was doing so with great enthusiasm. And as much as I had steeled myself for that exact thing, I was still disappointed that we hadn't been able to move past it. As the morning progressed, however, the rumors started to become foundations for financial developments that had very real, very tangible, very frightening potential results. Chief amongst these developments was the widening of our credit default spread (CDS). In layman's terms, that means that the broader market was implying that the realistic chances for Bear's becoming completely insolvent were increasing significantly. People out there, people who were the market makers for this sort of thing, really believed that there was a chance Bear Stearns would go bankrupt. And in what is a sick reality of the financial world, they were actually creating the equivalent of betting lines on the outcome. As the hours passed, the odds of our going bankrupt got better and better, at least in the minds of the Wall Street bookies that were tracking the whole affair.

An investment bank is not totally unlike a sports team in that every participant in the action has an effect on the eventual outcome of things. And each situation that arises causes each individual player to react differently. Part of my daily routine involved the issuing of structured products, products that were issued from the Bear Stearns balance sheets. In other words, part of my day consisted of the sale of debt obligations that Bear Stearns was responsible for. So when I issue these products, I need to know what funding rate to imbed into them so as to make them financially viable for the firm, and yet still financially attractive as an investment opportunity. And what's more, in the event that these products come back to us, if we're approached by a client who wants to sell them, we're obligated to buy them back. We're not legally obligated, but we prided ourselves on making a market on everything we created in the structured equities group. Thus we had an ethical obligation to buy them back if our clients felt that it was not the right investment for their portfolios. So we needed to know at what rate to buy them back in order to avoid a financial loss for the firm.

These decisions aren't made in a vacuum. Far from it, in fact. We consult people in several different departments—as well as our colleagues in London—in order to determine the most appropriate buy-back rate. As a result of the increase in our default spread, the rate we had to put on our buy-backs went up. Way up. To put this in perspective, standard buy-back rates were, before this week, about 200 basis points over LIBOR (LIBOR plus 200 bps). By Tuesday, we weren't terribly concerned just yet, but we were also anxious to make sure we didn't do anything to facilitate the financial ruin of the company. But as our default spread continued to widen, the amount we were having to give up over LIBOR was increasing, too. We were up to LIBOR-plus-350 bps by the end of the day on Tuesday. In other words, we were having to guarantee our clients higher buy-back rates in order to get them to buy the notes in the first place. Not a good sign, but we were still optimistic that we'd turn the corner and get past this nonsense. Once we'd cleared up these rumors, we'd get back to business as usual. But the general public was getting spooked. That much was painfully evident to anyone with even the most casual of interests. We needed to focus our collective attentions and energies on turning that corner and turning it fast.

As a way of trying to help the firm accomplish that elusive maneuver, Sam Molinaro went on CNBC and told the American public to believe him when he said that everything was fine. He denied that there were any problems with the firm's accounts, that no margin calls were coming in, that we had plenty of operating capital. He went so far as to call the entire situation "nonsense," echoing Ace's labeling of the rumors as "ridiculous" the day before. When pressed for an explanation as to why these rumors were circulating and growing, our CFO looked incredulous. "If I knew why it was happening, I would do something to address it," he said with a definite air of self-assuredness. He was hoping against hope that this appearance would put an end to the crisis once and for all. Given the situation, it was the best course of action at the time, based on what we knew about the situation.

His appearance, in a complete and utter backlash that ran counter to any semblance of rational thought that I could muster, basically reinforced in peoples' minds that there was really something wrong, something more than just a rumor. After all, if Molinaro himself is willing to take time out of the day and go on television to deny these things, it must be serious. Such is the post-Enron debacle logic of the American public when it comes to financial officers in major companies. You admit it, you're guilty; you deny it, you're guilty; you say nothing, you're guilty. If they were just rumors, we'd ignore them. At least that was what the public's prevailing logic suggested. So we're only denying them because they're true. Because if they weren't true, we wouldn't be commenting on them and we'd just allow them to grow on their own. There's no way we could win here.

Catch-22.

Amidst all of this impossible-to-refute logic that was rapidly destroying our firm, I happened to notice a very clear spike, or high point, in the put market, a market that specializes in sales that are as close to gambling as you can really come on Wall Street. That spike meant that serious investors were betting money on the fact that the price of Bear stock was going to drop. To understand puts, it's essential to think of them as bets that can be purchased, much like any market product like stocks or bonds. If an investor feels that the share price of a given stock is going to go down, he may buy a put option as a way of profiting from the decline in price.

Think of puts as a kind of future sale, but a sale at a price that can be locked-in beforehand at what is called the strike price. But the puts don't last forever; they have an expiration date attached to them. This investor who buys a put is absolutely convinced that the share price is going to go down below a certain price within a certain time frame. If the price of the shares have fallen in value to the predetermined strike price by the expiration date of the put, the investor wins his bet.

A put entitles the buyer to sell shares of stock at the strike price, regardless of how low the shares go. So if he buys the put on a stock trading at $10 per share with the stipulation that the price at which the put can be sold is $8 within the next week, he's betting that the company's stock will drop at least two dollars a share or more, so as to recoup the initial outlay premium he paid to buy the option. Let's say that over the course of the next few days, the shares drop to $6. Our investor's put is said to be "in the money," and he now has the opportunity to sell his shares back to the person who sold him the put at the exercise price of $8 (two points higher than it's currently selling), plus he can buy more shares at the existing $6 price if he expects the price to go back up. The put with the higher strike price is called an "In the Money" put, or an ITM put.

Another kind of put is an "Out of the Money" put, or an OTM put. I'm going to go back to the $10 a share stock to illustrate the difference. If you bought the put at $8 and then the stock hit $6 a share, you were "in the money" because the share price was sitting below the strike price (the $8 target on the put you bought). However, if you were thinking that the stock was going to absolutely go through the floor, you might buy a put that would only pay if the stock sank down to $3 a share. When the stock was selling for $10, that $3 put would be an OTM put because it is such a long shot to think the stock will sink that low. For that reason, OTM puts are far cheaper contracts to purchase than are ITM puts.

An OTM put does convert to an ITM put if and when the stock price drops below the strike price. So in other words, if I look at a stock that's trading at $10 a share and figure there's no way it's going to hold that value, I'll consider buying a put. The closer the strike price gets to $10, the more expensive the put, simply because it becomes more likely that that put will end up in the money due to simple market fluctuations. So I'm looking at that stock and saying there's no way it's worth more than a buck-fifty a share, and some day soon, everybody is going to wake up to that fact. So I might buy a put with a spike price of $3. Because that $3 target is so far from the current share price—you're talking about a 70% drop in value for the share to hit the spike—it's an OTM put that I can have for very, very little money. So I buy the contract. Now I wait. It's kind of like fishing at this point, because I've got to wait for that nibble. If I bet it right, then the stock's price will drop way down there. I got a bar-

WASHINGTON—MARCH 23: Erin Burnett (C), anchor of CNBC's *Street Signs,* speaks as Maria Bartiromo (L), anchor of CNBC's *Closing Bell with Maria Bartiromo,* and moderator Tim Russert (R) look on during a taping of *Meet the Press* at the NBC studios March 23, 2008 in Washington, DC. Bartiromo and Burnett discussed the collapse of Bear Stearns and its impact to the economy. *(Photo by Alex Wong/Getty Images for Meet the Press)*

gain on the put because it was so far out of the money. But then I wake up one morning and discover that the stock price has bottomed out at fifty cents a share, and my put is all of a sudden in the money. I sell the shares at my three dollar spike price and pat myself on the back for being such a brilliant speculator.

Puts gained a lot of public notoriety within the general populace in the days immediately after the September 11th attacks. With the chaotic aftermath of the attacks, the American economy was thrown into a huge tailspin. This is why President Bush told us all that spending was our patriotic duty, which became the reason for the evil ARM loans that killed our hedge funds. And what drove the economy downward? In part, it was the plunging value of the New York Stock Exchange. But what really interested investors, not to mention federal regulators, was the seemingly huge number of puts that had been purchased on specific companies: airlines that were directly affected by the attacks (American and United); reinsurance companies that were forced to pay billions in claims resulting from the attacks (Munich Re and AXA Group); and financial services companies that were directly affected by the attacks (Merrill Lynch and Morgan Stanley). And though the market shut down for several days following the tragedies, it reopened on Monday, September 17.

In hindsight, so obviously out-of-place were these puts that many argued after the fact that the government—or at least investors on Wall Street—should have seen it coming. Just like so many other disasters. We should have seen it coming. Interestingly enough, the Department of Defense thought that, in hindsight, so obvious were the signs that the United States was soon to be the victim of an attack that they sought to create a futures trading market based on the potential for terrorist attacks or other political events. The idea sprung from the Defense Advanced Research Projects Agency (DARPA), and was soon to become a public relations nightmare for the Pentagon. The idea wouldn't go away that easily, though. Intrade, an online futures trading site, allows traders to buy and sell positions related to terrorist attacks, presidential elections, pending legal decisions, even scientific experiments.

When the market reopened on that Monday, it was a day full of fear for investors. And a day full of amazing clairvoyance on the part of some nameless, faceless investors who had bet heavily on the decline of specific investments. And while it is strictly speculation, the coincidences involved in the particular investments screamed of insider trading. In other words, somebody knew something was going to happen, and they were dead set on profiting from it.

The targets of so much speculation were organizations with ties to al Qaeda, the terrorist network responsible for the attacks. The theory about the suspicious puts goes as follows: In the case of the airlines, the attackers could not have foreseen that the entire industry would be shut down. If they had, perhaps the put purchases would have been even heavier across the industry. However, they could accurately predict that the airlines whose planes were hijacked would experience some financial repercussions that would result in their stock prices' going down. Less than a week before the attacks, on September 6 and 7, there were 4,744 put options purchased for United Airlines stock. On September 10, there were 4,516 put options purchased for American Airlines stock. According to Bloomberg, those numbers were approximately 285 times the daily average. The day the market reopened after the attacks, United's stock, which began the trading day at $30.82, fell 42% to end the day at $17.50 per share. American Airlines didn't fare any better. Their stock dropped 39% over the course of the trading day, from an opening price of $29.70 a share to $18.00.

Regarding the reinsurance agencies, these companies are insurance companies for insurance companies. If a building—perhaps a skyscraper like one of the Twin Towers—were to collapse completely, the insurance company responsible for the building would be hit with a huge financial settlement. Because the potential losses for these firms was going to be directly tied to things like the collapse of the World Trade Center and other damage, the attackers would have had a pretty good idea that firms like Munich Re and the AXA Group would be on the hook for megabucks. And they were right. Estimates put total losses for the firms at $1.5 billion for Munich Re and $550 million for the AXA Group. On September 7, four days prior to the attacks, put purchases for these two specific companies came in at twice their normal daily average. By September 12, Munich Re, which trades on the Frankfurt Exchange in Germany (which was open on September 12, unlike its New York counterpart), had lost approximately 30% its value, plummeting from a high of 272 Euros on the 11th to a low of 197 Euros on the 12th. In New York, AXA Group had fallen to a low of $15.50 a share by September 21, down over $10 from its high of $26.59 at the beginning of the month.

One other industry that was potentially going to be negatively affected by the attacks was the financial sector. Morgan Stanley had offices in the

North Tower of the World Trade Center, and Merrill Lynch had headquarters nearby. Purchases of puts on Morgan Stanley totaled 2,157 from September 7-10. That is an average of 319 puts bought each day. Before September 6, the average number of puts purchased daily on Morgan Stanley stock was 27. Assuming the North Tower collapsed, the trader using his insider's knowledge would be able to guess that Morgan Stanley stock would drop substantially. It did, falling 13% from $40.59 to $35.28. Merrill also saw put orders skyrocket in the days leading up to the attacks. Before the 5th of September, 252 puts were purchased on Merrill Lynch in an average trading day. During the period of time from September 6 to September 10, there were 12,215 puts purchased on Merrill stock, an average of approximately 3,053 purchases per day. Merrill's stock slid 11.5% on the day the market reopened, dropping five dollars a share in that first day of trading.

Of course, the September 11th attacks are never really far from your mind when you live in New York, but I wasn't dwelling on the tragedies as I looked at the put market reports on my Bloomberg. Today, March 11, 2008, saw an exponentially higher-than-normal level of purchases of Bear Stearns puts, specifically puts with an expiration date of March 20 and a strike price of $30 a share. Nearly 60,000 contracts were purchased that day, with each contract for 100 shares of Bear stock. So there was a huge number of investors who were betting on the fact that our stock would be worth less than $30 a share within ten days, which would mean that the stock price itself would drop over 50% in that timeframe. A lot of people were betting a lot of money that the firm's financial future was worse than grim. We were headed for bankruptcy—or at least the very edge of that financial abyss—if these people guessed right. And judging by their puts—as indicated by those expiration dates of March 20—they thought the end for Bear was not only in sight, it was going to come very soon.

The frantic activity surrounding Bear stock within the puts market smelled like a rat to me. For this many people to be this confident, there had to be some kind of insider information. Or, even worse, some sort of rumor mongering going on. This was the same sort of activity that people noticed just before the September 11th attacks. And while I don't want to try to compare our loss to that horrific event, from an investment standpoint, the same sort of flashing red lights were going off. And given what I knew about the pre-attack put investments, it made me a little nervous that someone out there knew something we didn't. In much the same way that some people felt the United States should have realized these odd bets at the beginning of September 2001 were a warning sign of an impending attack, so, too, was I afraid that this put activity was the sign of an impending attack. But I wasn't worried about terrorists attacking the United States. I was worried about somebody attacking Bear Stearns.

In all fairness, another aspect of this activity could also have been based partly on Bear's creditors' seeking to hedge against a catastrophic failure on the part of Bear Stearns, which would have resulted in our defaulting on our repayment obligations to those creditors. The markets were moving very fast, and Bear's CDS was spiking up. By buying deep OTM puts—or puts that were way out of the money—our creditors could have helped to protect themselves, at least in part, from massive losses that would arise from a default situation.

As the activities continued and more and more puts were purchased, it occurred to me that there might be someone conspiring to play a big, fat joke on the boys at Bear. It was possible that all of this activity—the rumors, the puts, all of it—was designed to allow some prudent investor out there to make an absolute killing on the deep OTM puts. My feeling was that if these people—whoever they were—were buying puts that were OTM puts with incredibly low strikes, they could be the source of these rumors. They would have the most immediately visible motive for driving our stock price lower and lower. If they'd bought puts that were low enough, they could have gotten them for next to nothing. But if they could somehow manipulate the stock price way down, they'd make more money than they could count in a day. I realized, on some level, that this was more of the ridiculous conspiracy theories I'd been turning over in my head the night before, but at least it was something logical, something that fit into the models of economic theory. It made sense, in a twisted kind of way, especially in light of the fact that this entire situation had been perpetuated by rumors from the start. The rumors had become truth, and the truth was bringing down the firm. And, just like the day before, there was nothing any of us could do today that seemed like it was going to be able to stop this hellacious march towards the financial destruction of Bear Stearns.

While I was contemplating the bizarre scenario I'd concocted whereby Bear had somehow fallen victim to some kind of Wall Street scam artist who was waging a rumor attack designed to destroy the firm, Richard Bove, an analyst at Punk Ziegel, a small investment and research firm, made his declaration that the Bear business model was "not working" and that the firm would have to merge with a major partner in order to improve liquidity.

At the risk of overplaying the easy joke here, a punk is, according to my dictionary, "someone worthless or unimportant," and while I don't want to sound like sour grapes by resorting to juvenile name calling, Bove's comments about both our business model and our supposed liquidity issues did nothing but fuel the fire that was already burning, despite the fact that we couldn't explain what had started it any better than Bove could have. Some of us on the trading floor had a few choice names for Mr. Bove, and all of them were less-than-flattering at the time. The problem we were facing now, though, was that the rumors had created an entirely new reality in which we were forced to exist.

In that reality, Richard was right. Our business model was clearly not working at all, and the fire was burning out of control as money flew out the door. In other words, we started having actual liquidity issues rather than just the imaginary ones. We had liquidity problems that had been born of rumors. There suddenly appeared in my mind's eye an image of Richard Bove standing outside the Bear Stearns offices, holding a large torch. It makes sense, I suppose, given that the tertiary definition that my dictionary provides for the word punk is "dry, decayed wood that can be used as tender." Bove was helping to torch the place, no doubt about it.

It was welcome news, then, when Joe Lewis decided to say out loud and to everyone that would listen that he might be interested in adding to his already huge stake in Bear Stearns stock, which was estimated to be somewhere in the neighborhood of $870 million, making him the largest shareholder in the company. It was huge for us at the time, because Lewis was notoriously private about everything. The man was a gazillionaire, lived somewhere in the Bahamas and absolutely refused to do public interviews. He was like the Bobby Fischer of the investment world. And when somebody as mysterious as Joe Lewis announces something like that, average Americans put their ears to the ground and start listening to what he's saying. They don't care if he's telling them to buy an Edsel and fill it with cases of Billy Beer. He's an eccentric guy, reclusive. Like Obi-Wan Kenobi. So he must know something. At least that seems to be the theory for a lot of people out there. Call it the *Star Wars* effect.

There's something about eccentric, fiercely private people that makes them look like they're the second coming of the investing version of Jesus Christ from the perspective of the average American, and for the life of me,

I can't figure out what it is. My respect for Joe Lewis had nothing to do with where he lived or how high the walls around his house were or how often he was spotted in public. I just thought he'd made some incredibly smart financial moves over the course of his career, and the numbers bore that out. I respected him for his investing talents. So when Joe said he might add to his holdings, I perked up. The pessimist in me had to laugh at an old investor joke: *Hey, if you liked us at 100, you're going to LOVE us at 50!*

But then the optimist in me took over, if only for a few seconds. Perhaps Lewis was looking at this as a buying opportunity. The stock he'd put so much faith in was doing poorly, but that didn't mean we were done for. Many investment advisors will tell their IRA clients that it's imperative to contribute the same amount to your IRA monthly, regardless of what the market is doing. By doing that, the investor is able to take advantage of both good financial times and bad. Maybe Joe was just employing that same good old-fashioned long-term investor strategy. Or maybe it was just possible that Lewis was playing God for a day, speaking into existence an entirely new truth, an entirely new reality. One that declared Bear Stearns to be the financially viable institution that we knew it was in order to counteract the false rumors that had battered us so much and battered our stock price, to boot. In the end, our stock closed up 67 cents higher at the end of the trading day. I breathed a momentary sigh of relief. Maybe it had worked. Maybe Lewis's own optimism in Bear's future had stemmed the tide and we were going to make it after all. Maybe, finally, we'd turned the corner once and for all, and our firm had been saved by our *deus ex machina*.

Or perhaps it was more appropriate to refer to him as the *deus ex Bahamas.*

But Joe Lewis, our temporary savior who had magically appeared from a beach somewhere in the Caribbean to swoop down and announce his public support for Bear Stearns, was just like the firm itself insofar as the public perception was concerned. If he said something positive, it was only because he wanted to ensure that his own interests—namely his huge stake in the company's stock—didn't tank, so by saying something, he was trying to reassure the investors and quiet the ever-growing financial panic that was surrounding us. He certainly couldn't have actually believed what he was saying; that was just ludicrous to consider. Because if it were actually true and there was no reason to question Bear's financial state, then there wouldn't be any panic in the first place, and thus no reason for him to have said it in the first place.

Catch-22.

CHAPTER SIX

No News Is Good News

"For most folks, no news is good news.
For the press, good news is not news."

—GLORIA BORGER

Colleagues of mine ask me why I insist on a morning run of a few miles, especially given the fact that I'm always in the office by 7:30 in the morning every day of the week. They can't figure out how I find the energy to pull myself out of bed early enough to do it all. I always answer the same way: I tell them that it's a necessity for my daily existence. Running relaxes me and allows my mind to drift over all sorts of things going on in my life, even sometimes giving me the ability to figure a solution to some pressing issue regarding a derivative structure or a trade. And today, Wednesday, March 12, 2008 was no different. I was out for a jog that had started at 5:30 that morning. Because of my home's proximity to Central Park, my usual loop included a jaunt through the pastoral serenity of New York City's largest public open space. As I was headed for home that morning, I noticed a slight pain in my lower stomach. As I crossed Museum Mile, it was all I could do to keep myself upright. The pain, I was pretty sure, felt like what those with a burst appendix must feel right before they die. It was excruciating pain, centered on the lower-right quadrant of my abdomen. For the first time in I don't know how many years of running, I was forced to stop in order to regain my stamina. It was humiliating.

I'm sure the pain—both the pain of the cramp and the pain of being forced to stop—showed in every outward element of my being. My posture was that of a beaten man, hunched over trying to regain my ability to stand upright. My breathing was labored. Sweat was pouring out of my skin. And though I am not a vain person by nature, I was ashamed of myself for not being able to go further and I was ashamed of the figure I cast standing there hunched over as if I were vomiting on the corner. I was only a few blocks from my home; I should have been able to at least muster enough strength to go that far. This city isn't for the weak or the timid. Only the strong survive, and only the strongest of the strong survive working for top-flight investment banks. But this, this picture of utter defeat, was the kind of thing we told jokes about on the trading floor. This was pathetic. I managed to pull myself together enough so that I could limp a few more blocks.

The pain was still there, though; my stomach felt like a wet towel being wrapped around itself by invisible hands bent on ringing out the last remaining drops of moisture. The light at 80th and Lexington was red, which gave me a legitimate excuse to stop again. Almost legitimate, anyway. Red lights in Manhattan are a suggestion, not an actual legal command. And if there's no traffic coming, they're not even a suggestion. They're just decorative at that point. There was no traffic coming in either direction, but I stayed where I was for the moment, because there were, to the best of my knowledge, no other pedestrians in the immediate area who would see me, either.

As I stood there wallowing in my own shame, I turned over in my mind what it was that had brought on this fierce cramping. Nothing I'd done before my jog this morning was out of my normal routine. I'd stretched sufficiently, following the same regimen I always do. I'd drunk two full glasses of water, just like I always do. So I was limber and I was hydrated. There was no reason for this amateurish performance. Yet there had to be. There had to be a reason to explain why, after two decades of running, I was falling victim to a cramp, of all things, on a normal morning jog. I began the mental argument with myself, back-and-forth, as the light changed and I began to unconsciously walk—the shame!—across the street. The argument continued all the way across Lexington Avenue.

And then it dawned on me.

My morning routine, the one I so vehemently defended against my colleagues' suggestions that I was an "anal retentive geek," was based on the premise that it was my time away from the world, away from the news, away from the problems. Away from news stories like the one about the company for which I worked teetering on the edge of complete dissolution. I'd seen this morning's *Times* on a newsstand as I began my jog, and the headline had screamed at me: "Fed Offers Wall St. Banks New Loans To Ease Crisis." I didn't stop to read the article; I didn't feel like I needed to. It had been announced yesterday that the Federal Reserve Bank was going to be allowing investment banks to borrow money against CDOs, like the subprime mortgage bonds that had gotten us into this mess in the first place. So the Fed was in effect saying to investment banks, "It's okay that you've taken on debts with collateral that is now effectively worthless. Because we're going to give you money on that now-worthless collateralized debt." So the government was going to do nothing but continue this cycle of throwing good money after bad.

The news had scared me yesterday and it had really screwed up my entire night. My sleep patterns were thrown off as I ruminated in my head about the fallout from this decision. When I woke up, though, I'd managed to purge it from my conscious mind. Until I saw that headline again, and I was right back in the thick of it again. My run—usually my refuge from things like newspaper headlines detailing worrisome news—had been completely devoted to thinking about this new development, and those constantly reappearing thoughts had interrupted my normally steady breathing pattern. In the end, that is what had led to my cramps. As I crossed 3rd Avenue, I'd given up trying to resume jogging and resigned myself to walking. It gave me more time to think, anyway.

Average investors had rejoiced in the news that the Fed was taking this relatively unprecedented step. It was, they figured, an end to the mortgage bond crisis. If the Fed was confident that the mortgage bonds were worth something as collateral, then surely the bonds were going to make a come back. The Fed wasn't run by idiots any more than hedge funds were. These guys were smart enough to know that loaning money on worthless collateral was a bad move, so they must have seen something in the market that told them that mortgage bonds would be rebounding. The Dow Jones had closed up over 400 points the day before in response to this news. And on the surface, it all made sense. The Fed was offering cash—cold, hard cash—to investment banks in exchange for these mortgage bonds that had become cement blocks chained around us as we tried to swim to freedom. So naturally the market at large responded positively. The bond market, however, is not the market at large.

In that same *New York Times* article, which I did end up reading back at my apartment, Lou Crandell, an economist with Wrightson ICAP, said that the Fed was "creating a $300 billion bank out of nothing." And that's what scared me. If these bonds were as worthless as a lot of people seemed to think, then how was the Fed going to be able to use them to replace this $300 million? The whole scheme was rife with the potential to send inflation soaring and to possibly start the next Great Depression. The Fed, of course, said they were doing all they could to "minimize risk by accepting only securities that still had the highest triple-A ratings," which I found comical. The bond market as a whole met this whole announcement with nothing more than a big yawn in terms of prices, which indicated to me that other bond traders were nervous about it, too. But like a good northeastern WASP family, we bond traders didn't share our concerns with one another. If we didn't talk about it, maybe it didn't really exist.

These thoughts that had effectively ruined my morning run had stuck with me as I showered, dressed, ate breakfast and departed for work. As I left my apartment that morning, the pain had shifted from a debilitating cramp to more of a growing fear planted deep inside my body. In the back of the cab riding to my office, I focused my attention on the *Times,* hoping there was something there that was going to get me over this worry that was still gnawing at my stomach. One good thing about the variety of newspapers available at the typical New York newsstand is that you can almost always count on at least one of them to provide you with some ridiculous cause de célèbre to get behind as a way of distracting you from your daily troubles. Author Jay McInenerney had given his protagonist Jamie Conway the infamous Coma Baby in *Bright Lights, Big City.* Sherman McCoy's own legal troubles that were splashed across tabloids captivated almost the entire city of New York in Tom Wolfe's *The Bonfire of the Vanities.* Unfortunately, I had no such luxuries as fictional characters to distract from my reality; this was all too real, thank you very much.

Fortunately enough for me, though, in my realm of the real, I had Eliot Spitzer. His hanky-panky had, since the news broke, served as a welcome respite from the reality of Bear's financial troubles, and the story itself had become a guilty pleasure of mine. Today's headline—front page, of course—created quite the interesting mental image: "Spitzer Wrestles Over Response, Paralyzing Albany."

In my mind's eye, I saw our fearless governor as he entered the squared circle, staring menacingly at his opponent. Spitzer wore a mask with some sort of sequined flame appliquéd on the sides. It covered his entire head, lacing tightly in the back, and had two eye holes and an oval where his mouth was. Even his nose was covered, lest the governor's proboscis should offer enough evidence to identify his otherwise disguised visage. His opponent today was a pair of renowned competitors, Response and Albany, the former represented by the governor's young lady friend and the latter by the ever-loyal Mrs. Spitzer. As this masked horror entered the wrestling ring, though, Response began to literally shake in her boots, terrified by the very prospect of tangling with the enraged governor. So scared was she in fact that she wanted no part of Spitzer. She turned to her partner, Albany, hoping for support. Albany, however, was paralyzed with fear.

I was jolted back to reality by the cab driver asking for his fare. I fished a twenty out of my wallet and waited while he made change. As he counted out the bills—I swear to God that some of these guys make change at a snail's pace because they think you're going to get tired of waiting for your change and just give it to them—I thought about my brief mental exercise of lampooning Governor Spitzer. In truth, it was not a laughing matter. The state was, in effect, at a stand-still while we awaited word that he would be resigning his post as governor. His eventual exodus was an

WASHINGTON—MARCH 17: U.S. President George W. Bush (2nd R) meets with Securities and Exchange Commission Chairman Christopher Cox (L), Treasury Secretary Henry Paulson (2nd L) and Federal Reserve Chairman Ben Bernanke in the Roosevelt Room of the White House March 17, 2008 in Washington, DC. The sale of Bear Stearns Co. to JP Morgan Chase for two dollars a share and the uncertainty in the U.S. credit market, sent many foreign markets down and left the Dow Jones index with mixed results in trading today. *(Photo by Martin H. Simon-Pool/Getty Images)*

inevitability; it was just a matter of time. Of course, there were a lot of people saying that same thing about Bear Stearns. At this point, it was almost a race to see who would disappear first.

Because it was the beginning of the third day of what we were now pretty sure should be labeled a financial crisis, I felt that today was basically our make-or-break day. Once is a mistake, twice is a coincidence. Three times, though, and it's a habit. My grandmother used to say that about people's lying; I had adopted her words of wisdom for my own causes in this situation. I figured one day, Monday, had been an anomaly. The second day, Tuesday, had been a coincidence. If the rumors were still around today, which would be the "habit" day in my grandmother's lingo, I might be looking for a new job by the weekend. The tension on the trading floor that morning was palpable. Alan Schwartz was taking time out from a major media conference in Palm Beach, Florida, to go on CNBC to try once again to dispel the rumors, to calm investors, to reassure Wall Street. In short, he was going on television to save Bear Stearns. He was in Florida doing what he does best, namely acting as our *über*-banker, and he was an important part of the media investment banking business. Unfortunately, the network went out of its way to emphasize the fact that he was in Palm Beach as opposed to New York, without offering the benefit of an explanation. Many of us in the office were concerned about the appearance of last summer's redux of management being away during a time of crisis. This negative media coverage was yet another blow to our reputation.

David Faber, the CNBC host interviewing Alan, cut right to the chase. There was, he said, concern about "counterparty risk." He actually used his hands to make air quotes as he said the words. Counterparty risk is simply the risk that the "other side" of the deal—if you're the buyer in a transaction, then the counterparty is the seller, for example—won't make good on their end of the bargain. A lot of people refer to counterparty risk as "default risk." Faber said that there were stories he'd heard from what he called "reliable sources" that firms were refusing to put on new counterparty risk related to Bear. So Faber asked about rumors—there was that ugly word again—regarding Goldman's refusal to take Bear on as a counterparty.

The trading floor, at that exact moment, went quiet as a tomb. We all looked around, searching for that face that would say we'd misheard. None appeared in my line of sight. In the space of a few seconds, I went through a range of emotions, from absolute disbelief to anger. I ended up being very confused, as a television reporter had just said that Goldman Sachs was refusing to do business with us. I searched my brain for the appropriate response, the perfect words to encapsulate what was happening. I have advanced degrees in management, so perhaps my business lexicon is better than my everyday vocabulary. Whatever the reason, the only response I could muster was an obscenity.

"Oh fuck," I muttered.

On the television screen, Alan managed to bob and weave like a champion. He ducked the specific question and talked about how the volatility in the market was causing "pressure administratively on getting some trades settled out." He repeated the fact that our liquidity was strong, our balances hadn't changed, we still had billions in the bank. He was very, very sure to say that he was not aware that there was any firm who was "not taking our credit as a counterparty." He made that point crystal clear.

Alan was asked about the source of the rumors that had refused to die over the course of the week, and he claimed ignorance. This was nothing new. And it wasn't helpful. If the CEO of Bear Stearns was unable to explain why we were going bankrupt, then perhaps we had problems that were far bigger than any of had dared to fear. Without going so far as to say that the rumors were "nonsense" or "ridiculous," as those descriptors had been previously employed and managed to only worsen the situation, Schwartz just repeated the fact that our liquidity was strong, we had capital reserves, we were not out of money, there was no need to panic.

The spot featuring Alan lasted for three minutes and nineteen seconds. When it began, David Faber quoted our stock price as being up a point-and-a-half. Three minutes and nineteen seconds later, the price was "down," according to Faber, from its morning opening price. He didn't elaborate. Those of us watching from inside the Bear office were glad he didn't. We were all in too much of a state of shock to take any more negative news. Goldman was refusing to take on more counterparty risk from Bear? A million questions flooded my brain. The mind was willing, but the body wasn't able. I sat in my chair, numb.

Alan had assumed that his appearance on CNBC that morning was going to calm the situation. In retrospect, it seems almost childishly naïve to think, despite all that had happened, all the other attempts to stem the tide that had fallen flat, that he could say whatever the magic word was, whatever it was going to take to get this thing turned around. But Alan did his best. The results, however, were the opposite of what we'd all hoped for.

From my vantage point on the trading floor, I was able to gauge some of the reactions of the prime brokerage division. These are the guys who are, as their name suggests, the primary brokers for large clients. Hedge funds, large money managers and the like. The prime brokers are the go-to people for these clients, and they close out their trades, they keep their cash balances, that sort of thing. In essence, they serve as the liaison for these major investors; they are serving in the capacity of an investment advisor. And just like any investment broker, if their firm goes belly-up, they'll be fielding calls from their investors seeking their money. If the firm goes bankrupt before those investors can get their money out, though, it can take quite a long time for them to see it. So it is in the investors' best interest, if they suspect an impending financial crunch, to get their money out before the firm hits bottom.

After Alan's appearance, I was told that our prime brokerage guys were seeing significant amounts of money withdrawn from the firm due to the wide-spread belief that we were done for. It got so bad, the prime broker-age guys told us, that Mike Minnikes, who ran Bear Stearns Security Cor-poration, a major subgroup of the larger prime brokerage division, called Alan Schwartz and said something to the effect of, "You'd better do some-thing quick, because money is flowing out of here like water."

When Mike said, "You'd better do something," he meant something beyond going on TV again. Desperate times call for desperate measures, and we'd passed desperate times a few days ago. We were now in that unfortunate place where things like selling the firm weren't totally out of the question. We needed to raise some capital, that much was clear. And as basic a mandate as that is, our very survival had come down to whether or not we could find some sort of big brother figure who would bail us out. If this Goldman rumor proved to be true, our credit rating was shot. So short-term survival loans were not going to happen. A buy-out by another bank or dealer was the only viable option for survival at this point.

Beyond the immediate liquidity problems we seemed to be facing in prime brokerage, I wasn't aware of a lowering in our credit rating. David Faber's mention of it was the first I had heard of any other firm's refusing to deal with us due to counterparty risk. If it was true, it was serious. Bad serious. I asked around the office, but couldn't find anybody on the trad-ing floor who'd heard anything beyond what was just said on television. Those blank stares that had met mine when I first heard the words were looking for answers, too.

We later learned from a source at CNN that word of the supposed Goldman Sachs deal had come from a leaked email that had gone out from Goldman to some of its hedge fund clients. The derivatives department at Goldie was declaring that they would no longer serve as the go-between for investors who might be worried about Bear as a credit risk. If that news had stayed private, there's a chance we could have survived. But now that the news was public, the drive to the firm's destruction had just shifted into overdrive. We were in serious trouble.

To understand the level that we'd sunk to, you have to really understand the subtext of the Goldman email. As I explained, a counterparty is simply the other side of a deal. Every deal has a party and a counterparty. Which side is which is simply dependent on which side of the deal you're on. If you're buying futures, the person writing the future option is the counterparty. With Bear specifically, for example, we would often serve as a counterparty in terms of what are called repurchase agreements, or repo loans. A repo loan is a way of raising short-term capital very quickly. The way it works is this: An investment bank, say Bear Stearns, wants to raise a couple billion dollars really quick. But they only want to have it for a very brief period of time, basically overnight. So what we at Bear do is sell a bundle of securities to another investment bank, say Goldman Sachs. They pay us the money we're looking to raise and we give them the securities in exchange. The next day, we'll buy back the securities. They get their money back, we get our securities back, everybody leaves happy.

From that description, it's easy to think that we're all a bunch of Boy Scouts running around Wall Street, just giving each other money whenever someone needs it. But it's not quite so simple as that. The securities we're selling are typically worth more at the time of the sale than the amount we're actually getting for them. In investor banker language that's called a haircut. A haircut is a reduction, on the part of the buyer, in the market value of a particular investment. In this example, the security we're selling Goldman is the investment, and Goldman is reducing the value of it. So in other words, they're paying below-market prices for the securities, and we're happy to sell it to them at that price. The purpose of Goldman's paying the lower amount, and our willingness to accept it, is that it's a form of insurance for Goldman. If the value of the securities drops over the course of the loan—which, even though it's just an overnight thing, is possible—then Goldman doesn't want to be left holding securities that are worth less than what they paid for them, even though we're agreeing to buy them back. The name haircut comes from the fact that the margin spread we're trading at is so thin, it's the metaphorical width of a hair. So, a haircut is actually the "cut" that the lender takes out of the "hair."

On top of the haircut, Goldman will also charge us an interest payment, of sorts, on the cash. So when they're "renting" these securities for a lower price than what they're actually worth, they're also charging us a fee for the service. All of this is standard practice, so it's not as if Goldie is just singling Bear out. What it all boils down to is that a repo loan is very much a credit-intensive relationship. If the guys at Goldman are worried we're not going to be able to pay back the money—like if they think we're having something of a liquidity problem, say—they're not going to want

WASHINGTON—APRIL 3: (L-R) US Federal Reserve Chairman Ben Bernanke testifies before the Senate Banking Committee hearing on the government bailout of Bear Stearns along with Securities and Exchange Commission (SEC) Chairman Christopher Cox, Under Secretary of Treasury for Domestic Finance Robert Steel, and the President of the Federal Reserve Bank of New York Timothy Geithner, April 3, 2008 on Capitol Hill in Washington, DC. U.S. senators expressed concern Thursday that billions of dollars in taxpayer funds has been put on the line to back last month's emergency takeover of troubled investment bank Bear Stearns. *(Photo by Tim Sloan/AFP/Getty Images)*

to play ball with us. And when Faber mentioned a "deal" with Goldman, he was referring to a repo loan that had been declined the previous Friday for those exact reasons.

In the overall scheme of things, this was a horrific development. If Goldman Sachs was refusing to loan us money, even only overnight, that was a problem. A huge problem, in fact. But when Faber had said that he'd heard that the deal had eventually gone through, what was that? Either we'd been denied the loan or we hadn't, and if we had, then there was potentially something going on that wasn't being made public. But if Goldman had eventually given us the money, then why had they refused it in the first place? That CNBC interview was the first any of us had ever heard of the whole thing, but it was certainly not to be the last on that Wednesday. Later that morning, I was in a trader's meeting with the treasury division to discuss buy-back levels for the products I was creating. Yes, in my naïve state—or perhaps I was just focused?—I was still going about business-as-usual, trying to create new investment products for our investors. It was at that meeting that the treasury division dropped the bomb.

All of the traditional sources of funding for Bear Stearns had cut off any and all short-term unsecured loans to the firm. Like a drunk who's spent his entire day at the bar, we had been cut off.

In what had to be the zillionth ironic twist of this whole mess, we were suddenly put in the position of the ones who couldn't get a loan because of our credit rating. And our credit rating had been shot to hell because of the spike in defaults of subprime mortgages. The same mortgages that people shouldn't have been given in the first place due to their own credit problems. In other words, our credit crisis was brought on by our bets on other peoples' credit crises. The chickens had come home to roost. But that meeting was never made public, so only the people within the firm knew of the situation. At no time in the firm's history had it been more important for us to put up a good face than it was right now. And it had never been harder for me to put up a good face than it was right now. It was made a slightly less impossible task by the fact that our balance sheets showed a positive balance. At least for the time being.

But no matter what our bank passbook said, there was still the perception on Wall Street that we had liquidity issues; it was the confidence issue that David Faber had mentioned that was the crux of the whole situation. Because of investors' misguided perceptions about the firm, the confidence they had in Bear was shattered. And because that confidence had been shattered, the whole thing was rapidly becoming a self-fulfilling prophecy. And all of this rumor and innuendo made for great news. And CNBC took it and ran with it and had an absolute ball. All at our expense. And the further we fell as a result, the more the news networks talked about it. And the more they talked about it, the further we fell. The whole experience was death by media in real time.

The "reliable source" that David had referenced in his piece was a person referring to an email that had been sent out from Goldman Sachs to its major clients. Basically they were telling hedge funds and other major investors that they wouldn't be continuing to work with Bear in counterparty relationships. There were a couple of layers of meaning to this message. The outward meaning, the one that was "officially" intended by the email, was simply the statement of a policy. Goldman Sachs would no longer be assisting clients seeking credit swaps with Bear Stearns. Simple as that. They didn't have enough faith in our own credit to offer us overnight loans or to take us on in credit swaps, or any other transaction that would subject them to the possibility of default by Bear. That's the easy part to read. Honestly, that news alone was enough to send shockwaves through the entire trading floor of every investment bank in the world. But the subtext, God help us all, was powerful enough to send Mother Teresa to death row for crimes against humanity. It was that damning, the hidden meaning beneath the corporate message. It was our death sentence.

That oh-so-powerful subtext told the recipients of that email—some of the biggest hedge funds in the country, to be specific—that Bear's credit was worse than it appeared. So big a risk was dealing with Bear that they're saying in a public way that they don't trust us to cover our own debts, hint, hint. And just in case you missed it, Bear's credit sucks, hint, hint. And in the event it hasn't yet sunk in, you'd be an absolute fool to do any business with Bear Stearns now or in the future, a future that doesn't look like it's going to be in existence very much longer anyway. And we all know about a fool and his money, right? Is this hint settling in yet? Do you understand what we're telling you? Bear is finished as an investment bank, or at least as an independent one, so don't give them any more money. And if you have any money with them now, for the love of God, get it out fast! And just in case you missed it the first time, this is not a drill. Bear Stearns will not be in business next week and you will lose everything you have invested with them if you don't take it out as soon as possible.

At this point, my Bloomberg was going nuts with Bear headlines. The Bloomberg screen is actually quite a colorful affair, something of a kaleidoscope of complementary colors that work to create a picture that an interior decorator would probably describe as "sleek and modern, very new-age." News headlines stream up the screen in real time as the wire is picking them up. If you see something that catches your eye—for example, a headline indicating that the company you currently work for is about to go completely bankrupt—you can stop it and read the story. It's normally an enjoyable enterprise, reading the day's financial news in day-glo colors. But normally there aren't quite so many of those aforementioned headlines about the company you work for going completely bankrupt. Up until today, things like Eliot Spitzer, may God have mercy on his unfaithful soul, had knocked Bear out of the Bloomberg headlines, or at least from the top of the list. Such was not the case any more, though. Sex sells papers, but politicians cheating on their wives are a dime-a-dozen. You only get one shot at the collapse of a New York investment bank.

By the end of the day on March 12, 2008, Governor Spitzer had lost favor with the news agency; he'd dropped from the radar altogether, in an apparent attempt to allow him to figure out his future plans in some semblance of privacy. After he'd announced that he had done it and the press had discovered that there weren't any more forthcoming skeletons emerging from the closet, they lost interest. In his stead, Bear Stearns had assumed the place of honor at the top of the Bloomberg "top picks" page. What's more, we'd also assumed the number one ranking in terms of number of headlines over the course of the day. By the end of that Wednesday, Bear accounted for twenty-seven of the forty-three featured headlines. Some of the phrases used to describe our beloved firm in those headlines included "stock declines," "betting against," "proceed with caution" and, in what was to become quite the overused pun over the course of the next couple of days, "investors are bearish." At least the news guys were trying to have a sense of humor while some of us lost everything.

Thankfully, at least the inordinate number of investors' fears camouflaged what was the Bear scandal *du jour,* the cataloging of which was approaching wayward politicians in sheer number. Today's story was the fact that our former CEO, our own beloved Jimmy Cayne, he of Nashville bridge tournaments and associated smut, had closed on the purchase of two adjoining apartments in the Plaza, the former jewel of New York's elite hotel ranks that had been converted to condominiums. Apparently when your stock is setting some sort of speed record for declining prices, it's considered newsworthy when you spend $28.24 million to buy a 6,000 square foot place overlooking Central Park to spend your golden years. Had it been anyone else in the firm—or really, anyone else on the planet, for that matter—I don't think it would have registered with any of us. But in the end, it was just another piece of extra-spicy news that Bear didn't need right now. What we did need was good news. We needed to get out to the public the good news about Bear. And realistically, we needed someone to step up to the plate and buy us out.

I discovered, in light of the news about Jimmy's new home, that news reports were a double-edged sword. On the one hand, the good news was that only two of the headlines were about his Plaza purchase. The bad news was that the other twenty-five were about the fact that our company was in the equivalent of hospice care for investment banks. We were hooked up to every conceivable hospital life-support device known to mankind, and the medical staff had been instructed to keep us comfortable as we slipped the surly bonds. This was most definitely not good news, and the prospects for brighter days ahead weren't any better. Our stock price closed that day at $61.58 a share, down about a dollar-and-a-half from the previous day's closing. I didn't know it at the time, but it was to be the beginning of one of the worst single stock collapses in recent history. It's like we were being unavoidably sucked into a vortex. The momentum of our fall was pulling us down faster and faster. As I sat staring at my screens that evening, watching the firm's existence spiral faster and faster down the whirlpool that was sucking us in, I said to Captain Nemo, "I think it's over."

He agreed with me as we both shook our heads in utter disbelief.

CHAPTER SEVEN

Bleeding Out

Exsanguinate {eks-sang-gwuh-neyt} (v):
1. to drain of blood; make bloodless. 2. to bleed to death
—RANDOM HOUSE UNABRIDGED DICTIONARY

Jay Sebring is an interesting footnote to one of the more macabre chapters to emerge from the entire 1960's decade of peace, love and hippie folklore. Sebring, an internationally-renowned hair stylist, was a victim of the vicious attacks carried out at 10050 Cielo Drive in the hills northwest of Los Angeles, California, on the night of August 9, 1969. He had been romantically linked to actress Sharon Tate, wife of film director Roman Polanksi, and was visiting the house on that fateful evening. Accounts differ as to why the particular house was targeted, but the end result didn't really concern itself with the particular motives that had influenced the choice of locations. When members of Charles Manson's "Family" left the home that night, five people had been savagely murdered, among them Jay Sebring. Cause of death was not immediately apparent to the first detectives who arrived on the scene, but the brutality of the montage suggested that an epic struggle had taken place, a struggle characterized by a frenzied fight for life that had ended in blood-soaked death. In all, the coroner performing the autopsies on the five bodies counted a total of 102 stab wounds and 6 gunshot wounds. In Jay Sebring's case, the coroner's report lists cause of death as "exsanguination." The autopsy revealed seven wounds made with a long-bladed knife, three of which could have been in and of themselves fatal. Sebring was also shot once with a .22-caliber pistol, a wound which could also have been fatal in and of itself. But the cause of death, exsanguination, meant that Mr. Sebring had literally bled to death; his body had finally shut down due to the fact that there was not enough blood to keep it going.

If you'd polled the group of us working on the trading floor at the Bear Stearns headquarters in New York City on that Thursday morning, March 13th, 2008 I'd bet you a lot of money that most of us couldn't have told you what exsanguination meant. What's more, I'd go double-or-nothing that none of us actually cared what it meant. But despite the fact that we might not get that question right on a TV game show, on that morning on the trading floor, we all knew, in a sense, what it felt like to die of a complete loss of blood. We knew what the word meant, and you better believe that we cared. What had begun the day before as a comparatively slow drip-drip-drip of money exiting the firm's coffers had become a full-on deluge by Thursday. Our blood supply—our money—was draining out of our veins faster than anyone could have imagined. We were dying, just like Jay Sebring, of exsanguination. As the body of Bear Stearns lay on the street with a crowd of onlookers gawking and pointing, the blood continued to flow out. The heartbeat grew fainter. The light flickered. And we all knew how it felt.

Before I'd arrived at the office that morning, however, for the briefest of instants I had thought that maybe the fates had smiled down on Bear and delivered us from our distress. The front page of the *Times* that morning showed Spitzer in what was to become a typical pose—lips curled under teeth, eyes cast downward, looking like a man beaten—announcing that he was stepping down from the office of governor in order to begin the familial healing process. "I am deeply sorry that I did not live up to what was expected of me," the governor was quoted as saying in his resignation speech. The Pentagon was doing damage control in regards to whether or not detainees were being unfairly tortured during interrogations. The Democrats were worried that racial issues would start to play a larger role in the election process, as Barack Obama continued to build on his popularity in his quest to be the nation's first African American president through the Democratic primary race against Hillary Clinton. All very interesting on some level, but there was a major bonus from the perspective of Bear Stearns employees: We weren't on the front page. It was the noticeable absence of any banner headlines about the firm that, momentarily, buoyed my spirits and allowed me to believe, just for a second, that things had returned to normal somehow.

I turned the pages, looking for news. Even in the business section there was little mention of Bear. French authorities were still investigating the scandal involving Société Générale, and had taken some poor broker into custody. I felt for the kid; he was 29 and was too young to know what he was doing, when you really thought about it. But such is the world of high finance. No room for pleading ignorance. In this world, you're expected to know what to do and what not to do, and you're expected to be able to do what you're not supposed to do without getting caught. In the end, if you got caught, you were expected to know how to deflect the blame to somebody else. It was a cruel world where survival of the fittest was the law of the land, and this kid looked like he'd gotten caught with the non-dominant genetic mutation.

Even after looking through the whole section, the whole paper, for that matter, the only mention of our troubles that I could find was buried in an article about investors' lack of confidence in the Fed's plan to save us from ourselves. And we weren't even mentioned specifically in the article; it was more a guilt-by-association thing. I felt an odd sensation creeping through my being. It took me a second to realize it was relief.

NEW YORK—MARCH 12: New York Governor Eliot Spitzer (R) announces his resignation as his wife Silda Wall Spitzer stands next to him March 12, 2008 in New York City. New York Lieutenant Governor David Paterson will take over for Spitzer when his resignation goes into effect Monday, March 17, 2008. *(Photo by Chris Hondros/Getty Images)*

But that mysterious feeling of safety was short-lived.

Once on the trading floor, I checked the Bloomberg. Two major developments had surfaced, and their news was a yin-yang sort of symbiosis, with two potentials competing for overall supremacy. It was being widely reported that investors were treating Bear stock as if it were an infected patient in quarantine. Arm's length was the standard distance, and for a lot of investors, the further they could get from anything associated with Bear stocks the better. All in all, this wasn't news, really. Not by my ranking of things, anyway. Our stock had been a hot potato all week; the fact that investors were proceeding cautiously didn't trigger any sirens in my brain. Basically I took this as status quo at this point. I'd grown accustomed to seeing reports about poor performance and liquidity problems and that sort of thing. Headlines that would have sent me into a full-blown panic attack and convulsions on the floor a week ago were met today with a shrug of the shoulders and a "what are you gonna' do?" attitude. The times had changed in the hallowed halls of Bear Stearns.

But the other headline that caught my eye and perked up my attention was the one informing readers that Darius Yuen had been hired as a new Senior Managing Director in charge of our equity capital markets in Asia. To a degree, this was the level we as a firm had sunk to, at least in my mind. News of somebody being hired was reason to celebrate, at least privately. So desperate was I for any life raft I could cling to that I found one wherever I could. And I found one in Darius Yuen.

This was going against my own efforts to hire people. It was definitely becoming harder to get people to join Bear. The last thing you want where there is counterparty risk is that counterparty to be the form you are working for. For example, one lady we were going for passed on and instead took an offer with Goldman Sachs. Okay. Hard to win that one. But another guy we were going after was going to relocate from London. He ended up declining our offer, though, and I was surprised to learn that he had gotten engaged while contemplating our offer. Ultimately he made the right call, on many levels.

No, it was the other side of the equation that really made me happy. It was, in a manner of speaking, the counterparty in this pairing that I chose to focus on as a distraction from the financial ruin that was piling up around me. It was Yuen's acceptance of the job that buoyed my optimism. I have no idea what Yuen was going to be making, but I had to assume it was enough to lure him away from one of Europe's major banks to lead what amounted to a tiny presence in Asia. If this guy had the confidence that Bear was going to ride this storm out, then maybe it was going to happen.

In retrospect, the association of BNP Paribas and Bear Stearns, even in something as benign as hiring a new SMD, was an interesting one, given that the two companies followed very similar trajectories at different times. BNP Paribas had, in August of 2007, run into a little trouble of their own relating to the United States subprime mortgage crisis. Yep, the same one that had caused two of Bear's hedge funds to collapse at about the same time. And the same one that was bleeding us dry at this very moment. As a result of the possibility of a complete meltdown of BNP Paribas and the resulting global financial shockwaves that meltdown would create, the European Central Bank intervened. The ECB offered low interest credit lines that totaled 96.8 billion, an amount at the time that was equiva -lent to approximately $130 billion. The parallels at the time were, for the most part, lost on me, because I wasn't privy to what was about to happen with the Federal Reserve Bank. But in hindsight, it was just another one of those things that you couldn't make up, even if you wanted to.

In the end, though, Darius Yuen signed a contract with Bear that would have put him on the Bear payroll beginning in May, and he would be reporting to our newly-appointed Asia CEO, John Moore. Neither Moore nor his newest charge had any idea that Bear would cease to exist in any recognizable form long before their new partnership would take root in Asia. It sounds like a stroke of hideously bad luck for Mr. Yuen, but noth-ing could actually be further from the truth. After the carnage was com-plete and Bear had been absorbed by JPMorgan, Darius was under a contract that had to be honored. That meant that he'd been guaranteed salary and bonuses for 2008 and, if he negotiated well, 2009 already locked in. Our sales guys call that getting "G'd Up." You get your guarantees up-front just in case something goes horribly wrong.

So JPMorgan inherited this new employee that they didn't hire and, quite possibly, didn't want to hire. JPMorgan already had quite a presence in the Asian market before they acquired Bear, so there's no telling whether or not they had any need for a Senior Managing Director over there. But there's that whole guarantee issue. Because Darius got G'd Up, he's enti-tled to his bonus and salaries. So he's getting paid no matter what. For a lot of guys, the prospect of sitting on the beach somewhere for a year or two while you collect money from a firm that didn't hire you but had to honor your contract anyway isn't a bad way to make a living. Whether

JPMorgan took Darius on or not, I don't know. I have to say, though, if he's sitting on a beach somewhere right now reading this, I mean this with all sincerity, Darius. Well done!

Back in New York, the mood in the office was growingly increasingly frantic, especially in the corner offices with the windows. Mike Minnikes' suggestion from the day before that Alan needed to do something prompted our CEO to board a plane bound from PBI to Kennedy post-haste. It's never a good sign when your chairman unexpectedly cuts short his attendance at a business conference. Of course, it's also never a good sign when your firm is collapsing around you and the non-executive chairman is at yet another bridge tournament, this time in Detroit. But Jimmy was no longer in the decision-making chair; that honor belonged to Alan, and it was now or never time for Bear Stearns. Whatever last tricks Alan had to pull out of his hat, now was the time to pull them out. There was nothing to lose now. One prime broker mentioned that she'd received a few

NEW YORK—MARCH 26: A protestor stands outside Bear Stearns headquarters March 26, 2008 in New York. Hundreds of housing activists stormed the lobby of the Bear Stearns skyscraper in Manhattan, overwhelming security and staging a noisy rally, protesting the government-backed sale and bailout of the investment bank. *(Photo by Chris Hondros/Getty Images)*

emails she'd received from clients, clients who were withdrawing assets by the hundreds-of-millions and, in some cases, even billions of dollars. Ordinarily, I would have reacted with shock, horror, disbelief. Today I had no reaction. I was absolutely numb to the destruction that was becoming more apparent with every passing second, as there was nothing I could do. It was just like the news headlines that were announcing Bear stock as a bad play for investors. It was all just status quo, hum-drum stuff that didn't even elicit a response from my central nervous system. I had managed to completely disassociate myself from the world around me, because I felt that was the only way I could actually face the future, the future that was growing increasingly bleak with every passing moment.

I'm not sure what it is about times of sheer horror that makes clocks seem to stop. When a single major event happens that disrupts a person's sense of safety and general well being, time seems to drag by at an almost stand-still pace. And while every trader on the planet wishes he could stop time—for example when something isn't going right so you can adjust your strategy—it's an impossibility. So why the hell is it that when your own little world is crashing down around you, time, in its infinite quest to make a joke at your expense, stops? You want it to go by fast, to get through this, to get to whatever inevitable end has been preordained for your future, to get to your final destiny. But it insists on dragging it out, forcing you to endure it blow by blow, each punch sending you closer to death but still leaving you with just enough strength to hang on so you can continue to endure this misery. This nightmare that none of us could seem to wake up from just wouldn't end.

What made this free-fall all the more frustrating for everyone associated with Bear was the fact that we were a week away from announcing our earnings report for the first quarter. We were scheduled to announce on Thursday, March 20, 2008 and we had a self-imposed quarterly quiet period during which there was an information blackout so as to prevent the appearance of any wrongdoing. Basically it was a way of ensuring that nobody said anything that could be misconstrued by investors regarding what our earnings would be, and thus potentially manipulate our stock price. Though the Securities and Exchange commission requires a quiet period prior to a company's initial public offering (IPO) for investors, to do so prior to the release of regular quarterly earnings reports is, legally, up to the discretion of the company. However, because that time prior to the announcement is filled with anxiety, many companies choose to voluntarily remain quiet, so as to avoid any added anxiety or the perception of any kind of attempts to manipulate our stock price by members of upper-level management. So regardless of what any of us might have wanted to say or could have said in order to save Bear, our hands were tied. We couldn't say anything, so the frustration level grew. By this point, truth be told, anything we'd said probably would have been nothing more than window dressing anyway. We were no longer sliding down the hill to bankruptcy. We had fallen off the mountain altogether, and were now plummeting to the ground.

It was the general feeling on the trading floor that afternoon that Bear was being taken asunder by forces far beyond our control, and there was nothing any of us could do to rectify the situation. The quicker we all got on board with that fact, the sooner we'd all accept that we were dead. Fate had conspired against us, first with rumors then with our quiet period, to destroy the firm entirely. It was like swimming in surf, when the undertow takes you further away from the beach. You can swim as hard as you want, but it's not going to counteract the natural suction that is pulling you backwards. In the end, the more you exert yourself, the more exhausted you become, thus making your predicament all the more dire.

People who know about these sorts of things tell you that when you're stuck in undertow, you should actually relax. Allow the current to take you to where it will and then, once it subsides, you can resume swimming back to the beach. By not fighting the current—which is a futile fight in the long run—you reserve your strength for that time when you are free of the undertow's grip. But in the financial world, you're not just worried about the waves and the current. If you stand still too long, the sharks will get you, too. So there's really no point in not fighting. But there's really no point in fighting, either. You're dead no matter what you do. It's quite the emotionally uplifting business, investment banking is.

I phoned up a colleague in London to discuss the situation in New York. I told him that it felt like the market at large wanted blood, a sacrifice of sorts. It reminded me of the summer before, after the hedge funds had collapsed, and the world around us demanded a sacrifice. Warren Spector had been named the sacrificial virgin who would die so that the rest of us might live. Spector had died for our sins, making him some sort of Bear Stearns Christ figure, I suppose.

In much the same way as the financial world had demanded a sacrifice in the wake of the hedge funds' collapse, these days the market seemed like it was aligning itself to bring down a major player in the world of investment banking. My colleague agreed, to a point. He said that he could feel the same vibe of the market's demands for blood, but he was sure it wouldn't be Bear. "You guys are in pretty good shape financially," he reminded me. And he was right. We had billions in capital reserves, a fact that had been repeated so often that it was bordering on becoming a cliché this week. Too bad nobody believed it anymore.

After I hung up with London, it was as if a switch had been flipped. My phone bank lit up with calls from clients wanting information, news, reassurances, anything that would assist in mapping their way out of this financial quagmire. By now, the liquidity rumors had become old hat, and in a need to stay current and hip, they had morphed into ones regarding Bear's inability to close on trades due to our internal liquidity issues. It was, I suppose, a natural evolutionary process, the rumors changing their content from strictly about liquidity to the effects of that liquidity problem. I fielded the calls as quickly as I could and assured the callers that I knew nothing of any substance that would give any credence to these wild stories that were flying everywhere. And despite the survival instinct that was guiding my every action these days, I was being honest insofar as I knew. I asked the guys in prime brokerage point-blank, and they assured me that they were still clearing trades. I related this intelligence to our clients and colleagues. But the rumors persisted. And it just kept getting worse. Our cash balances that had been as high as $11 billion on Monday were hovering perilously close to zero. And when that number became reality, when the needle on the tank hit empty, we were done.

Alan Schwartz arrived at the office in the early afternoon, and was immediately all business. His normally friendly face was drawn; he looked like the man that he was, one who was in the thick of a battle that he was losing badly. He assembled the firm's top executives—the President's Advisory Council (PAC), which consists of roughly the top hundred executives in the firm—in a conference room, and though I was not on the guest list to that particular party, I managed to get the basic idea of the meeting, which was predictably enough a request for anyone in the room to do whatever was in their power in order to keep the firm alive.

I learned later that it was at that meeting that Alan phoned Jamie Dimon, the CEO at JPMorgan, in hopes of negotiating some sort of deal that would salvage the firm. It was a last-ditch effort to save the company, but it was also a very calculated move on Alan's part. It was widely reported that Morgan was a natural choice to be a Heaven-sent savior, given that they were the clearing house for all of our transactions. Every investment bank has a clearing house, the purpose of which is to settle trades at the end of the day. The clearing house is a third-party entity, so in any transaction, you've got the buyer and the seller, plus the clearing house. The clearing house clears trades, collects margins payments, reports all trading data and handles the processing and clearing of all trades at the end of the day. So you have to think of a clearing house like a checking account of sorts, and the investment banker is the actual check writer. The clearing house itself is basically the one writing the checks for the clients.

In Bear's case, JPMorgan was, at least tangentially, our clearinghouse, our checkbook; in the past, we'd kept a cash balance with them that was designed to pay for trades that we made on behalf of our clients. I say tangentially because, despite widely-distributed reports about Morgan still being our clearing house, the fact is that they had sold the business to Bank of New York—Mellon. Just like we bought mortgages, other banks bought clearing house services. So in fact it was not JPMorgan but rather BoNY Mellon who would pay out on our coupons to clients that held them.

Regardless of who was holding the cash for us, much like the relationships in the professional world that had gone sour for us, this one, too, was very much dependent on our faith and credit. Had JPMorgan still been our clearing house, it would have made perfect sense, then for them to bail us out, given that, as our clearing house, they had to show us they had faith and credit in us. And what better way to do so than by giving us money to survive? But given that they had sold that element of the business, the plot thickened, so to speak, in terms of why JP was so anxious to bail us out. Or at least so willing to do so.

In the end, JPMorgan was basically the only firm out there who was in the position to hand over gobs of operating capital to Bear in a hurry. And what's more, because they had been our clearing house, they had to assume we were good for the money. It was kind of like a parent giving their own adult child money to survive. It's just what you do when you're in that position, even though it had passed the point when you really felt like you had some sort of parental obligation. But what it really boiled down was that nobody else was lining up to give us the money, so we had no choice other than to go to our good friends at JPMorgan, in hopes that our former clearing house would be able to cauterize the wounds and stop the bleeding once and for all. Jamie Dimon was, hopefully, going to be our medical savior.

While Dimon and his band of would-be rescuers contemplated the offer that Alan had thrown their way—the details of which I was not made privy to—Alan pulled out his final card, and it was the absolute epitome of a desperation bid. I heard via the interoffice grapevine that he had called a major client, a hedge fund manager, and begged him to go on TV to announce that he had full faith in Bear's credit and cash positions and that he was continuing to do business with the firm now, and that he had equal confidence in Bear's financial future. Though I was never told explicitly who it was that Alan had sought out, I do have my thoughts about the likely recipient. But in the interest of allowing the innocent to remain so, I'm not going to speculate, just in case Alan was calling in favors none of us knew about.

NEW YORK—MARCH 26: Protestors chant and carry signs in the lobby of the Bear Stearns' head-quarters March 26, 2008 in New York. Hundreds of housing activists overwhelmed security and stormed the lobby of the Bear Stearns' skyscraper in Manhattan, staging a noisy rally and protesting the government-backed sale and bailout of the investment bank. *(Photo by Chris Hondros/Getty Images)*

Regardless of who it was that Alan was soliciting for help, it was something he never would have done had he not been staring down the barrel of a gun that was not only loaded, but that had just been fired. He was, in essence, calling a client, a major client, and telling him that the firm was as good as dead. He's telling this investor who has God only knows how much money tied up in Bear investments that the firm, the firm handling his huge sums of cash, is losing all of it. I'm sure he phrased it more gently than that, but that's the basic message that was conveyed. He's saying to the guy that at this point, he is the only person in town who effectively has the power to save the firm, and, just as a chance by-product, save his own personal fortune while he's at it. Alan had been CEO of Bear for all of two months, and he was forced into making this type of phone call. This was, I'm sure, not exactly the picture he'd had of his life before he took the job. This was worse than baptism by fire; this was being burned alive at the stake.

In the end, though, it didn't matter, because the client in question refused to make the television appearance. Again, I doubt it would have done anything, but it certainly didn't hurt too much to try at that point. The artery had been opened and there was nothing left to cauterize the wounds we had sustained to this point. The Bear was dying of exsanguination. By the end of the day, our stock price had slipped to $57 a share, down from the over $61 a share opening price. A four point-and-change drop. I thought this latest development was embarrassing. In fact, the price was a six-year record low, a news tidbit the Bloomberg was advertising to anyone who was connected to the network. But that slump wasn't even the tip of the iceberg in terms of what was about to happen to the share price. In just a few days, a $57 share price would seem like an exorbitantly high price to pay. And as so many of us associated with Bear saw our net worth drop by massive percentages, we longed for a $57 share price.

I left the office that evening unsure of what to think about anything. Outside on the sidewalk along Madison, there was a bank of television reporters and photographers, all no doubt hoping to get a picture of the body before it was declared officially dead. It felt somehow like a *Law and Order* episode filming there. I avoided the cameras, hoping to postpone my fifteen minutes, and hailed a cab. I sank into the backseat, trying to somehow hide from all of this. I used to do the same thing as a kid on long road trips with my parents. When I'd get bored watching the world pass by outside the car windows, I'd lie back and just zone out. It was kind of a Zen thing, I suppose. I'd try to become one with the car's interior, melting into the upholstery. And at that moment in that cab, for the first time since I had been awake, my mind was truly quiet. I rode that wave of relaxation all the way uptown.

At my apartment, I steeled myself for re-entry into the world of reality, the world where I had responsibilities to my family. It was a funny time to be dealing with all of this, as my sister-in-law and niece were visiting from British Columbia. They don't work in the financial world, so I am not sure if my recounting of that day's rather dramatic turn of events sounded like just another "normal" day in my crazy existence, or if they actually realized the magnitude of the events that were unfolding around me. As I walked in the apartment, the kids were the first to greet me. I was home earlier than usual, so they were excited by my unexpected arrival. My wife looked momentarily surprised, a look that was followed by a hint of concern, like she knew something terrible had happened at the office. As a former investment banker, Chartered Financial Analyst (CFA) and strategist, she was in tune with the markets and she knew exactly what was going on at Bear.

I gave her a pathetic smile, which was the best I could muster at the time given the circumstances. Once we were able to chat alone, I told her the outlook was bleak at best, and that more than likely Bear was going under. I told her the firm was literally bleeding to death, at an astoundingly rapid pace. In fact, if the firm was still in business by the end of the day tomorrow, quite frankly, I'd be surprised. She didn't flinch.

"What's the worst case scenario?" she asked in a reserved tone.

I told her that, worst case, Bear could be out of business and, assuming that happened, a lot of other major firms could go down, too. If that happened, we'd have to move to our home in British Columbia and chill out until the storm subsided.

She sighed heavily. Then she smiled. "If that's the worst case scenario, then I think I can handle it." She even giggled a little, as if to point out that I was actually talking about what a tragedy it would be for us to be "forced" to temporarily move to our home near the glacier. And that was it. That was the extent of our crisis planning. Now it was just a matter of what came at us next.

I wish I could have mustered the same feelings for the firm. While I knew in my heart that I would bounce back from this crisis and that my family would remain intact and that we would go on with our lives, the prognosis was not so rosy for Bear Stearns. It was past the time we could have saved the firm; the lifeblood had drained out of it. It was now just a matter of pulling the sheet up over the patient's head. Doctors have targeted 40% as the approximate maximum amount of blood a person can lose and still live. And while things like averages are tricky instruments to use in the real world, the average human body contains about 5.5 quarts of blood. So if that average human lost approximately 2.2 quarts of blood, he'd be past the point of saving, at least according to medical opinions. To carry the metaphor a step further, if an investment bank lost 40% of its capital reserve and there seemed to be absolutely no way to stop the outflow of cash, it, too, would be past the point of saving. In both cases, the victims would have been said to have died of extreme loss of blood. Just like Jay Sebring.

CHAPTER EIGHT

A Sucker Born Every Minute

"The uniform, constant and uninterrupted effort of every man to better his condition, the principle from which public and national, as well as private opulence is originally derived, is frequently powerful enough to maintain the natural progress of things toward improvement, in spite both of the extravagance of government, and of the greatest errors of administration. Like the unknown principle of animal life, it frequently restores health and vigour to the constitution, in spite, not only of the disease, but of the absurd prescriptions of the doctor."

—THE WEALTH OF NATIONS

When strolling through midtown Manhattan, it's not uncommon to see shoppers lined up outside stores like Abercrombie and Fitch on Fifth Avenue. People cuing up to get inside, just so they can spend exorbitant sums without really telling you why. Unconsciously, of course, they know why they're buying what they're buying: It's cool, it's fashionable, it's hip, it's hot. Their brain has been imprinted with the belief that a specific brand or a specific style is the fashion of the moment, and they're desperate to be a part of the movement. And Abercrombie is not the only one. Case in point, any true Christmas celebration in New York involves the requisite trip to Macy's on 34th Street with its accompanying miracles, and any fan of Tom Hanks will require a stop by FAO Schwartz up near Central Park to watch the employees dance on the huge piano on the second floor. But it's not just holidays when the people-watching is world-class around these parts. It's an every day affair.

So every so often, when the kids aren't overscheduled with activities and my wife and I don't have any plans, sometimes we all like to head down to that part of the city and just watch the world go by. We'll grab a café latte from the ING Coffee Shop on 49th Street, which I frequent because it's close to my office (and I am nothing if not a creature of habit), and then take a walk uptown. It's really a spectator sport, living in New York, one of the self-proclaimed people-watching capitals of the free world. And while those shoppers are so busily spending their hard-earned dollars in the opulent stores dotting Fifth Avenue—after all, who can resist that little blue box from Tiffany's or the ostentatious glamour of Bergdorf Goodman?—just a block away, some of the brightest minds in the advertising world are hard at work trying to convince you to stop thinking for yourself and start thinking with your wallet.

Madison Avenue has traditionally been the home to many of the world's premier advertising firms. Names like Young & Rubicam and Doyle Dane Bernbach still retain addresses on Madison, while the other major firms that once populated the street have moved on, replaced, ironically enough, by upscale boutiques that no doubt once employed their services. The guiding principles behind advertising as a general practice are derived from the idea that if some commodity is made to seem valuable to a consumer, the consumer will in turn want it. Things get a little more complicated when you start talking about necessities, such as clothing. Take, for example, jeans. Regular, standard blue denim jeans. A staple for many of us. The kind of thing you wear when you're working in the yard or running the kids around town on the weekend or whatever. So how do you justify charging $200 for your designer's version of a pair of jeans, when somebody else is charging $35 for another brand? The simple answer is advertising.

By telling people how great your jeans are, the ones that you're charging $200 for, some of those consumers will eventually start to believe you. And all it takes is the right segment of the population to believe your jeans are truly worth the price because the *faux* leather tag on the waist says something different than the "lesser" jeans of your competitor. You find that little pot of gold, and all of a sudden you're setting your kids up with multi-million-dollar trust funds that were financed by the sales of your brand of blue jeans. And the truth of the matter is, the same thing holds true for stocks that are bought and sold on the New York Stock Exchange.

The official trading day on the floor of the New York Stock Exchange begins at 9:30 AM Eastern Standard Time. I use the word "official," so as to differentiate between the standard trading day that happens "between the bells" and those periods of time known as pre-market trading and after-hours trading. Pre-market trading begins at 8 AM, and after-hours trading goes from 4 PM—6:30 PM. The main bread-and-butter of the investors working the floor, though, begins at 9:30 on weekdays. And for publicly-traded companies, it's that window from 9:30 in the morning until 4 in the afternoon that fortunes are made and lost, there in the chaos of the paper-strewn mosh pit of humanity that is the floor of the Stock Exchange. The time leading up to that opening bell, though, is not necessarily one of quiet solitude and reflection on the part of company honchos. I would venture to guess it's much like the floor of the United States Senate just minutes before an important vote, with whispered offers of support in exchange for votes spreading throughout the chamber. The difference with the Stock Exchange is that the votes aren't such a secretive affair. Just the opposite, in fact. If you've got news that will help your stock price, you want to shout it from any rooftop that you can find, and you want to get that news out to as many people as you can. Press releases make the rounds, as firms lobby on behalf of their company in the hopes of eeking out a few extra points in the stock price. Advertising firms call this form of advertising a consumer stimulant, as you seek to trigger an immediate response from the potential buyers, like a cup of coffee in the morning. Chief Executive Officers call it financing their retirement.

No matter what you choose to call it, this is advertising time. This is the time to tell your would-be consumers why they should buy your stock. Why your stock is desirable. Why, if people own it, they should hold on to it. Why, if people don't, they should pay as much as they have to in order to acquire it. The law of the land is that if you've got something somebody else wants—be it a pair of jeans, be it a house, be it a share of stock—they have to pay for it. And they have to pay a price you're willing to accept. So the more desirable your commodity seems to them, the more they're willing to pay for it. And even better, if you play your cards right, fewer people want to sell it, because they start to believe that what they've got really is that special. The combination of fewer numbers of potential sellers coupled with greater numbers of potential buyers is an equation for a jump in your stock price. But the key to getting your message out and ensuring the ideal market conditions to bring about that jump is to differentiate yourself from all the other stocks for sale. And given that there are over 2700 individual securities listed on the New York exchange alone, that's not necessarily an easy job.

The time before that opening bell rings—and, quite frankly, much of the time during the trading day itself—is devoted to educating the consumers about your stock. Name recognition is key. The specific sector your company falls into, say financials or capital goods or technology, isn't as important in the overall scheme of things as the fact that people know your name. It's vital to establish that knowledge in the minds of consumers, because when they pick up the phone and call their broker, you want the name of your company to be the thing at the front of their mind. So during that period before the opening bell on Wall Street, it's a beehive of activity. Firms are jockeying for position on cable morning shows dedicated to the financial markets and announcements are flying all over the place. There's an overwhelming amount of information coming in daily, even hourly. This influx of information, which is spread even further and faster via the Internet, has created a niche market for television personalities seeking to cash in on the widespread exposure that so many Americans have to the stock market. Between 401k plans, IRAs and individual investment accounts—not to mention the hundreds of billions of dollars invested by hedge funds and other conglomerates—the combined capitalization of all the publicly listed companies trading on the NYSE topped $25 trillion in 2007. That incomprehensible amount of money has made careers for many people on networks like CNBC, the cable network favored in the Bear Stearns offices. People like Jim Cramer, for example, the host of CNBC's wildly popular "Mad Money" segment.

So important is this guy that he was once referred to as "one of the most influential voices on Wall Street" by Carl Quintanilla on *NBC Nightly News.* Perhaps. But consider the advice Cramer gave in an email answering a question about whether an investor should pull his money out of Bear stock: "No! No! No!" wrote Cramer. "Bear Stearns is not in trouble. If anything, they're more likely to be taken over. Don't move your money from Bear." And I agreed with him. Indeed, at this stage of the game, it was looking like it would be hard for Bear Stearns to survive as an independent entity. If we were taken over, as Cramer was suggesting might happen, we'd return to being a stable firm again.

Unfortunately, many people thought that Mr. Cramer was referring to Bear as a stock pick. But when I and a lot of my colleagues watched the replays, it sounded to us like something completely different. It sounded to us like Cramer was commenting on Bear's safety as a functioning, working, solvent broker and dealer. One that would continue to trade and clear their client's funds. Even if things got really bad—and it seemed like things were getting worse with each passing hour—Cramer knew that an entity as critical to the functioning of the US market would get taken over before the market took it out. As Wall Street gurus go, Mr. Cramer was not alone in his endorsement of Bear. George Soros—that amazing economic and political sage—was, as we later discovered when he discussed his own fund's performance numbers, getting long Bear stock. He really put it best when explaining what looked like a great value trade ended way offside. He said that he had forgotten to take into account Bear's unpopularity with "the establishment."

So with the opening bell a half-hour away on Friday, March 14th, 2008, our shares were clinging to a $57 price, down from our 52-week high of $154.17. I couldn't think about how much money I'd lost as a result of that drop; it hurt my head too much. During my tenure at Bear, this was the lowest the share price had sunk. But we were still in business, to the best of my knowledge, so I did what I always did. I read reports on the monitor, and noted without too much surprise that the news wasn't particularly good. Subprime losses had topped $195 billion. Bear stock was still a pariah on the Street. Same old same old. While I was reading the reports on the Bloomberg, I was also watching the market reports on CNBC out of the side of my peripheral vision. I listened to see if there was any major news coming out that I would need to have in order to do what I needed to do. The news I got that morning blew me—and the rest of the trading floor—out of the water. It was, perhaps, intended to serve as an advertisement for Bear stock before the market opened, a way of pumping it up. A way to reassure people that all was well at Bear, that we were operating on an all-systems-go mindset and there was nothing that was going to stop us this time. If that was the intention, it failed miserably.

Bear Stearns had secured a $30 billion line of credit provided by JPMorgan, a loan that had been guaranteed by the New York Federal Reserve Bank. JPMorgan would be extending a facility (Wall Street-speak for a line of credit) to Bear Stearns for a period of up to 28 days.

It was like hearing a knock at the door at 4 am and opening it, only to see two police officers. You know they're not there to sell you tickets to the Policemen's Benevolent Association Ball, and your stomach drops through the floor. Your body starts to tingle. You get tunnel vision for a minute. After the initial shock began to wear off, I looked around the room, trying to make sure I'd heard it correctly. Everyone on the trading floor was doing the same thing. We were all looking for confirmation of the news. I shot my eyes back to the Bloomberg screen. Like magic, it appeared: "JPMorgan, New York Fed Agree to Provide Funding to Bear Stearns." The sight of that news headline made me sick to my stomach.

The Federal Reserve System is much like the court of appeals system in that there are several elements that go into making up the single body. Just as there are thirteen different circuit courts that make up the United States courts of appeals system, there are twelve federal reserve banks in the country that together make up the Federal Reserve System; the largest of these twelve banks is the Federal Reserve Bank of New York, which is located at 33 Liberty Street, a couple of blocks north of the New York Stock Exchange. The Federal Reserve Bank of New York's jurisdiction covers all of New York State, Fairfield County in Connecticut and the northern counties of New Jersey, as well as Puerto Rico and the US Virgin Islands. The Federal Reserve—"the Fed" in everyday language—was created by the Federal Reserve Act of 1913, and was originally designed to assist in avoiding future bank panics. Several such panics in the early 1900's—especially the panic of 1907—had eroded faith in the commercial banking system across the country, and it was decided that a governmental agency needed to be created in order to lend a sense of security to banks. The idea was that by providing a central bank from which commercial banks could borrow money, those banks would not find themselves in a position of running out of money if a panic were to ensue.

The Fed is also the central banking institution in the United States, and it is the policy-making body that determines, among other things, the interest rate at which commercial banks can borrow money which they in turn lend to their customers. This is what news reports are referring to when they say that the Fed lowered interest rates, such as was the case immediately after the September 11th attacks when spending became our patriotic duty, future repercussions be damned. When the Fed lowers interest rates, the lower interest rate is passed on to commercial lending institutions, like your bank. In turn, the bank passes on a lower interest rate to you, the consumer who is taking out the loan. The hope is that you'll be so excited about getting to borrow money for such a cheap interest rate that you'll race out, get a loan and spend, spend, spend.

The Federal Funds Rate is the interest rate that a depository institution charges another depository institution for borrowing funds at the Federal Reserve Bank for a brief period, a period which is usually not longer than overnight. The way to think about it is that the Federal Reserve Bank is, in fact, a reserve. It's kind of like that extra gas tank. Every bank in the

A SUCKER BORN EVERY MINUTE

United States is required to keep a balance at the Federal Reserve as a fall-back in the event of larger-than-expected withdrawals from the bank. Though the specific amount varies depending on the size and type of bank in question, usually a commercial bank is required to keep a reserve equal to 10% of the value of its demand accounts, which is the name given to accounts that are open for withdrawal by a depositor, things like checking accounts and savings accounts. Because the cash is available on demand, they are collectively referred to as demand accounts. That 10% does not all have to be on deposit with the Federal Reserve; banks have the option to split the balance between the Federal Reserve and their own private vaults.

So let's say a bank has demand accounts totaling $1000, which means they're required to keep a reserve balance of $100. They've got $50 of that in their own vault, which means they need to have a balance of $50 in the Federal Reserve. Now somebody walks into the bank and takes out a loan for $25. That money comes out of the bank's vault, which means their reserve is now down to $25 in the vault and $50 at the Federal Reserve. They need to borrow $25 to keep their balance at the required minimum, so they call up another bank that has more than they need in their Federal Reserve account and have that bank transfer $25 to their Federal Reserve account. So now the bank in question has $75 in the Federal Reserve to go with their $25 in the vault, thus bringing them back to within the legal minimums. The interest rate charged by the lending bank is that rate set by the Fed.

Though both the Federal Funds Rate and LIBOR are rates that affect the rate charged to banks for borrowing money, the two are calculated very differently. LIBOR is determined by the various interest rates charged by banks with the highest of credit ratings. The Federal Funds Rate, on the other hand, is manipulated through the purchase and sale of government-backed securities—US Treasury bills (T-bills), notes (T-notes) and bonds (T-bonds). If the Fed wants to lower interest rates, they buy up securities, which puts more cash into circulation. Because more money is available, fewer people need to borrow it. Thus interest rates go down. If the Fed wants to raise the rates, they sell securities, thus removing cash from circulation and raising interest rates.

So banks are paying interest to borrow money to allow them to loan money to their customers, and the lower the interest rate those banks are charged for borrowing money, the lower the interest rate they in turn charge their clients. On the surface, it sounds like a pretty simple system. Keep interest rates low, let people borrow money, expect them to spend it, the economy grows from all of this spending, everybody wins. But not so fast. Just like an economy that is completely stagnant (not growing at all) is a bad thing, so, too, is an economy that expands unchecked. Either extreme is potentially dangerous. Remember that the price of commodities is based on how many people want to buy them. Let's go back to the $200 blue jeans example. There is a set number of denim manufacturers that can only produce a finite amount of denim in a given time period. So that amount, the number of actual jeans available for purchase, remains constant. But if every person on the street is suddenly walking around with wads of hundred-dollar-bills in their pockets, and if the folks on Madison Avenue are doing their jobs right, then all those c-notes are going to be converted into super-stylish and super-expensive blue jeans. But remember the constant number element of this equation. You've got more people who want to buy than there are people who want—or, in this case, who have enough of the specific commodity in their possession—to sell, due to the fact that there is only so much denim that can be produced.

Now Adam Smith's invisible hand comes into play with the free market economy, and the price of jeans goes up due to a sudden increase in demand working against the constant figure that is the available number

NEW YORK—MARCH 17: Traders work the floor of the New York Stock Exchange on March 17, 2008 in New York City. Stocks have been volatile on Wall Street following news of JP Morgan Chase acquisition of Bear Stearns & Co, for $2 a share, with help of $30 billion in financing of Bear Stearns assets from the U.S. Federal Reserve. (Photo by Michael Nagle/Getty Images)

of jeans. Suddenly the price of jeans has gone to $500 because it's a bull market in jeans, so now the average person is back to not being able to afford them. This is what is affectionately referred to as inflation. Of course, most of us can make do with run-of-the-mill blue jeans. But when this sort of condition is present in the economy, it's not blue jeans that see prices go sky-high. Remember that most commodities are bound by limited supplies. Things like food, gasoline, basic materials. All of these things suddenly cost more. And because of the interrelated nature of the economy as a whole, when the price of basic goods goes up, the cost for services goes up, too. So suddenly everyone is having to pay more for everything, while employers are trying to keep costs—things like the salaries they pay their employees—in check by not raising them. The end result is that everything costs more and everyone is making comparatively less. Not a good way to be.

So keeping the economy out of a recession—negative growth within the economy, meaning the economy is completely stagnant—while simultaneously avoiding inflation—meaning the economy is growing too fast—is a delicate balancing act. And the job of overseeing that delicate balancing act falls to the Fed, and specifically to the chairman of the Federal Reserve. Now you can understand why so many of us on Wall Street hold our collective breath whenever the Chairman of the Federal Reserve is set to announce a change in interest rates. While the job of keeping the economy's growth at a reasonable level is the Fed's most publicized job, a less talked about element of the Fed's job description is that, as a lending institution, they are to act as a "Lender of Last Resort," or LOLR.

That title strikes me as somewhat apocalyptic, with the "last resort" tag attached to it. And much as the name suggests, when you get to the point of calling on the Fed as your lender of last resort, you're in a pretty hellacious situation. They only pull out an LOLR loan for situations that have the potential to really destroy the national economy. And it's only been used a few times in the history of the institution's existence, which means it's also one of those factoids that nobody really knows about. It's like your grandmother's good china; they only break it out for big occasions. I'm talking about the sort of thing we had during the Great Depression. That's the kind of serious trouble that they're trying to avoid by invoking the LOLR provision within the Fed. Or something financially apocalyptic like when the fifth largest investment bank in the country is about to cease to exist due to the fact that they're literally running out of money.

The deal that was struck at the zero hour just before Bear turned into the pumpkin being pulled by mice was an attempt to avoid worldwide financial calamity, and there is not a shred of dramatic exaggeration in that claim. I can't overemphasize the fact that the financial disaster that was looming on the horizon was one of Armageddon proportions and, we'd long ago passed the time for traditional solutions and think tanks to determine the best course of action. Alan Schwartz publicly acknowledged that our cash reserves had "significantly deteriorated" and that we were in grave financial trouble. Monday's rumors had become Friday's news. Schwartz had to dig deep into the well of potential solutions to find a way out of this. And that's just what he did.

The thrust of the action by JP was that they were giving Bear what was in essence a twenty-eight day loan that was being bankrolled by the Federal Reserve Bank of New York. The Fed was giving JPMorgan money to in turn give us. Simple as that. We had turned into the ugly sister who needs a date, and we had to rely on our better looking sibling's own social contacts to provide us with companionship. And the ugly sister always gets the short end of the deal, no matter what.

It was, quite possibly, the single most humiliating moment for a trader to endure, despite the fact that it was entirely out of our hands. This was far worse than the painfully low stock price we were sporting at the opening, and I was really scared that $57 was going to look like a king's ransom in about thirty minutes. The Bloomberg lit up like a bonfire with headlines relating to Bear, all of which basically retold the same story. About that time, a memo circulated the trading floor, one that had been penned by Alan Schwartz as an interoffice memo addressing this new development. While reading it, I couldn't help but notice that it included a little mention of the fact that Bear was "investigating alternative strategic options" with JP. We all knew what that meant; it didn't take a Greenspan-ologist to read that subtext. I immediately turned to the woman behind me on the trading floor and said, "JP is going to buy us this weekend. 'Alternative strategic options' means we're being sold," I explained. She nodded grimly, acknowledging that what I was saying was true and that he had, in fact, read that sentence correctly.

The market opened with great fanfare at 9:30 that morning. In a space of no more than twenty minutes that seemed like the blink of an eye, Bear stock had lost half its value. Apparently being the ugly sister was as undesirable to investors as it was to high school students, no matter what favors you might offer in exchange for a date to the prom. I watched helplessly as my net worth was literally relieved of millions of dollars in restricted stock options. Somewhere in my mind, I heard Jim Cramer imploring his faithful to Sell! Sell! Sell!

Numbness overtook my body. The firm, I knew, was lost. There was no way to hide from the fact and there was no way to alter this course. Bear Stearns was done. The only thing I can liken it to is watching a train wreck. You're standing there on a hill, looking down at two locomotives racing towards one another. There's nothing either one of them can do to stop the collision, because once they realize what's going to happen, there's not enough distance to stop either train. The combined forces of the two trains heading in opposite directions meet at the point of impact, ripping each one apart with noises that are typically reserved for the most frightening of nightmares. All the engineers can hope for is to jump off the trains and survive to drive another day.

Because I'd been there in the heat of the moment before, I could picture what the floor of the exchange looked like. It would be reminiscent of a Biblical battlefield. Order chits would be flying like leaves blowing off trees in a hurricane. By the end of the day, it would look like a blizzard had blown through the building, as the discarded pieces of paper would drift into piles beneath perspiration-coated telephones and the air would smell like tension. You can't explain that smell any better than Potter Stewart could explain obscenity, but, just like you know pornography when you see it, you know the smell of tension when you smell it. I've been there and I've smelled it. And now, from the trading floor inside Bear Stearns headquarters, I could see all that was transpiring on the floor of the exchange in my mind's eye. I could smell the tension, hear the yelling, see the panic, feel the sweat. It was like I was there, and it was only ten o'clock in the morning, God help me. This is the big one, kids. Smoke 'em if you've got 'em. Remember Wall Street Rule #1, everybody. Cover your own ass.

I'm not Catholic and have no real idea how I learned the prayer, but as I sat there and watched 85 years of Wall Street history crumble around me, the words popped into my brain: Hail Mary full of grace, the Lord is with thee. Blessed art thou amongst women and blessed is the fruit of thy womb Jesus. Holy Mary mother of God, pray for us sinners, now and at the hour of our death. Amen.

My phone went off like a fire alarm. People calling, calling, calling, all of them wanting to know what's going on, what's going on, what's going on. What do you tell them? "I'm really sorry, sir, but there's no easy way to say this. You just so happened to have put your money in the pocket of the ugly sister, and the only way she could get a date was by asking her hot sister to find her somebody desperate for a little action in the backseat." And while I didn't use that exact explanation for my clients who called, it would have made about as much sense as the more politically-correct and financially-minded explanation I did use. The whole situation was so confusing to me, so confoundedly frustrating, that I couldn't properly express it.

This line-of-credit, the stop-gap measure that was supposed to solve the problem that hadn't really existed in the first place had done nothing but worsen it. When we started the week, we had no liquidity issues. But because people had said that we did have problems with our capital, it became true, even though it wasn't true when people started saying it. But because they'd said it enough, it became true. So we were forced to find capital to offset the losses we'd sustained because somebody decided we didn't have capital when we really did. So when we finally got more capital to replace the capital we'd lost, people took that as a bad sign and pointed to the fact that we'd had no capital and had to get a loan to cover it, even when we did have the capital they said we didn't have.

Like I said, the ugly sister always gets the short end of the deal, no matter what.

So as our situation stood as of noon Friday, March 14, we had endured a week that had seen our capital reserves drained due to rumors, and then refilled due to an archaic Depression-era law, the use of which had apparently scared the life out of every investor on the planet into selling their stakes in Bear stock. And to make it all just a little more vivid of a nightmare for us, the stories about other investment banks not trading with us that had been relegated to rumor status only a couple of days earlier were now full-blown truths, too. Investment banks, even the ones who had always traded with us, weren't taking my calls. The Bear Stearns treasury department, and thus the entire firm itself, had no way to fund itself; there was no short-term borrowing to be had from anywhere. So we were forced to resort to calling in our own IOUs that had been circulated.

When the equity market closed at 4 PM, the entire floor erupted into a cacophony of clapping and cheering. Not out of joy, of course, but rather out of relief that this indescribably horrible day had ended. The only two good things I could say about March 14 at that point were that it was Friday and that it was over. At that point in the day, the carnage was effectively complete; our stock closed at $30 a share, down $27 from its opening price. I looked around me at the faces of the abused souls that had spent their day in defense of the firm and in defense of their children's college funds. In the end, they were largely unsuccessful on both fronts. Many of them had lost millions of their savings that had been tied up in stock options. And they all knew, too, that their financial futures were at best uncertain; it was clear enough to all of us that we might not have a job to report to on Monday. But despite all that, they'd survived the onslaught and, at the very least, were still upright and able to move on their own power, so technically it could have been worse. But not much. They needed something. I needed something. This day—hell, this entire week—had been a disaster of monumental proportions, and that ordinarily called for a trip across the street to Maggie's Place, what we called our "Disaster Recovery Site."

But I was not in the mood for Maggie's. My small group typically liked to go across the street to the Madison Lounge inside "The Roosie," the Roosevelt Hotel at Madison and 45th. I normally get to bug them in a good-natured way about their upscale tastes, but tonight I didn't care. The day was over and anywhere would do. A little-known fact about the Roosie is that it's actually owned by, of all entities, the government of Pakistan. President Musharraf himself stays at the Roosevelt when he's in town. The Madison Lounge, though, reminds me a lot of the old Oak Bar at the Plaza or the Blue Bar at the Algonquin. Not so much in appearance, mind you, but in terms of its ambiance. It's a great old New York-style place, with a long wooden bar and leather-covered stools. There's a portrait of President Roosevelt above the fireplace down at the end of the bar, Teddy looking quite menacing in his Rough Rider uniform. It's the perfect place to celebrate achievements, because it's the sort of place that makes you feel like you're successful, just because you're inside. You sit and sip your martini, and just soak up the ambience of the place. It has an amazing restorative quality for me.

Most of the other groups had gone to Maggie's Place which, unlike the Roosie, is more the beer-on-tap kind of place that you go because things didn't quite go your way and you're looking for a little commiseration with like-minded souls, plus enough booze to get you on your way without costing you a fortune. And on the day when your world had dissolved into a dizzying whirlpool of self-destruction, Maggie's was exactly what a lot of those guys were looking for. The camera crews were again outside, and a few of them had even clued-in to the fact that Maggie's was a popular joint for a lot of us Bear folks. There was more than one trader on the floor who could walk into Maggie's and before he'd even made it as far as the bar, his drink was already poured and waiting for him. It's that kind of place with that kind of following. And given its location, a lot of that following was made up of young investment bankers and Wall Street people who were blowing off a little steam after a long day in the trenches.

Back at the Roosevelt, my own little group found that there wasn't much to talk about once we'd gotten our drinks and staked our claim on a twelve-square-foot plot of wooden floor near the back of the bar. Eyes were misty, with far-off stares that were seeing nothing. Faces looked drawn, pale; shoulders slumped noticeably. We mostly talked about what we thought would happen next. We knew that things would be changing quickly. It was going down this weekend. The scene of the crime would be inside the Bear Stearns headquarters. It would be tough and nasty, and the outcome would be ugly. There was no doubt about it. Who would buy us? Who would want us? Why did this happen? There were a lot of questions floating around the bar that night, and we attempted to work through them in hopes of providing answers. We were a team that specialized in solving problems, but not like this. We weren't trained to tackle these kinds of issues. This was it. This was the big one.

"I'm pretty sure we're going to get bought by JP," I said finally. The conversation continued from there with no prodding from me, and the soft hum of a full bar's worth of different conversations was soothing. We talked about what we'd do if we got let go, we talked about how it was nothing more than rumors that had put us in this situation and how unfair that really was, we talked about Eliot Spitzer and how his career trajectory seemed to be following ours. Small talk, like the bar in general, was soothing to my over-taxed and frazzled nerves.

Later that night, after I'd left the assembled mourners, about that time when you test fate by saying that things can't get any worse, the Fed dropped another bombshell on us. The terms of the facility that they had so kindly arranged with JPMorgan only the night before dictated that the line-of-credit was good for "up to 28 days." After approximately twelve hours of existence on the public record, the line-of-credit was being modified somewhat, as the Fed made another announcement: Our facility would expire at 6 PM on Sunday, March 16. We had just under forty-eight hours—the rest of that Friday night, all of Saturday and most of Sunday— to find a way out of this mess. When I heard the announcement, that was it. I was utterly speechless.

CHAPTER NINE

Brother Can You Spare a Dime?

"Revenge is an act of passion; vengeance of justice.
Injuries are revenged; crimes are avenged."

—SAMUEL JOHNSON

A study done in regards to foreclosures arising from the subprime crisis at the beginning of 2008 found that about half of all homes that
fall victim to foreclosure are left in less-than-move-in condition by their
former owners. Apparently as a final act of revenge on the companies making money off of others' financial problems, the homeowners have resorted to creative ways of making the job of taking over the home a little
harder. Real estate agents report opening front doors of foreclosed homes
only to discover paint poured on carpeting, holes punched into walls, rotting food and other unpleasant gifts left by the former owners. The agents
who are charged with reselling the home find it an unconscionable act of
vandalism; the perpetrators see it as a way of evening the score. The message is that you can kick the homeowner out, but don't expect them to roll
out the red carpet for you, their conquerors. In response, many banks have
resorted to cash payments of up to a few thousand dollars, held in escrow
pending the exchange of ownership, in return for the homeowners' leaving the home as clean as possible.

While it might seem a petty action on the part of the owners who are
being foreclosed upon, many people find that their brains are hard-wired
to seek revenge; all it takes to trigger the response is the right condition.
For example, if your home—the only home you've ever owned in your life,
the home you worked your fingers to the bone in order to keep, the home
you bought with a mortgage you knew you couldn't afford but that some
smooth-talking mortgage broker talked you into buying because he needed one more mortgage to meet his quota for the month—is suddenly taken

away from you by the same people who convinced you that it was not only your right to own, but also your duty to buy. That simple act of revocation might just trigger even the most mild-mannered person to commit acts previously deemed incomprehensible. It's impossible to say until you've found yourself in the position. I've yet to have to walk that mile, so I'm in no position to judge.

Much of the need for revenge in this type of situation resides in the psychological perception that the entity taking peoples' homes away from them are callous and uncaring. And while this may or may not be an accurate representation of those doing the foreclosing, the fact of the matter is that they're only doing their jobs. Much like police officers, these people are simply doing what their job requires of them. But like police officers, they're often seen as profiting from human suffering, degradation and misery. And they seem to do so with a distinctly noticeable lack of concern for the people whose lives they are in charge of. But the fact of the matter is that it's professional behavior, not some sort of latent sadism, that allows these people to behave the way they do.

Observers have noted the same sort of professional behavior on Wall Street, where it's not entirely uncommon for parties facing financial problems to reach out for help from other, more solvent firms. Such was the case in 1998, when Long-Term Capital Management (LTCM), a hedge fund founded by John Meriweather in 1994, faced imminent collapse. Meriweather, the former vice-chairman and head of bond trading at Solomon Brothers, partnered with some pretty heavy-hitting names in the financial world, including Myron Scholes and Robert C. Merton, who shared the Nobel Prize in Economics in 1997. So this was not a question of people who didn't know what they were doing getting together and starting a fund. This was a group of men who knew their way around the markets, and they were veritable Zen masters of investment strategies. In the larger financial world at the time, most investors had never heard of these potentially hyper-lucrative things called hedge funds, and they had no idea of the immense risks that the funds took on. That was all about to change.

The fund started with over a billion dollars in investors' money, and the managers proceeded to invest in bonds, relying on Meriweather's expertise in the field. However, a desire to increase return (what some people call "greed") led them to invest in other areas, areas in which the managers were not so experienced. They were highly leveraged in a lot of positions, and when things went south economically, the fund went downhill fast. The downturn started in 1998, with a series of European and Asian market downturns. Because LTCM had invested heavily in those markets, their balance sheets took a tremendous hit; so while their asset values were dropping, their liabilities—specifically the money they owed on the original purchase prices—remained constant. By September of 1998, LTCM had lost approximately $1.85 billion in capital. Over the course of the next few weeks, the value of the fund's equity sank to about $600 million. And they were still highly leveraged. Not a good place to find yourself as a hedge fund manager.

Enter, stage left, the boys from Goldman Sachs. Goldie paired up with AIG and Berkshire Hathaway, and were offering to buy out the partners of LTCM for $250 million. In addition, they wanted to inject $3.75 billion into the fund's operating capital and absorb the fund into Goldman's own umbrella. LTCM rejected the offer. So in stepped our old friends from the Federal Reserve Bank of New York. The Fed put together a bailout package in hopes of averting a wider financial crisis. The fear then was that if a hedge fund collapsed, it could trigger a larger market panic. Of course, these days, hedge funds collapse daily, so it's old news. But at the time, like I said, most people had never heard of hedge funds, so the idea of a fund collapsing was a terrifying prospect.

The basic premise of the buyout scenario was that all the major investment banks would contribute to the fund as a way of keeping LTCM afloat. In exchange for their financial contributions, each bank would receive an ownership stake in the fund that would account for 90% of the total fund, dispersed proportionately to each individual firm based on their contributions. The list of contributors read something like a list of benefactors to a major philanthropy published in the charity's annual report. Goldman, Merrill, Morgan Stanley, Solomon Brothers and a host of other major Wall Street players were listed in the equivalent of the "Gold Circle" level, with contributions in the $300 million range. Société Générale occupied the "Silver Circle" at $125 million. The "Bronze Circle" of $100 million donors included Lehman Brothers and Paribas.

Noticeably absent from any of the contribution levels was Bear Stearns.

Publicly, Bear fell back on the excuse that it wasn't our job to bail out other peoples' financial mistakes. After all, part of investing—especially in hedge funds—was the potential for loss, and if these people had made unwise investments, what business was that of ours? We certainly wouldn't expect other investment banks to rescue us in a similar situation; if Jimmy Cayne had only had a crystal ball in those days, maybe things would have turned out differently. But whatever the reasoning, it was a professional posture, much like the prison guard refusing to bend the rules. The rules of the game of high finance included high risk and, quite possibly, massive gains. You also ran the risk of equally massive losses in the event things didn't work out so well as you might have hoped. In the end, you took the good with the bad, and that's the way it went. Dog eat dog, and all that.

On a more pragmatic level, Bear executives were concerned about the impression the bailout was going to create for the larger market. In other words, they were afraid that this bailout, rather than staving off financial panic, was going to in fact increase the likelihood of that panic. And they didn't want to be any more exposed than they had to be. The boys at Bear were being good practitioners of Wall Street Rule #1 and covering their own asses. The larger financial community, however, didn't appreciate the maverick response from Bear Stearns regardless of how pragmatic we might have thought we were being. And though there was no formal punishment or censure they could slap the firm with, it was an act not forgotten. In the end, the panic that Bear had been so scared of never materialized. The firms who had assisted in the buyout were actually rewarded with a small profit that had resulted from the liquidation of LTCM's positions. All those investment banks ended up better for their involvement in the buyout. But it didn't matter. Bear had not elected to participate. And no matter what banks had made what profits, their memories held fast to the refusal of Bear to come to the aid of another in times of trouble. And if you think a pissed-off woman is tough to deal with, you've never seen a room full of investment bankers scorned. Hell really hath no fury like investment bankers scorned.

One of the firms with the strongest memory of the slight by Bear was Goldman Sachs, whose Chief Operating Officer at the time was Hank Paulson. Despite his successes at Goldie—he eventually rose to the level of CEO of the firm—it was not until 2006 that Hank gained some semblance of notoriety in the larger public body of humanity. It was May of that year that Paulson was nominated by President George W. Bush to be the new Secretary of the Treasury. In that position, Paulson was in the position of developing financial policies for the United States, and one of his most notable acts in that capacity was the creation of the Hope Now

Alliance. The Hope Now Alliance was created in 2007 to help those home-owners facing foreclosure as a result of the subprime mortgage crisis. And though the Alliance's actual successes have been downplayed amidst much criticism by homeowners and lawmakers alike, Paulson's concern for those homeowners stuck in that financial quagmire was apparent. It is entirely possible that those in the establishment of the financial world—Mr. Paulson included—still held a grudge against Bear for our refusal to help out in the LTCM crisis. Human nature is hard to shake sometimes. After all, it was just business, especially for an appointed federal official in charge of domestic economic policy.

But I'm sure it wasn't just Paulson that remembered the neglect exhib-ited by Bear during the LTCM collapse. I have no doubt that every firm on the planet remembered. And when it came time for Bear to ask for hand-outs, we found a pretty cold reception. We could live with that. It was business, after all, and if we were going to live by the sword, it made sense that we would also die by the sword. It was part of the deal we'd all signed on for. But when it turned into perceived favoritism angled specif-ically against us, it turned into something more than just business as usual. It turned personal.

At 6 o'clock on Sunday night, March 16, 2008, our deal with JPMor-gan was set to expire. The Federal Bank of New York—the same ones who had facilitated the bailout of Meriweather's hedge fund ten years earlier—after dropping the deadline bomb on the previous Friday, was poised to drop yet another one. They were going to loan JPMorgan $30 billion in order to facilitate that firm's acquisition of Bear Stearns. My prophecy on Friday was, unfortunately, proving to be accurate. The firm was being pur-chased by JPMorgan.

I went into the office late Sunday afternoon to see what was going on and to see if there was any new information I could get to help explain this whole mess, as I still wasn't sure what was actually happening. My super-visor had made a presentation that afternoon to the JPMorgan equities derivatives division, who would become my new bosses in the event that the JP execs deemed me worthy of hiring once they'd taken over the firm. There were a group of equities guys there, trying to explain our funding situation within the equities area. Among everyone assembled in the office, there was an aura of impending doom. A feeling of disaster hung in the air; there was no question that something terrible was about to happen. Soon after I arrived, all the negativity in the room became real. All the impending doom, all the feelings of disaster, all the senses of a hideous out-come for Bear combined into a single, awful announcement: JPMorgan was buying Bear Stearns, lock, stock and barrel for $2 a share. The business, the building, the whole thing. All for $2 a share.

A cup of coffee at Starbucks was now actually more expensive than a share of our stock.

BSC, the trading symbol for Bear Stearns common stock, had achieved the title of "fallen angel." On Wall Street, a fallen angel is an investment—a bond or a stock—that has fallen to an all-time low. And $2 a share fit the bill for BSC. That share price meant that the total sale price for our beloved firm was around $236 million for the whole she-bang. Our stock price had lost about 70% from the IPO price from 1985. So without adjusting for inflation and all of the associated cost-of-living increases in that time, the original Bear Stearns investor had lost seventy cents on every dollar he'd put in to the company over the course of 23 years. Certainly not the poster child for encouraging investment in the stock market.

As soon as the announcement was made, those assembled around me looked visibly ill. The shockwave that travelled through the office was palpable. There were no words to accurately describe what we were feel-ing. Where in the hell did they come up with $2 a share? The building alone should have been worth a minimum of $10, not to mention the busi-ness itself. We'd been around for 85 years. We had offices on three conti-nents. We were Bear Stearns. Somebody needed to tell these people that we were worth a hell of a lot more than $2 a share. About this time, peo-ple who hadn't yet made it to the office began to filter in as word spread. The ones who lived too far away to come in to the office began calling. Everyone was asking the same thing: How did they get $2? The same question started coming in on email, too, from colleagues both across the country and in Asia. Word was spreading fast.

I huddled with several of my colleagues to see who knew what. None of us, until that point, grasped how dire the firm's financial situation was and we didn't understand the forces that were working against us. But we did figure that the $2 share price was indicative of something horrific on our balance sheets, what we call "toxic waste" in investment banking. We listened in on the conference call from JPMorgan's executives who want-ed to discuss the buyout. We all expected to hear about some kind of toxic waste on the balance sheets. But there was nothing. Not a damn thing. There wasn't a single negative item they had to discuss about our balance sheets. In fact, one JPMorgan representative went so far as to say the firm was "happy with the conservatively marked positions." So what the hell?

We were left with no explanation for the ridiculously low share price. Our speculation gradually shifted, though, from the cause of the bargain-basement price paid by JPMorgan to worries about what the week ahead held. Bear was done, that much was a given. But we were sure the market wasn't done with its sacrifices. And the ripple effect could wipe out half the investment banks on Wall Street in no time flat. The resulting economic whirlpool would put all of us not just out of work, but into bread lines.

Our overarching fear was that the Bear sale would trigger a huge sell-off in the equities market. And then, God only knows where the crosshairs would land. After Bear had gone down, somebody was going to be next. Our general feelings were that Lehman was next on the block for Monday, and Merrill would be Tuesday's victim. And as it turns out, I learned from a friend at Lehman that while we were learning of our $2 share price, the Lehman guys were preparing to face the same kind of assault, as they feared that the market would turn its sights on them after Bear was dead and buried. Nobody would be safe once the Bear had been killed. A worldwide financial disaster was, at that very moment, as real a possibility as it had ever been in my mind. And as real as I ever hope it to be in the future, for that matter.

But that worldwide financial panic would not happen. Other investment banks would not be dealt the same fate as Bear Stearns had suffered. The other firms on the Street were safe. It's not that they were somehow immune to investor panics spawned by rumors. And it's not that they were somehow immune to those investors pulling their money out of those firms. The fact of the matter was that the Fed had done something that guaranteed the financial well-being of every investment bank in the country, an action that would preserve their financial resources regardless of what rumors circulated or how much investor money was withdrawn.

Five minutes after Bear was officially left for dead and had been purchased by JP, the Fed announced that they would be opening what is called the discount window to every investment bank in the country as a way of forestalling any future bank runs. In other words, they wanted to avoid another Bear Stearns collapse. A colleague told me that Alan Schwartz nearly put his fist through a wall upon learning of this announcement; he'd been pushing for this exact thing for almost a year, to no avail. Why would the Fed do this now, after Bear was effectively finished, when such a move could have saved the firm? This is, to my mind, how the Fed dealt with the moral hazard in the market; this was the point of the lesson they were trying to teach all of us.

The discount window is another action the Federal Reserve Bank has at its disposal to deal with money-related issues. In essence, the discount window allows banks to borrow money for a short period of time, money that they might need to help with a liquidity problem they might be experiencing, for example. And up to this point, the discount window had only been open to commercial banks. It was a sort of last line of defense against bank panics. But now it was open to investment banks, too, just in case any of them should need massive infusions of short-term cash in the next several days as a way of staving off bankruptcy. Aside from causing a spontaneous remodeling in part of Alan's office, the move by the Fed put investment banks on the same footing as commercial banks in terms of borrowing money. Now securities brokers would be able to borrow money at only .25 basis points over the rate charged to commercial banks, a difference that usually hovered around .5 basis points. And on top of that, the Fed drastically lowered the overall lending rate. So suddenly investment banks could borrow money from the Fed at what were ridiculously low rates.

And the Fed added the bonus of a time extension for paying back the loan. Whereas loans to commercial banks used to have to pay back their loans in 30 days (which had been extended from an overnight deadline just a year before) to 90 days. This was the first time in history that investment banks were given access to the discount window. A whole lot of economists found fault with the fact that the Fed was allowing borrowers to use high-risk CDOs as collateral for these loans. CDOs like those mortgage bonds that seemed to hang on like Mercer staph and caused even more damage. If these investment banks defaulted on their loans—like that would ever happen—then the taxpayers would be stuck holding the tab. That's the thing about the risk associated with these pesky mortgage bonds: Somebody always ends up paying the tab when things go wrong, and it's usually not the person who's making the money off them.

There was a sudden transformation of sorts, whereby investment banks were bestowed with a new kind of existence, an existence that made them exactly the same as commercial banks when it came to borrowing money from the Fed. Before now, investment banks had been forced to borrow money from commercial banks; now they could go straight to the cow for their milk. From a legal standpoint, now that the investment banks and commercial banks were basically one and the same in terms of their abilities to borrow money, the Glass-Stegall Act was no longer in effect; because it had created investment banking as a separate entity from commercial banking—and because that separation had been torn down—Glass-Stegall no longer applied. There was no longer any distinct difference between investment and commercial banking; the two bodies—commercial and investment—were now in direct competition with one another. When Glass-Steegal was in effect, investment banks had to go to the commercial banks for loans; now they could go straight to the Fed, bypassing their commercial counterparts. It was at that exact moment that we all realized Bear had been sacrificed by the Fed. All indications were that the Fed had waited until Bear had gone completely under before opening the discount window. Had we been granted access to the discount window, Bear would have survived. Five minutes. That's all it took. If they'd made the decision five minutes earlier, all of this would have been avoided. We would have been wounded, we would have been bloody, we would have had a long road back to stability. But Bear would have remained alive. None of us assembled believed that it was an accident that the announcement had come so quickly after our firm's demise.

In the end, what all this last-minute maneuvering meant was that the Fed was coming to the rescue of banks that didn't need rescuing. And what's more, they were only coming to the rescue of those banks after they'd basically assured the demise of Bear Stearns. They had loaned JPMorgan the nails and the hammer and the coffin. Now it was just up to them to put us in the ground for good. So from the point of view of a lot of Bear employees, justified or not, this mess had taken a turn from being a business transaction to being an act of revenge on the part of a few people who thought they'd been done wrong by Bear in the past. And a lot of those people were in positions of economic power within the whole structure. And human nature, which is hard to shake some times, is also a two-way street.

They were gunning for us, no doubt about it; they would extract their revenge from the hides of the Bear Stearns employees one way or another. It didn't matter that the majority of us hadn't worked for Bear at the time of the LTCM collapse, it didn't matter that a lot of us hadn't even been in investment banking at the time, and it certainly matter that Bear had already suffered as much as we had. Somebody was going to pay, by God, and that somebody was going to be Bear Stearns.

The mood in the office was one of stunned anger. We felt like we'd been singled out by the rest of the financial community. We were paying for the sins of our forefathers. We'd been crucified. I couldn't stand being around the place any longer, and I left about ten o'clock that night. I remember nothing of the taxi ride home; I was completely numb by now. When I finally made it home, I had a glass of red wine and went to bed, naively thinking I might be able to sleep. I kept getting out of bed to check the Asian markets to see what was happening as a result of the news of Bear's sale. Already emails were coming in from colleagues in the Far East. They wanted to see what was happening, they wanted to see how I was doing. They wanted gossip. The Bear Stearns collapse had become a very public event, a spectator sport. And people were lined up to watch the final destruction in what could only be called, if one were of the mindset to make jokes at a time like this, Bear baiting.

Monday, I knew, was going to be a really, really bad day.

CHAPTER TEN

To the Victors Go the Spoils

"Veni, vidi, vici."

—JULIUS CAESAR

When Julius Caesar wrote to the Roman Senate that he had come, seen and conquered the forces of the Pontic army in 47 BC, it was more than simply an announcement of victory. It was a declaration of supremacy, a declaration of absolute and complete domination over another. The story of that victory places two opposing armies—the Roman forces led by Caesar and the Pontic army led by Pharnaces—at either end of a large valley in what is present-day Turkey. The valley held significance for both armies, as Pharnaces' father had defeated another Roman force at this very spot twenty years earlier. After pre-battle preparations had been made and the fighting ensued some time in May of that year, the massacre was bloody and quick. According to Caesar's accounts of the battle, from start to finish the time elapsed was approximately four hours. What was left of the Pontic army after that brief time fled in a mass retreat. Caesar's succinct and pointed announcement to the Roman Senate mirrored the quick victory in length and purpose: I came, I saw, I conquered.

That battle was only a small part of the larger Alexandrian War, the final outcome of which saw Julius Caesar ascend the throne as the undisputed ruler of all of Egypt. Each battle along the way became a piece of that larger puzzle. Each victory built upon the victories that had come before, and eventually Caesar had acquired enough victories to become the all-powerful ruler of the region. Today, while battles are still fought and wars waged by world leaders, we don't see the same sort of empire-building that predominated ancient times. With a few notable exceptions—Adolf Hitler's annexations of portions of eastern Europe and more recently Saddam Hussein's invasion of Kuwait, for example—most world rulers today are satisfied with the way the world's borders have been drawn. The same cannot be said, though, for corporate America.

Takeovers in the business world are a common occurrence, but the terminology is sometimes misconstrued. Basically there are two types, friendly and hostile. And already the misnomers start flying. The problem with these two broad terms is that they don't adequately describe what is actually happening in the process. A friendly takeover doesn't necessarily mean that everyone gets together and has a few cocktails and pats each other on the back, and a hostile takeover doesn't necessarily involve a flaming arrow through the window announcing the aggressor's intentions. Quite often, in fact, a friendly takeover can be quite contentious and a hostile takeover can be exactly what a company's shareholders want.

Any takeover attempt of a publicly traded company has to, at some point, involve that company's board of directors. In a friendly takeover, a bidder makes an offer directly to the board. If the board finds the offer is acceptable, meaning that they feel it serves the shareholders' interests better than the current situation, then they vote to recommend allowing the takeover. The recommendation goes to the shareholders, who are expected to vote in favor of it, given the endorsement by the members of the board who are elected to their position with the expectation that they will be keeping the interests of shareholders at the forefront of their minds. Things get a little sticky, though, if the board rejects the offer but the bidder doesn't want to take no for an answer.

When the board of the target company rejects the offer up-front and the would-be acquirer continues to pursue the takeover, it is said to be a hostile takeover. The problem with that term, though, is that it conjures up images of pistols at twenty paces or perhaps a rock thrown through a window with a note attached to it declaring malicious intent. Or better yet, some sort of made-for-TV wrestling cage match, perhaps featuring none other than the masked Governor Spitzer and his paralyzed foe Albany. But the fact of the matter is that a hostile takeover—just like a hostile witness in a trial—simply means that the bidder is not acting in the manner that was expected of him. This is not necessarily bad from the standpoint of the shareholders, as I've said. The sometimes hidden truth about takeovers is that what is labeled a hostile takeover can often be seen as a beneficial thing for the target firm, at least from the perspective of the shareholders. And there are plenty of examples that illustrate this point.

Perhaps the best-known case of a hostile takeover—also known as a "corporate raid"—that shareholders were in favor of was the case of RJR-Nabisco and the epic battle that ensued when that company resisted the takeover attempts of Kohlberg Kravis Roberts (KKR). The attempt was at the time the single largest takeover in the history of Wall Street and was, at varying times, friendly, hostile and just plain ugly. The action took place in the late 80's, and centered on an attempted leveraged buyout (LBO), which is typically a hostile takeover that is unsolicited and unwanted by the target company. Ironically enough, I learned later that KKR was at one point interested in buying a 20% share of Bear, a deal the firm was negotiating with then-CEO Jimmy Cayne. The deal, due to a host of conflicting issues, fell through.

An LBO is what it sounds like—using leverage to buy out a company; the purchaser issues bonds in order to purchase a company. Oftentimes the assets of the company being taken over are used as the collateral for the bonds. So the better the company looks on paper, the easier it is for it to become the target of a leveraged buyout. Because of that contradictory situation—the more successful you are, the better your chances of falling victim to an LBO—a lot of investors see LBOs as the most mercanary of all takeovers. These are the sorts of things that keep CEOs awake at night. As one venture capitalist colleague put it, "I work with people who specialize in LBOs. They're my friends. But calling them 'LBO friends' just sounds like an oxymoron."

Corporate officials fear LBOs for the simple reason that the takeover wrests control from the current officials and oftentimes drives the company into financial straits from which it is impossible to recover. The takeover artist who formulates the deal, though, makes out like a bandit and doesn't care if the company stays afloat or not. Thus the "mercenary" descriptor. But from an investor's point of view, especially a less-than-educated investor in terms of the finer points of what all these acronyms mean, the deal sounds pretty good. You see what the target company is worth, you figure that income won't be going anywhere anytime soon, the collateral is more than enough to cover the debt, you can't lose. The takeover company issues bonds and sells them to investors. And they clearly wouldn't be doing this if it weren't going to make money for everyone, right? It's a can't-miss deal. Who are these board of directors people anyway? They clearly can't see what an incredible opportunity is sitting right there.

Like Mom always said, if it sounds too good to be true, it probably is. Consider the fact that the usual debt ratio in an LBO is 90% debt to 10%

equity. So when you buy a bond, there's not a whole lot of equity backing it up; you're leveraged to the gills, just like our friends in the hedge fund game. And just file away in the back of your mind for a second the memory of how those hedge funds fared with leveraged assets. So because the debt load is so high, the bonds are rated as sub-investment grade, or what a lot of people call "junk bonds." This is not to say that the bonds themselves are worthless; it's just that they're often such a high risk investment that the default rate is much higher than average. Junk bonds have made many a man wealthy beyond his wildest dreams. Junk bonds have also been the financial ruin of plenty of suckers out there, too.

From the perspective of the average investor who's loaded down with bonds financing a takeover, the biggest problem with an LBO is that ungodly wide debt ratio. 90% debt generates a lot of interest payments, so when the company that is taken over is finally absorbed and the takeover company is forced to start making those interest payments on their debt, the money can run out fast. Case in point, in 1988, Canadian real estate developer Robert Campeau bought Federated Department Stores in an LBO that featured a whopping 97% debt to only 3% equity. Even by LBO standards that's outrageous. The interest payments became so great that Campeau's firm was unable to meet their financial obligation. The market didn't cooperate either, as retail sales dropped. The end result was a rapid downward spiral that ended in Federated's bankruptcy. Investors took a bath on that one; Campeau's corporation faded from existence.

So fearful are some companies of LBOs and the potential financial pitfalls they bring with them that they have taken a page from the playbooks of the United States Air Force and its old Cold War-era U2 spy planes, the pilots of which were supposedly issued cyanide capsules and poison-tipped pins that were to be used to commit suicide rather than face capture and interrogation by enemy captors if they were shot down over enemy airspace. Gary Francis Powers, the only U2 pilot to be shot down, did not carry through with the suicide pact. His capture effectively ended the U2 spy plane program. But the concept of the poison pill lives on in corporate America, and as odd is it sounds, companies have been known to literally sabotage their own balance sheets in order to make themselves appear less desirable to LBO specialists. It's their own version of avoiding capture by the Russians.

Going back to the RJR Nabisco deal for a second, it started out as an attempt by the CEO of the firm trying to buy his own firm. Ross Johnson, president and CEO of RJR Nabisco, together with his management team, attempted to buyout the public shareholders of the company and take the company private in order to help the company's stock recover from the stock market crash of October, 1997. However, you don't buy a company like RJR Nabisco without people taking notice, and that's what Hank Kravis and George Roberts at KKR did. They noticed. And they had similar ideas. Only their ideas included making themselves wealthy through an LBO, which happened to be one of KKR's specialties. They are a financial investment firm that is in the business of buying and selling businesses. So that's what they set out to do.

Johnson's attempted takeover was friendly and well-intended, at least on the surface. He no doubt wanted what was best for himself and his ego, but he also wanted what was best for the company as a whole. So his buyout offer was not what you would call hostile. And typically firms like KKR that specialize in LBOs don't like to do hostile deals, because they figure all a hostile takeover does is upset the shareholders and make their own jobs that much more difficult. In fact, Morgan Stanley, one of the investment banks advising KKR, actually suggested a hostile takeover before the deal went through; KKR declined to pursue that option. It was going to be a friendly deal all-around. Everybody would make money, everybody would love the final product.

At this point in the game, it sounds a lot like you've got two sides that are basically playing nice; there's no real conflict here. Friendly takeovers coming from both sides, everybody is going to win no matter what. It sounds like all we need to do at this point is figure out who's offering the most money and start planning the second home in St. Barth's. Things got a little ugly, though, when Ross Johnson's group announced that they would pay $75 a share for RJR stock. And while that might sound like a pretty good price (especially when your own stock is trading at a whopping two bucks a share), it was the equivalent of stealing the company. It was that low an offer. The board, despite the fact that Ross was the firm's CEO and they liked him as both a person and as a professional, vetoed his offer. The amount was far too low, and Johnson knew it.

Johnson was not to be denied, though. So the takeover attempt was taking a hostile turn. Then comes KKR with another offer. This one is a friendly offer, remember, because KKR doesn't like to do hostile. They were willing to up the ante to $90 a share. Basically what you had going on at the time was a bidding war similar to ones waged by two parties wanting to buy the same house in some ultra-exclusive resort community. Ross and company, working with investment bankers from Solomon Brothers and Shearson Lehman Hutton, countered yet again, this time offering $112. They were, at least on some level, admitting that their original offer was so ridiculously low that they felt the need to overcompensate, perhaps. The collective wisdom of the group was self-assured that they could not be outbid on this one, especially not with a leveraged buyout. The numbers just didn't justify it. There was no way an LBO could afford the debt ratio required to outbid this latest offer. They kicked back, lit their cigars and waited for their approval to come through.

You've got to realize, though, that the KKR team didn't get where they are by giving up, and they also didn't get where they are by being dumb. These guys have some of the sharpest business minds this side of hedge fund managers, and they went over the offer from Team Johnson with as fine a tooth comb as they could get their hands on. And in their search, they found a loophole. So they came back to the table with an offer of $109 a share. It was a lower offer than Johnson's, but it was the offer the board finally accepted. In fact, the friendly takeover-turned-hostile had turned friendly once again. Funny how these cycles come around full-circle. But it was an LBO. Could there actually be such a thing as a friendly leveraged buyout?

In the end, why did the board settle on a lower offer? It makes no sense, on the surface, that an offer that is clearly and obviously less than another offer should be accepted. But the guys at KKR discovered that Johnson's offer didn't have what is called a reset. That means that the value of the offer could change over time. If the market changed drastically, there was no adjustment made to the share price, so the shareholders could end up getting far less than they'd been promised. The KKR group guaranteed a $109 share price, regardless of market fluctuations, and that guarantee is what earned them the nod. Interestingly enough, the board of RJR Nabisco actually welcomed the KKR group with open arms. Like I said, perhaps it was the mythical friendly LBO.

And it wasn't just the guarantees that kept Johnson from closing the deal. A major turn-off for a lot of people in the ever-important court of public perception was the deal that Johnson had written for himself in the proposed deal, and which someone made sure to make public. Draw your own conclusions as to who it was that leaked that information, but suffice it to say that Johnson stood to make an immediate $200 million off the deal. If he had succeeded and managed to turn the company back into the profitable firm he claimed he could, he'd be standing on top of about $1 billion in five years. In financial circles, we call that a golden parachute— your safety net of unfathomable amounts of money that relieves you of those pesky nagging worries about the actual future of the company you've just acquired. On Wall Street we call that a good capitalist. But when you're the average guy reading about it in the newspaper, you call him a greedy bastard. In some circles, the two terms—"good capitalist" and "greedy bastard"—are interchangeable.

On Monday morning, we still weren't sure what to call the guys at JPMorgan.

▲ ▲ ▲

Monday, March 17, was St. Patrick's Day, and the New York City celebration of the holiday is legendary, and included a parade with the ubiquitous bagpipe players so common to Irish celebrations. The parade makes its way up Fifth Avenue, beginning at 44th Street. The location of the Bear Stearns headquarters on Madison Avenue means that our office is near the staging area for the parade itself, and it is an annual tradition that the bagpipe players come in to the office and offer a display of their musical talents to those working on each of the floors in the building. This year, though, it was a different crowd outside our office. As the day progressed, we would end up losing a lot more than just the bagpipes. We ended up losing our shirts, too.

CNBC had set up their remote broadcast cameras directly in front of our office, using the Bear Stearns sign above the door as a backdrop for their coverage of the firm's demise. The cameras and the lights and all the associated support elements that go into the production of a remote television broadcast created a circus atmosphere outside the building; it was quite the juxtaposition, this yoking together of the firm's destruction and the world of make-believe that is associated with television. The presence of all of the equipment and curious onlookers outside kept the bagpipers at bay, and their absence wasn't lost on any of us. We all missed them, and would have traded the CNBC cameras for the bagpipes any day.

The takeover of Bear Stearns by JPMorgan, I suppose, has to be called a friendly takeover, simply because there was no resistance to it. We had no choice in the matter, so we didn't fight them on their ridiculously lowball offer. What were we going to do? It's not like our current economic position put us in the prime spot to be driving a hard bargain. Ross Johnson's offer of $75 for RJR was attempted robbery; $2 is so simply insane a price that it confounds the mind to even consider it. But like I said, we had no choice; our only other viable alternative was bankruptcy. And to call bankruptcy a viable alternative is about as much of an oxymoron as referring to guys who specialize in leveraged buyouts as friends. JPMorgan had come, JPMorgan had seen. Bear Stearns had been conquered.

The news of the new share price had become public knowledge instantaneously throughout the world, and the precipitous drop of $28 a share in Bear stock drove the Dow Jones Industrial Average down drastically, despite the fact that only a week earlier the Dow had seen its best day in terms of gains since July of 2002. The drop in the value of the Dow Jones resulting from Bear's collapse is a point that requires a little explanation, as Bear Stearns wasn't ever even a component of the Dow. The Dow Jones Industrial Average (DJIA) is one of several stock market indices that track performance of stocks as a group. It was created by the publisher of the *Wall Street Journal,* Charles Dow, and first published in 1896. Its purpose is to gauge the performance of the stock market as a whole by tracking the performance of 30 of the most widely-held stocks in circulation. In literature, they call this synecdoche, allowing a part to represent the whole. The same concept applies with the Dow. The part, the 30 stocks that comprise the DJIA, represent the whole by offering a basic idea of how the market is behaving at a particular day. And truth be told, it's a pretty accurate indicator.

The Dow includes a variety of companies, firms like Alcoa and Exxon-Mobil and Home Depot. And while there are a few representatives from the financial sector, the majority of Dow components have nothing to do with investment banking. So it perhaps seems odd that a drop in a stock like Bear could affect so drastically the overall average of the market that way. In other words, why does the value of Coca-Cola stock reflect what's happening with Bear Stearns? The answer to that lies in the fact that we live in a world with an economy that is so intricately interwoven that a rise or fall in one segment of the market oftentimes results in a similar move in another segment.

For example, when Bear's stock falls, other financial groups don't look like such the safe haven for bargain-seeking investors because, all of a sudden, that sector of the economy looks pretty fragile. And what's more, the guys at Lehman were already preparing for their own bankruptcy proceedings in the event that the market turned on them after it had finished with us. But they didn't have liquidity issues, right? Neither did Bear when those rumors started. In other words, once Bear went down, all the banks looked bad from an investment point of view, because we had just shown the world how quickly a major firm could go under. And when those financial services stocks start looking bad, other things start looking bad, too. People get worried. Panic sets in. And if the Bear experience taught us nothing else at all, it's that panic doesn't need rhyme or reason; it just is what is. And when it is what it is, it's bad. People don't necessarily understand why they're doing what they're doing when they're panicked. They just know that they need to do something, and there's safety in numbers. So the herd mentality takes over and you see huge sell-offs in the market. All because somebody started a rumor a week earlier.

This kind of thinking had been stewing in my overtaxed brain all night; I'd thought of nothing else. I even recall a brief dream sequence about financial markets crashing. I had slept next-to-none that night, and my wife had actually gotten a few minutes less sleep than I. We were both up and in the kitchen by five o'clock Monday morning. We didn't talk much; there really wasn't much to say. I went for a quick run—I felt like it was vital to keep up some semblance of normalcy during what I was sure was going to a day full of abnormal events—and went to the office. Everyone had arrived early. Gathered in small groups, talking quietly about what had happened and what they thought they were going to do. And there was a lot of reminiscing, as you can no doubt imagine, about first days at the office, best days on the trading floor, funnies memories, that sort of thing. Everyone was attempting to appear upbeat and happy, just another day at the office. I didn't yet realize that humor was going to be the life ring we all clung to in order to get us through this nightmare of a day. By seven o'clock, my phone was ringing non-stop.

It's a pretty good indication that something major has happened in your life when literally half the people you've ever met in life throughout your travels around the world are suddenly, spontaneously, calling you to see how you're doing. The specific language they choose while talking to you is an indication as to the sort of major event that has recently transpired. Tones of good-natured happiness and jokes like college buddies recalling war stories are usually a sign that you've just received some sort of well-publicized and quite substantial cash windfall. Alternatively, tones of supportive sympathy like you would use with a seven-year-old—"Hey, buddy, how you holding up? Things are gonna' look up, sport."—are usually reserved for major illnesses or other personal catastrophes.

BEAR TRAP

The calls I was getting, though, were characterized by a tone usually reserved for those times when blood-covered witnesses of mass killings congregate immediately after the event, or survivors of some kind of atomic blast stumble upon the charred remains of their family. On that Monday morning, I fielded more personal phone calls that began with "Holy shit!" than I can even begin to count. Literally. That phrase. For whatever reason, "Holy shit!" was deemed the best opening line for a conversation about the utter and absolute collapse of the investment banking firm that I had worked for. It was as if some memo circulated around to all my friends, suggesting they use "Holy shit!" as the perfect ice breaker today. There is, I'm sure, some kind of political statement on the demise of the English language in modern society buried within that fact. But at the time, I was too busy answering phone calls to think about it.

Everyone who was calling at this point was good-natured and well-meaning. These were, for the most part, friends of mine that I'd worked with in the past or met during my travels or even gone to school with all those many years ago. This was different from the night before, when colleagues were calling in hopes of getting some sort of quasi-legal inside scoop on what to expect from the market the following day. This wasn't finger-pointing and rubber-necking at the scene of a disastrous accident. This was sincere and genuine concern for my well-being. I really did appreciate all of the contact from well-wishers and supporters. I do think that many of them were actually surprised by my response, which was basically one of gratitude mixed with happiness. Given the situation, it was obvious that this would be a sort of Shakespearean brave new world. All of my thoughts about the future were now rapidly accelerating in terms of their immediacy. My future was now. So my general response to the crisis was that it could be an opportunity in the making. The loss of money didn't bother me that much. The golden handcuffs—the name given to financial incentives like restricted stock options designed to keep an employee loyal to a particular firm—were gone. They'd been unlocked, removed, obliterated. What I felt was an overwhelming sense of liberation.

Of course I was also experiencing a bit of shock by the whole thing— just like everyone else around me—as we tried to make sense of the massive destruction of wealth that had taken place. But in my mind, I was moving ahead. For whatever reason, I am an optimist, and nothing—not even destruction on this level—was going to change that. As I spoke with people, I found that there was a wide range of reactions to the situation.

There were some, like me, who looked at it for what it was and basically said, "Okay. This is done. What's next?"

I tried to keep my optimism in check, though; I didn't want to appear overly excited. I knew that there were plenty of people in the office who didn't share my view and, truth be told, I felt profound sorrow for those people who had been blind-sided by this. There were senior guys at the firm who spent their entire careers at Bear; it was all they knew. And Bear Stearns was a magical place. There will never be another place like it, and we all knew that truth at that moment. That was yet another level to this tragedy; not only was the firm gone, but the philosophy of the firm was gone, too. We were all going through the Kübler-Ross grieving process—denial, anger, bargaining, depression and acceptance—and all of us were at different stages in the process.

Through it all, I was able to keep the whole thing in some semblance of perspective. I'd traveled the world. I'd lived in South Africa. I'd seen some bad stuff in my days. I'd seen human suffering on a level most people can't imagine in their worst nightmares. I'd seen poverty the likes of which aren't known in this country. I knew what it was to be truly low. So to compare our situation at Bear to the living conditions for 99% of the rest of humanity, this was nothing. The majority of my colleagues would bounce back very quickly from this setback. And for most of us, when we thought about it, that's all it was. A setback. Taking risks and placing bets are part of the investment banking game. That's what we do on a daily basis, what we get paid to do. Generally we win those bets. Today we lost. There would be a tomorrow, though.

The humor that had been so present early in the morning, the laughter amidst the tears, was still the dominant theme on the trading floor by the late afternoon. I realized then how vital humor—and the accompanying laughter and smiles and all that—really is to existence. Humor has been shown to serve as a sort of internal defense mechanism in humans subjected to massive amounts of stress. "Gallows humor," they call it. I called up my friend Vinnie in Treasury and asked how he was doing. "I'm sitting here on Death Row," he said. "How about you?" Another colleague, my counterpart in London who oversaw the derivatives structuring for that office, said that he was "living the dream, man." At least we still had our collective sense of humor.

And while I realize that my situation on the Bear Stearns trading floor pales in comparison in terms of the anxiety felt by a condemned man marching to his own death, I do have to say that the stress of that day was as heavy a weight as I've ever felt in my life. So perhaps it was in the same vein as those same men who relied on humor to distract their minds long enough to get through their own executions that I, too, fell back on humor to relieve a little of that inordinate amount of stress. The room around me was buzzing with calamitous predictions of financial ruin. The Bloomberg was running rampant with stories of Bear's demise. The firm was now officially dead. The Dow Jones was dropping like a rock.

But I had to laugh at the fact that I got three consecutive emails from ex-girlfriends. I really did laugh. I said to the woman behind me, "I think this falls under the category of, 'You Know You've Really Messed-Up Big Time When...'" It was, for me, a sign that Bear's demise was officially international news, because each of these women live in different parts of Canada. And what's more, none of them work in finance, so the news had crossed over to more general media, too. But I did take it as a good sign that they seemed genuinely concerned about me.

By the end of the day, the Dow Jones had actually climbed back up a few points from its opening. Apparently investors thought that the financial gods would be happy with the blood sacrifice they'd gotten. One dead bear might just satisfy the deities' blood lust. Only time would tell. For me, it had been a day spent picking up the pieces and trying to explain why they'd all fallen down in the first place. Before leaving the office for the night, I wanted to do two things. First, I emailed most of my email address book, just to make sure I hadn't missed anybody over the course of the day's communications. I told them that I appreciated their concern and assured them that I was actually looking forward to whatever the future might bring, including the possibility of a job with JPMorgan. There was nothing more for me to say.

Second, I called my wife. I hadn't had a chance to talk to her all day, and I wanted to make sure that she was doing okay. Before I let her talk, I let forth with the reassuring explanations of how I knew we'd land on our feet and I wasn't worried. My wife, ever the cool customer, just said, "Yep. Okay. Let's move on." And that's just what I did. As I left the office that night, I was reminded of the words of the French playwright Prosper Jolyot de Crébillion: "Fear created gods, audacity created kings."

The Bear might have been sacrificed to the gods of Wall Street. But I wasn't afraid, so I didn't need gods.

CHAPTER ELEVEN

Business as Usual

"The goal of Rapid Dominance will be to destroy or so confound the will to resist that an adversary will have no alternative except to accept our strategic aims and military objectives."

—SHOCK AND AWE: ACHIEVING RAPID DOMINANCE

I was in high school when the ABC network aired "The Day After," the Cold War-era apocalyptic story of full-scale nuclear war between the United States and the Soviet Union. The story centered on the destruction of the seemingly benign and non-strategic town of Lawrence, Kansas, as a result of the fictional war between the two superpowers. Among the host of trivia tidbits associated with the movie is the fact that Lawrence was chosen by the writers specifically because of its proximity to the exact geographic center of the United States, as well as the fact that it didn't seem like a typical target for an enemy attack in a time of war. The suggestion was that, in the event of an all-out nuclear war, there would be no safe place anywhere in the country to hide. The show aired over two nights in November of 1983, and garnered a Neilsen share of 62%, with approximately 38.55 million households tuning in to watch nuclear Armageddon play out in their living rooms. That figure places "The Day After" in the company of some of the best-known television programs ever: the final episode of "M*A*S*H," Alex Haley's "Roots," the Who Shot J.R.? episode of "Dallas" and a smattering of NFL Super Bowls.

The network had hoped for exactly that sort of audience size, and they realized the controversial and potentially horrifying nature of the subject matter that they were presenting to that audience. So they took a host of precautions before, during and after the airing. Case in point, in the hopes of avoiding an alarm much like the one Orson Wells managed to create with his "War of the Worlds" broadcast 50 years earlier, ABC set up special 1-800-numbers staffed by operators specially trained to calm viewers who might be having panic attacks as a result of what they were seeing on their television screens.

The feeling around the Bear Stearns office on Tuesday, March 18, would have made a perfect audition piece for "The Day After." People wandered around the office in a daze, their faces exhibiting much the same blank expression that Jason Robards had while his character stumbled through the remains of the town at the end of the film. We all had that sense that there was no future worth living at this point. Reality had set in; Bear was dead. The carcass was rotting on the street as people hurried past, lest they catch whatever it was that had killed the Bear. The metaphor of war's incredibly destructive outcome that was suggested by the ABC miniseries was very apropos of this situation, as we all felt like the losing army in an all-out battle just like the one portrayed in the movie. We had just signed an unconditional surrender, giving the entirety of our powers to our conquerors, the forces from JPMorgan, and we were preparing ourselves to receive them as our captors. And much like Lawrence, Kansas, seemed an unlikely target for nuclear weapons, so, too, did Bear Stearns seem an unlikely target for invaders. But that's where we found ourselves now, and today was the day that we accepted that as our new reality.

I'd gotten a call that morning from my counterpart at JPMorgan asking for a meeting with me. The members of the Fixed Income gang from Bear were already having their meetings. They were dealing with the JP guys in a civil fashion. Not with open arms so much, but rather with an attitude of getting on with things and moving forward. Maybe they hoped that by avoiding any kind of conflict with their superiors, they could perhaps ensure a future for themselves under the protective umbrella of the occupiers. But not all of them went along so merrily. One of my colleagues in the FI department likened the invasion to opening the door to a bunch of termites, and then allowing them to go all over your house and devour the entire thing.

So despite my inclinations to the contrary, I went with the flow of the tide and set up the meeting with the JP Structured Products area. But literally within minutes of my making that meeting, my boss asked me to cancel the meeting. Number one, he told me, we were not 100% sure this thing was going to go through, and he was concerned about giving away some of our trade secrets in the event the deal did fail to go through. Alternatively, assuming the deal did go through, we wanted to control the process as much as we could, and hopefully get through the merger with as much of our group still intact as we could. So we would coordinate, he told me. Bear Stearns was made up of fighters, and the inner fighter in all of us hoped that we would be able to resist being taken over for as long as possible.

So I really had nothing to do in terms of my actual job, so I monitored the markets. In so doing, I noticed that there was some action with Bear stock this morning. The stock was trading in the $4 to $5 dollar range—oh, how the mighty had fallen—despite the fact that the bid price was $2. I took this as a good sign. Perhaps it meant that the merger wasn't going to go through. If people were willing to pay $5 for a share that had already been publicly announced to be worth $2, maybe there was yet another potential savior on the horizon. At this point in the proceedings, I was willing to cling to any news that even suggested the possibility of a positive outcome. Jimmy Cayne and Joe Lewis were pounding the pavement, looking for help on Wall Street, what investment bankers call a white knight. In investment banker-speak, a white knight is an entity—it can be a company or individual—that offers to do a friendly takeover when the target firm is in the midst of a hostile takeover attempt. We clearly fit the description of the latter; we just needed the former to save us from what looked like an increasingly ugly future. The rumor circulating the office was that Jimmy had contacted somebody at Deutsche Bank. Whether or not Deutsche was even remotely interested in taking over Bear was immaterial; giving a name to the potential savior made the whole thing more believable. And those rumors, coupled with the movement in the stock price, were enough to allow me to believe, if only for a few minutes, that maybe everything was actually going to work out.

As it turned out, though, my hopes were not only short-lived, they were the result of what can only be called the polar opposite of a white knight. After some investigation, I discovered that the price fluctuations were brought on by bond arbitrageurs. An arbitrageur is like one of those guys on late-night television offering risk-free money. These guys make trades that offset each other in order to make their profits; they're all about making money that is as free from risk as it is humanly possible to be. For example, they'll find the same commodity for sale in two different markets with two different prices. They'll buy up the lower priced commodities and short sell the higher priced ones. As everybody gets on the same page and the two prices get closer to one another, they start raking in the money off their trades. It's that simple. It's just a matter of finding the right kind of situation to execute this sort of trade. And the current situation with Bear was that right kind of situation.

In the case of the Bear Stearns bonds, arbitrageurs were counting on the fact that Bear wouldn't declare Chapter 11 bankruptcy. Had that happened, everybody would have suffered, bond holders and stock holders alike. The tri-party agreement between Bear, JPMorgan and the Fed saved creditors and punished shareholders. In the end, this was the best way to ensure the financial viability of the entire system at large. Because of the risk in the economic climate surrounding Bear, our Credit Default Spreads were trading somewhere in the realm of Geosynchronous Earth Orbit. Whereas our CDS had traded at about 30bps above LIBOR before this whole mess, by now we were lucky to be getting 1000bps above LIBOR. And what that means is that anybody who's shopping for a bargain in the world of high finance is going to be looking at Bear debt, because it can be had for prices lower than anybody ever thought possible. So hedge funds and other arbitrageurs were out there buying up Bear bonds like they were going out of style. If JPMorgan bought Bear, then Bear's debt became JP's debt. And JP had no financial problems whatsoever, so once that debt transferred over, it was as good as guaranteed. This was a sure bet.

But buying bonds doesn't necessarily have an effect on the stock price. Just keep in mind that these guys who were buying all the Bear bonds were counting on the fact that we wouldn't go bankrupt. The avoidance of bankruptcy was best accomplished, at least in the minds of a lot of arbitrageurs, by our being bought by JPMorgan. Again, that happens, no sweat; bond arbitrageurs make out like bandits in that scenario. But throw into the mix the fact that Jimmy is out there courting a white knight to come save us, and you can see where there might have been some concern. If JPMorgan got wind of the fact that we were looking for help elsewhere, they might pull their funding. After all, they weren't really in the market for a big fight here. And if they pulled their funding and no white knight came in, we were headed to Chapter 11 without question. And like I said, we declare Chapter 11, suddenly all those investors who were snatching up that oh-so-cheap Bear debt would be left holding even more worthless pieces of paper that were associated with Bear. So this whole deal wasn't a sure thing yet, and what it boiled down to was that the arbitrageurs were doing their best rendition of investors being sure to practice Wall Street Rule #1.

The best way to cover your own ass in a situation like this is to make sure you're in a position to control the outcome. And the only way to accomplish that with a situation involving a publicly traded company is to have enough stock to force decisions to be made the way you want them made. You control the stock, you control the outcome of shareholder votes. Simple majority. Easy as that. So these guys were buying Bear stock in addition to Bear debt. They wanted to make sure that they acquired enough of our shares to force the JPMorgan deal through, regardless of what Deutsche wanted to do. If they could buy enough Bear stock to create a voting majority, they'd make sure that the deal went through to ensure their bonds wouldn't default. In other words, they were trying to take the hostile takeover that was possibly going to turn friendly and make it friendly on their own. If they had enough stock to build a majority amongst themselves, it would have been impossible for the merger to fail, regardless of any outside factors.

But why not just pay the $2 share price? They certainly could have bought the stock for that price. So why bid the price up to $4 or $5? The answer to that is two-fold. First of all, they were willing to pay a higher price, simply because they knew they were going to make back the losses plus a very tidy profit on the bonds. So basically it was a situation where they knew that one of five lottery tickets would pay off, but they had to buy all five to guarantee the win. They were willing to accept the losses they took on the other four in order to assure themselves of that one big payout. Secondly, and probably more importantly, they had a vested interest in excluding other investors from coming in and buying it. Because the share price was publicly $2, if they were bidding $5, then nobody in their right minds would come in and pay above that amount, because they'd automatically be losing over $3 a share. But when you stood to make a huge profit on the sale of bonds if the JPMorgan deal went through, as these arbitrageurs did, that $3 loss on every share of stock didn't bother you in the slightest. This was the perfect example of buying yourself insurance and reducing the risk that somebody would come along and undercut your chances by buying up shares when you weren't looking.

And while all of this was going on, just to add a little more drama and intrigue to a situation that was already suffering from drama and intrigue overload, there was talk circulating around the office about the employees banding together and defeating the merger. I realize that this image might conjure up visions of angry villagers with pitchforks and torches storming the castle, but I assure you that it was nothing quite so violent. Remember that this is corporate America, where shareholders really do wield quite a bit of power when it comes down to decisions like this. And because of the way that Bear bonus structures worked, we employees as a group represented a pretty major force in terms of shareholders. Together we held about 30% of the public-issued Bear stock. Bear is something of an anomaly in the world of investment banks in that the company is one-third owned by the employees; therefore, it wasn't entirely out of the question for us to take up the battle against the merger and save our firm. Granted, for this scenario to work, we would have had to create an international company-wide union more powerful than the Teamsters ever dreamt of being—and we would have had to put the thing together basically overnight—and then we would have also had to have found another major player or two willing to join forces with us. It was a long shot to say the least. But it was not inconceivable for us to work together and defeat the merger. It just wasn't likely.

The whole thought was really nothing more than a passing fancy, basically, regardless of who thought we could do what. The fact of the matter was that the merger with JP was a done deal, regardless of what the arbitrageurs did in terms of buying up huge blocks of stock. When everything was said and done, it was the Fed that had made this deal happen. The Federal Reserve Bank of New York had more or less sponsored a contest, and they were awarding one prize. The prize was ownership of Bear Stearns, and the eventual winner of the contest was JPMorgan. For anyone else to come in and try to usurp JP from their pedestal, they would have had to bring with them the blessing of the Fed. And only JPMorgan was holding that divine marker. So there would be no other challengers in this tournament. It was over and done with before most of us had time to realize what it was that had happened in the first place.

And it probably sounds like the grumblings of a bitter employee to say that the Fed somehow bestowed upon JP this absolute right and screwed everyone else out of their chances, but consider JP's market cap after the deal was announced. Market cap—the abbreviated version of market capitalization—is the total value of a company's outstanding shares. The figure is determined by taking the number of shares that are outstanding and multiplying that number by the current price of a single share of stock.

It's used as a way of determining a company's size; a "large cap" company, for instance, typically has a market cap over $10 billion or so.

In the case of JP's market cap, their value skyrocketed by over $15 billion once the deal had been announced. $15 billion was, arguably, the total enterprise value (TEV) of Bear Stearns. TEV is the total dollar amount of a company's market cap, interest-bearing debt and preferred stock all added together, with excess cash subtracted. So the equation looks something like this: TEV = (market cap + debt + preferred stock)—cash. Preferred stock is differentiated from common stock in that preferred shares don't have voting rights, but usually receive dividends paid out before common shares. In essence, then, this was nothing more than a transfer of wealth to JPMorgan. It was like opening a card from your grandmother and finding a $15 billion check in there, made out to her favorite grandson—JPMorgan—just because she thinks it's a nice thing to do for her favorite grandson. It wasn't like this was even a Christmas present. This was just the Fed saying to JP, "Hey, we like you guys. And to show how much we like you, we're going to give you Bear Stearns." In essence this was a transfer of wealth from Bear Stearns shareholders to JPMorgan shareholders, a transfer facilitated by the federal government.

I remarked to a colleague at the time that it felt like we were living in some kind of totalitarian regime, some sort of place where decisions were made for you, and those decisions weren't based on any kind of fair or equitable treatment. They were just made. And we, the ordinary citizens, the Proles in this new Orwellian world, had to live with those decisions. We'd had our free will taken from us; we no longer had the ability to resist. Oh, brave new world that has such people in it!

But what was most comical about the whole situation was that we were told to tell our clients that everything was business as usual. Seriously. With a straight face, we were supposed to say that it was just business as usual around the ol' hacienda at 383 Madison Avenue. A colleague actually put "business as usual" on his Bloomberg marquee, which appeared whenever someone sent him a message on his Bloomberg. The first time I said it to a client on the phone, I felt like the puppet of the dictator who'd been making decisions for us. It was as if I was out there in my military fatigues, the city burning in ruins behind me, a mushroom cloud climbing up into the sky, a bank of microphones and television cameras in front of me. The world was waiting for me to say what was going within the borders of our country. And there I was, gesturing slowly and calmly, assuring those around me that there was nothing to see here. Disregard that loud explosion you heard and ignore the fires raging around me. It's all just as it should be. Nothing wrong at all. That was the party line, despite the fact that the JPMorgan treasury department had already told us that we were strictly prohibited from buying back bonds from our clients until the following Thursday.

JPMorgan at that point was only guaranteeing our trades, not our debt obligations. There was a very real, very understandable concern on the part of the JPMorgan treasury that there was going to be yet another panic by investors holding Bear bonds, investors who would want out of their deals and would want us to buy back our paper, as was our custom. No matter what the bond arbitrageurs had formulated, the potential for another panic was very real, given the week we'd just lived through. One rumor, and it was off to the races again. As it turned out, though, most of our clients realized that the merger was most likely going to go through, and as a result, their once A-rated Bear bonds would transfer to AA-rated JPMorgan bonds in June.

So I did what I was told. Everything was on the up-and-up around Bear, by-howdy. Yep. Business as usual. Just don't ask me to do anything that looks like usual business, and we'll call it business as usual. Nothing to see here, folks. Move along. Nothing out of the ordinary. So ordinary and run-of-the-mill were the goings-on in the office that day that our legal department took it upon themselves to send out an email to everyone, lest any of us should fail to realize how normal the day was. In addition to serving as our notice that JPMorgan now controlled every action we took on behalf of the company, the email basically outlined the dos and don'ts for us in the coming days. Tops on the list was that we were not allowed "to solicit or encourage anyone to make a competing offer for Bear Stearns or any if its assets." So much for the white knight idea.

The list went on, detailing several other things we weren't allowed to do without the express permission of JPMorgan Chase. No names, just the company. It was safer that way, because there was nobody to hold accountable, nobody to blame. You can't blame "JPMorgan Chase," because you don't know who he is. So these rules came down from some nameless deity, and they were quite pointed. Case in point, without permission from the aforementioned nameless deity, we expressly prohibited from "taking any action or willfully failing to take any action that is intended or may reasonably be expected to result in any of the conditions of the merger not being satisfied." Apparently this JPMorgan Chase person, whoever he was, had some paranoia issues and wanted to make sure that, if nothing else, he adhered to Wall Street Rule #1.

And at the end of the day, an email appeared in my inbox. Senior Managing Directors of Bear Stearns would be meeting with Jamie Dimon, CEO of JPMorgan, on Wednesday afternoon to discuss the merger. Things were just about to get interesting around the office. Business as usual was about to take on a whole new meaning.

▲ ▲ ▲

A great many companies throughout the world have what looks a lot like a very complex family tree that a genealogical expert might have labored over for several years. It has boxes and lines and arrows, all fanning out the further down one goes. This is what is known in the business world as an organizational—or just "org"—chart. At Bear, we pretty much blew our noses on org charts. Bear Stearns is what a lot of people refer to as a "flat" firm. That is to say, we didn't have a formal organizational chart. You could look anywhere you wanted in the office, anywhere in any employee handbook you might be able to unearth, anywhere. And anywhere you chose to search, you wouldn't find an org chart. We despised the things at Bear. It was part and parcel of our reputation as the maverick of Wall Street. It was, admittedly, nothing short of organized chaos to a lot of minds, a lot of minds that rely on things like structure to get them through the day; this kind of environment that we had at Bear wasn't for everyone. But for those of us who were drawn to the craziness, we wouldn't have had it any other way. We loved the fact that we were all over the place. Ready, fire, aim. That was our mantra.

Of course we knew we worked for somebody, and we all knew who those somebodies were. There were 400-plus Senior Managing Directors at Bear, for example. All of us knew our titles, and all of us knew approximately where we fit into the pecking order. Each one of us—all 400-plus—had our personalized business cards, raised black lettering on a white background, very stark, very plain. And each of us had the words "Senior Managing Director" in a small, italicized font directly below our names on the left hand side of our cards. And each of us had control of a small group of traders that we molded and trained and mentored. But there wasn't a big piece of cardboard sitting on an easel showing how everyone fit into this grand puzzle that we all liked to call an investment bank. We just knew where we stood, and we all liked it that way.

Apparently nobody informed the guys at JPMorgan about our preference for the system we'd lived under while at Bear. Every meeting at JP started with an org chart. Everybody had an org chart and everybody wanted to show you their org chart. And they wanted to show you where they fit into the whole thing and where you, if you were lucky enough to garner an invitation to join the firm after the merger was complete, would also fit in. As Senior Managing Directors, we were all relatively confident that we'd get a shot with JP, whether we wanted it or not. And it was with that sense of self-confidence mixed with aversion bordering on revulsion that we all filed into the auditorium on that Wednesday afternoon to listen to a presentation from our conquerors: Jamie Dimon, the CEO of JPMorgan, and his chief lieutenants, Steve Black and Bill Winters, the co-heads of investment banking at JP.

True to form, they all mentioned their titles and where they fit into the neatly-constructed organizational chart that defined the very existence of JPMorgan. Was this what my future held for me? I had already worked at a big bank before Bear, and I'd vowed never to go back to that sort of system again. And all of those organizational charts? As it was now, I barely fit in at Bear Stearns, the land of misfit toys. How was I going to fit in at some Colossus Bank? I shuddered at the vision I had of my life for the next ten years.

After a second of contemplation of this horror, I decided that I'd suspend my criticism until I heard their offer. I promised myself that I'd keep an open mind. Who knows? Maybe this could be OK. Maybe they'd offer me enough money to make that grey suit look good. And as it turned out, JPMorgan allows business-casual attire in the office, which means no neckties. Things were suddenly looking up, at least dress code-wise. All three men spoke about how happy they were to be joining forces with such a great institution as Bear Stearns, how their whole team—each individual member of which no doubt had their own specific places on their organizational charts—was working to ensure a smooth transition and what their overall plans were in terms of merging the two firms together. It all sounded pretty basic, pretty much the "don't hate us, we're here for you" kind of thing.

And truth be told, they did a good job of it. They were respectful of all of us at Bear. This was a thankless job, giving the consolation speech to

the losing team. But they said all the right things, all the things we needed to hear. Whether we believed a word of it or not wasn't really all that
important. It was important for them to say the right things, otherwise
they would have had a full-scale revolt on their hands. And they did say
the right things. They weren't talking like salesmen. They were very con-
ciliatory. They apologized for what had happened to our firm and assured
us that they would strive to make the whole thing work out. Jamie Dimon
himself temporarily ingratiated himself to a lot of us by referring to the
whole arrangement as a "shotgun marriage," likening Bear to the pregnant
bride and casting JPMorgan in the role of the unhappy groom being forced
to take responsibility for his actions. He acknowledged that Bear had not
been the epitome of a willing seller and that JPMorgan had not been the
epitome of a willing buyer. The whole arrangement was forced on both
parties, at least in part, so now it was up to us to make the best of the situation, regardless of how bad a situation we thought it was. Basically he
was saying that it was what it was, and we had to live with it and move
on. So let's move on.

As I looked around the auditorium, my mind was going in a thousand
different directions. But one thought came to the forefront of my mind:
Sitting together in this room full of Senior Managing Directors, there was
represented a sum in the billions of dollars of wealth that had been vapor-
ized in the matter of a weekend. Billions of dollars. Poof. Gone. Adios.
No mas. And, right there in that same room, there were these men, these
guys in dark grey pinstripe suits. This was indeed going to get ugly at
some point. You could sense it in the air. People's blood was boiling.
JPMorgan didn't create the situation; but, unfortunately for them, they
would be receiving the brunt of the angry outbursts from the assembled
SMDs as if they'd been personally responsible. Was it an irrational way
to be thinking? Most likely, but you have to understand that few of
us really had the capacity for anything other than irrational thought at
that point. We were three days away from complete annihilation, and it
stung.

And then Jamie Dimon opened the floor to questions.

The first person who was called on set the tone for the rest of the meeting: "How dare you come to our house and call this a merger?" he screamed
at Dimon. There was a mild shuffling of bodies in seats, a way of offering
a silent agreement en masse, as this voice expressed what we were all thinking, but were too afraid to voice to this titan of the business world. And

besides, if we were lucky, he would be our new boss, grey suit and all. And we didn't want to upset him just yet.

Dimon remained cool in moments following the initial barrage. If he was shaken by it, he certainly didn't show it. But if he thought he'd won us over, he'd be re-thinking that assessment. He parried like a good fencer. He knew he had one shot to get this right, and if he screwed it up, he'd be dead in his tracks. "It sounds like you're trying to blame JPMorgan for what happened here," he said. "We're not to blame. We're here to help you."

He got lucky. The anger subsided. For a moment. The next few questions centered on constructive concerns about going forward, integrating existing employees, other issues related to merging the two companies. A lot of questions were lobbed at Dimon in regards to the two-dollar share price and how exactly that price was determined. It sounded a lot to one interrogator like a "fire sale price." The JPMorgan team claimed something to the effect that $2 was the price they were told to pay by the Fed. I can't say for certain that this was what they meant to say; it was, however, the message that we all got. It was obvious they were invoking Wall Street Rule #1. This line didn't seem to be burdened by things like the truth, but nobody called them on it. It was a losing battle at best.

And then a question from the back of room, this one from one of our brokers, that wasn't really so much a question as it was an accusation: "You call this a shotgun marriage? I call it a shotgun marriage to a rapist!" We all sat there for a second, waiting for something. We weren't sure what was coming, but whatever it was, we knew it wouldn't be good. It was one of the more uncomfortable moments of my life, sitting there waiting for Dimon to respond. But the voice from the back of the room didn't give him a chance: "You say you didn't do anything. But you were just walking down the street and there she was, naked on the street." He was finally silenced by a round of boos from the assembled crowd, people who, like me, felt that this sort of behavior was way out of line and unprofessional, regardless of the circumstances. But by that point, the meeting was devolving into nothing more than angry screaming; the tone was getting uglier with each passing second, and there was no sign that it was going to improve any time soon.

For their part, Dimon, Black and Winters did a great job keeping the peace in the room; it was the Bear employees who were upset and acting like it. Their anger was understandable. Like I said, we had, as a group, lost billions of dollars as a result of this meltdown, and these guys on the stage had profited from the same meltdown. It wasn't fair. And they all knew it, just like we all knew it. But there was nothing that any of us could do to change the situation. It wasn't really their fault. In fact, if we'd been JPMorgan employees, it's entirely possible we'd think Dimon and Company were the smartest guys on the planet. But we weren't. We were Bear employees. And we'd just been served with our collective notice that we were under new management.

At the end of the day, I knew that I'd had a front-row seat to Wall Street history sitting there in that auditorium on that Wednesday afternoon. But I knew, too, that it wasn't over yet. Not by a long shot. This thing still had a little way to go before it went down in the history books.

CHAPTER TWELVE

The Devil Is in the Details

"As I walk through the valley of the Shadow of Death,
I take a look at my life and realize there's nothing left."
—COOLIO, *"GANGSTER'S PARADISE"*

According to Roman Catholic doctrine, the determination of the exact date for Easter is quite a complex proposition. First of all, the day must be a Sunday. That's easy enough. But the Sunday in question must be the first Sunday after the Paschal full moon following the vernal equinox. Told you it was complicated. Let's take it in reverse. You start at the spring equinox, March 21. That date is set in stone. The Paschal full moon is the name given to the first full moon following the vernal equinox. The name itself is derived from the ancient Hebrew word for Passover, "pesach." So you go to the first full moon after March 21, and then jump to the next Sunday. That's Easter.

I'm not a terribly religious person, but I remember enough from required courses in high school and college to know that Easter is the day that Christians believe Jesus rose from the dead and ascended into Heaven. That Sunday, according to the ecclesiastical scholars, was three days after the crucifixion, which, with some quick math, we find took place on a Friday, according to those same scholars. Thus Christians around the world celebrate Good Friday on the Friday immediately preceding Easter. The Christian hope is that, because God sent His son to die for all of humanity, their own sins will be forgiven; the death of Jesus Christ is seen by Christians as a universal sacrifice designed to ensure that the sins of believers will be forgiven. So, in essence, Easter is a celebration of death. Maybe that's why I always thought it felt a little odd to wish somebody a happy Easter.

In the umpteen-zillionth instance of unintentional irony in the history of Bear Stearns and its untimely demise, the first full moon after the official vernal equinox actually fell *on* the vernal equinox. So Easter 2008 was on March 23. Now count back from that Sunday three days—Sunday the 23rd, Saturday the 22nd, Friday the 21st—and you get to Good Friday. The day of the crucifixion. The day that the acquisition of Bear Stearns by JPMorgan was, for all intents and purposes, finalized. The day that Bear died for the sins of Wall Street. But of course, as with everything else in this twisted mess, it wasn't accomplished easily. And it wasn't like Bear didn't go down without a fight. We'd basically given in at this point in time, but the old Bear still had a few gasps of air left; we weren't knocked out completely just yet. What made the whole takeover complicated at this point was a little jurisprudential snafu, a debt some junior associate will no doubt be repaying for the duration of the rest of his career.

After the little get-together on Wednesday afternoon with the Bear Senior Managing Directors, Jamie Dimon had somehow come to the conclusion that he might just be something of a *persona non gratis* around these parts. I can't say for sure where he could have gotten that impression; I suppose it's possible that the accusation that he was a rapist might have somehow given him an inkling. Whatever the source of his newfound understanding, we began to hear rumors about Dimon's wanting to maybe back out of the deal. Maybe it wasn't such a blessing to have to work with these people at Bear. Maybe they really did deserve the reputation of mavericks. Could it be more trouble than it's worth? Might the disruption of managing Bear not be as important as focusing on the work to be done at JP?

Word spread around the office pretty quickly about the very colorful SMD meeting in the auditorium, which no doubt further incensed Dimon and made us look even less grateful in his eyes. And rumors once again started making the rounds, building on the already talked-about possibility of Dimon pulling out of the deal. But now the rumors were being taken as fact. Dimon was literally threatening to pull the deal off the table that night. At Dimon's command, Bear was going to be left to go completely belly-up, regardless of what the Fed had dictated to him. His feeling was that if this was the thanks he was going to get—being called a rapist—he'd let us die and wouldn't lose a minute's sleep over it. Dimon was actually quoted in the *New York Times* as saying that he'd "send Bear back into bankruptcy" if we didn't give in to his demands.

What Jamie was doing was pretty much exactly what the Fed had done to us in the first place. He was pushing Bear into accepting his terms. He wanted to pay $2 a share for the company and that was that. If we didn't like it, we could go find ourselves another buyer. The only problem with that scenario is that there was no other buyer lurking in the shadows out there. So Dimon had all the bargaining chips and there wasn't a damn thing we could do about it. Bear was done. Cooked. Without a leg to stand on. The nails were going through the hands of the Bear on the cross.

But suddenly, just like Kristen the call girl had been our Madonna of the Bloomberg only two weeks earlier, a young lawyer from a relatively prestigious law firm was about to be unwillingly thrust into the spotlight in order to save us from this playground menace. And that young man's oversight was going to give all of us one last little taste of the sweet nectar of vengeance, this time at Jamie Dimon's expense. The lawyer's name wasn't released, so only a few select individuals know his name. I myself am not part of that great and solemn fraternity who were privy to his name, but whoever he is, I would one day like to find him, buy him a beer

NEW YORK—MARCH 26: Employees watch with interest as protestors march in the lobby of Bear Stearns headquarters March 26, 2008 in New York. Hundreds of housing activists overwhelmed security and stormed the lobby of the Bear Stearns skyscraper in Manhattan, staging a noisy rally and protesting the government-backed sale and bailout of the investment bank. *(Photo by Chris Hondros/Getty Images)*

and shake his hand for making me smile when I thought I would never smile again. All because of a single solitary little sentence.

According to the *New York Times* report on the incident, the sentence in question was buried in legal jargon and was "inadvertently" left in. Long story short, the esteemed law firm of Wachtell, Lipton, Rosen & Katz (herein after referred to as "the law firm") was asked to explain why it was, according to the contract representatives from the law firm had written up in consultation with representatives from JPMorgan (herein after referred to as "the client") and which contract the client had approved in witness whereof the law firm approved the contract in its final form, that JPMorgan would be responsible for Bear's trading obligations for one year, regardless of whether or not the deal went through.

Immediately fingers were pointed in opposite directions. Everyone involved blamed someone else. The lawyers blamed the investment bankers, the investment bankers blamed the lawyers. According to the Times, regardless of who was actually at fault, Dimon was "apoplectic" upon learning the news. And understandably so. This was not the kind of news he was hoping to get; in fact, it was just about the diametric opposite of any kind of news he wanted to get at that exact moment.

Those of us who were still sitting around on the trading floor at Bear Stearns, in stark contrast to the vein-popping fit of rage that was consuming Jamie, were in collective fits of laughter bordering on hysterics. We knew it wouldn't change the fact that our firm was done, but it was one last cheap shot at JPMorgan. And the fact will no doubt secure me an uncomfortable place in Hell, but I derive a great deal of pleasure from knowing that somewhere in the frozen tundra of Wacthell, Lipton's version of Siberia there toils a lawyer who may never be allowed out of his dungeon.

And true to our prophecies, this little hiccup didn't solve anything that really mattered in terms of JPMorgan giving us the money we deserved. But what it did do suddenly was put Jamie and the boys from JP on the defensive. All of a sudden they *had* to take us on. If they were responsible for our trading obligations, then they were sure as hell going to make sure they acquired ownership of the company. If they'd just taken on the obligations and let us go on our way, only to be bought by another company, that would have been equivalent to Spitzer paying his little strumpet to go play with some other lucky guy. Spitzer put his dollars down and he was going to get laid; Dimon had put his dollars down, too, and he was going to get Bear. Simple as that. But with this revelation, JP was not in the position they had been before, namely the position of being able to call their own price and demand it. And most importantly, they were no longer in the position of being able to expect to get that priced. The bully had gotten a black eye at the hands of an angry mob of ninety-eight pound weaklings who had suddenly found their voice and their strength. Because JP was stuck with us, we were suddenly thrust into the position of being able to ask for a few concessions ourselves. And tops on that list was a higher offering price per share of Bear stock. In fact, that was pretty much the only thing on that list.

Bear stock holders were about as angry regarding the current situation with the share price as Dimon had been about the oversight that made JP obligated to cover our trades. Because of that anger, Jamie spent a lot of time in those days fielding phone calls from investors who were threatening to vote down the proposal if he didn't up the share $2 share price that had been imposed when he thought we had no room to negotiate. But now things were different. Mind you, we weren't in the position to go up and say we wanted $80 a share. As much as I hate to admit it, JP still had us by the metaphorical short hairs. And Dimon was still furious at us and wanted us to do our penance. If he'd gotten his way, I'm pretty sure that his offer would have stayed at $2 and we would have found ourselves in the middle of the biggest game of chicken that Wall Street had ever played host to.

Cooler heads prevailed, though, and Jamie was convinced—perhaps against his will—of the fact that to continue on this course of "my way or the highway" was going to do nothing but create a public relations nightmare that he'd never wake up from. He finally agreed to sit down and negotiate with Bear shareholders. Actually he requested the meeting himself. Remember the importance of a person's reputation on Wall Street; without it, he's nothing. Dimon had worked too hard to build his, and he was too smart to throw it away on something like this. If this deal fell through, his career would follow a similar trajectory. So in terms of the negotiations for the takeover of Bear Stearns, he'd reached a point where he wanted to appease the masses. And truth be told, he had to appease them, because there was a very real chance they could vote him down and he'd be in a very bad place.

Back on the trading floor, we were contemplating the fact that Bear had been crucified. Hanging there on the cross. Dead. *My God, why hast Thou forsaken us?*

▲ ▲ ▲

We didn't have time to reflect on philosophical self-righteousness or partake in finger-pointing. We didn't even have time to pray. We were in the middle of yet another turning point—this one, though, potentially a positive one—in this crisis that had engulfed all of us and consumed our very existences. For the first time in a long time, at least for the moment, things were beginning to look up slightly. If Dimon backed out of the deal, another company could come in and buy Bear with absolutely no risk whatsoever. For example, if Morgan Stanley or Goldman decided that they wanted to play a little game of "screw your neighbor," the neighbor in question being JP, they could have come in and offered a higher share price and bought the company, but then stuck JP with all of the trading obligations, as they were legally obligated to take them per the contract they'd written up. It would have been the steal of the century. Hell, it would have been the greatest deal ever conceived of in the history of Wall Street. It

NEW YORK—MAY 29: People look at a painted portrait of Bear Stearns CEO James Cayne created by New York artist Geoffrey Raymond, on which people and Bear Stearns employees have written messages to Cayne expressing their anger about the collapse of the investment giant, in front of Bear Stearns headquarters May 29, 2008 in New York City. *(Photo by Spencer Platt/Getty Images)*

would have ranked up there with the Louisiana Purchase in terms of all-around bargains.

But it wasn't to be. Nobody wanted to jump into that viper pit and roll around. Not with the atmosphere on the Street like it was at the time. You want to talk about burning bridges, if some investment bank had come in and done that, it would have made Bear's refusal to take part in the Long Term Capital Management bail-out seem like nothing at all. But in the Bear Stearns offices, a brilliant derivatives lawyer was pushing the Bear management to realize that they were the ones now holding a pair of hole aces; they had the power in the negotiations now. He also pointed out that, because this information would become public quite soon (which it did, thanks to both the *Wall Street Journal* and the *New York Times*), if they chose specifically not to act on it and just let JP go with a good chuckle and a two-dollar share price, the shareholders would be in the position to actually sue the Bear executives for failure to do their legally obligated duty to act in the best interest of the shareholders. And there's nothing like a good old fashioned threat to get people's attention.

I also heard through the inter-office grapevine at the time—and later the rumor was confirmed in media reports—that Alan Schwartz was entertaining the idea of having the financial advisory firm Lazard LTD investigate what he referred to as "strategic opportunities" for the firm. In layman's terms, that means that Alan was looking for an opportunity that would somehow create a deal we would all be happy with, and which would help to shore-up Bear's existence in what was becoming an increasingly difficult market. Clearly time ran out on this option—insofar as it was an option at all—and Bear ended up with the financial equivalent of a neutron bomb.

So the negotiations went on. Most of us figured that the executives would end up getting us share prices up in the teens, with a few optimists daring to dream about low twenties. We had the building on Madison Avenue, which is quite a pricey little domicile, even by Manhattan standards. We had our Prime Brokerage.

And we had Bear Energy.

Bear Energy was a division formed in 2005 with the express purpose of taking advantage of the energy-related commodities market for major investors. Bear Energy was a little-known subsidiary of Bear, but despite its relative obscurity, the division was profitable to say the very least. With the price of oil constantly rising, all energy-related commodities were seeing prices reaching unheard of levels by early 2008. And as a result of some savvy investments on the part of the guys in Bear Energy, that little obscure division was sitting on about $1.6 billion of unrealized gains based on daily commodity prices, gains arising from positions they'd maintained in the energy market. In other words, Bear Energy was worth a whole lot of money, and JP was about to absorb all of that profit for pennies on the dollar.

Despite all of the finger-crossing and praying and hoping, and despite the existence of a billion-and-a-half dollars pouring into the bank account of Bear Energy, for whatever reason, we ended up being rewarded with a $10 share price. That was the best our negotiators could get us. Granted, it was better than $2 to be sure, but JP was still getting a ridiculously good bargain in this deal. JP bought 39.5% of the company's shares at that price, so they didn't need too many major investors to get on board with them in order for them to get their way. They got verbal assurances from a few major shareholders—one of them being Jimmy Cayne, who was no doubt anxious to make sure he could afford his new apartment in the Plaza—and the whole thing was, for all intents and purposes, over. Of course, Jimmy had every reason in the world to feel safe. Rumors that had circulated the office for a few days were confirmed by the Bloomberg reports: Jimmy had employed the services of a personal bodyguard—an *armed* bodyguard—after the collapse of the firm. It was never reported if he'd acted in response to a specific threat, or if he just felt that he was somehow in danger. Regardless of his reasons, the thought of Jimmy employing some meathead as hired protection earned a laugh or two on the trading floor.

And as more and more major shareholders added their names to the list of people who would be supporting the purchase, it became a done deal. Everything except for the crying, as my dad used to say. Everybody down, hands behind your head. The chase is over. You're now officially in custody. Bear would be absorbed by JP for the whopping price of $10 a share. We were told it was better than the alternative. Ten dollars was quite a lot more than two, especially when you multiplied it out over the hundreds of thousands of shares that a lot of us still held. Jamie Dimon would get his company. Jimmy Cayne would get his apartment. The rest of us would just get mad.

Some people—the same optimists who were gunning for a $20 price—found some solace in the fact that we were getting five times the amount we'd originally been promised. But the majority of us had a more pragmatic view of the situation, regardless of what such a view might do to our job chances. Call it what you wanted, but we firmly believed that this was wealth destruction by any measure, destruction that was being brought on by outside forces. To outsiders, we were overpaid crybabies from the get-go. We got annual bonuses that were more than a lot of people made in ten years. But we worked hard for those bonuses and, regardless of the public sentiment towards exorbitant CEO salaries, we deserved those bonuses. They were based on our performance, which means that we got bonuses based on how well we performed on behalf of our clients. The more money they made, the more money we made. So it wasn't like bonuses were handed out without regard to how well we did our job. And the majority of those bonuses were tied up in restricted stock options, so we couldn't sell them right away. What basically transpired in this whole deal was that somebody gave us money then tied our hands behind our back. Then, while we were bound, somebody else came and took 90% of our income while we were unable to defend ourselves. And the person who'd tied us up in the first place tried to convince us that we were lucky that they didn't take more money.

In the end, what it all boiled down to was that this whole mess was really nobody's fault; we were just the ones paying the price. The word had come down from the mountain that somebody—an investment bank, specifically—was going to pay. This behavior on Wall Street, this culture of risk-taking at the expense of innocent by-standers, was not going to be tolerated any longer. We were engaging in a game, basically. A very high-stakes, potentially financially crippling game. At the end of the trading day, investment bankers walk away from their failures the same way they walk away from their successes. They're making money regardless; it's not their problem that a client lost millions. After all, the market's a risky proposition and investments can lose money. The disclaimer each and every one of our clients was forced to sign told them that much. And that reality, that absolution from any kind of real responsibility, led some investment specialists to take unnecessary risks.

Those of us at Bear weren't the only ones engaging in this risk-taking. Far from it, in fact. But we were the ones who paid. We were that Christ figure you so often hear about in scholarly studies of literature. We were crucified to pay for the sins of the many. Our death was allowed to simultaneously serve as a warning to the larger investment community of what could happen if a bank insisted on pushing the risk envelope, and as a blood payment to the community of individual investors who had been hurt and who continued to get hurt in the mortgage crisis and ensuing credit crunch that was wracking Wall Street at the time. And it had all come to a head on that Good Friday.

Bear's lifeless body hung from the cross. Crucified, from the Latin words *crux,* meaning "cross," and *figere,* meaning "to attach." Or, as became the joke around the Bear office that day, crucified, meaning "to completely fuck over mercilessly and without shame."

Happy Easter.

CHAPTER THIRTEEN

What Do You Say When It's Over?

"Every act of creation is first of all an act of destruction."
—PABLO PICASSO

According to Greek mythology, King Minos of Crete waged a war with Athens, a war in which the armies of Minos defeated their Athenian foes. As a reward for his resounding victory, Minos declared that once every seven years, fourteen Athenian children—seven boys and seven girls— would be sent to him to be fed to the Minotaur, the half-man, half-bull monster that lived in the Labyrinth created by Daedalus. The third time this tithing came up, Theseus volunteered to be sent in the place of one of the boys so that he could go in and slay the Minotaur, thus ending the forced sacrifice of Athenian children. In the end, Theseus defeated the Minotaur, killing and beheading the beast. He escaped with the children and sailed home to Crete, where he was treated to a hero's welcome.

According to Plutarch, who recorded the story for posterity's sake, the ship on which Theseus sailed home was preserved by the people of Athens in the harbor as a memorial to his heroic deed. As boards rotted out on the ship's wooden hull, they were replaced with new ones. After some time, the entire hull of the ship had been replaced and the question arose: Given that all of the boards had been replaced over the course of time and there was, at this point, nothing about this ship that was intact at the time that Theseus sailed it, is this still the same ship that he sailed? In other words, when did the ship cease to be the old ship and become a new one?

And thus was born the Paradox of Theseus, a question asked when pieces of a whole are replaced over time, but the entity is still considered to be the original. If the entire ship is composed of new materials, is it still the same ship? Or, when discussing business mergers, if an investment bank is taken over and absorbed and altered by another investment bank, is

175

either of the two firms still the original investment bank? That question weighed on my mind in those final days of Bear's existence as we tried to create something new out of the absolute and utter destruction of the old.

On one of my last days as a Bear employee before the official paperwork being signed to complete the merger with JP, I'd been invited to a meeting with the JPMorgan head of equity derivatives. I found him to be a likeable enough guy, despite my misgivings about the whole situation. I realized, on some level, that this whole thing was no more his fault than it was mine. But he was still one of them, so I felt the need to proceed with caution. As it turned out, he and I seemed to have a lot in common, starting with our love of working with derivatives. Like me, he'd worked overseas; he'd done a long stint in Asia several years earlier. We made small talk for a few minutes, two prize fighters circling in the ring. Was this budding friendship going to be the real thing, or was this simply my adversary's way of lulling me into a false sense of hope? I didn't want to divulge too much personal information to this guy, this enemy who had yet to prove himself to be anything other than my foe. After the idle chitchat, we got down to business. My table on the trading floor. My people. My loyal band of young Turks that I'd built over the years. What about them? Would they be getting job offers with JPMorgan?

"Yes," he told me. "All your people will be getting jobs."

I heaved a sigh of relief. I had worked much of my time at Bear molding young structurers, trying to teach them the tricks I'd learned from my elders when I'd been in their position, just starting out on the trading floor, unsure of what way was up, let alone how to price and sell derivatives. They and their future careers had been a major concern weighing on me during the entire time this fiasco had been going on. I wanted them to get jobs with JPMorgan, jobs that would allow them time in a seat doing what they'd grown to love. They'd worked like hell for it, and they deserved the opportunity. And a seat on the floor at JPMorgan, my own personal feelings about guys in grey suits aside, would position them to call their shots when their time came to do so. For now, a job on the JP floor would be a nice safety net. A sort of golden parachute for these guys to enjoy until they decided where they wanted to go and when, on their own terms. And now I was being told that they'd made it officially. Each and every one of them would have the opportunity that I wanted so much for them.

"I've got to tip my hat to you," my new JP friend continued. "Based on my discussions with all of the traders that worked under you, I have to believe that each and every one of those people is fully prepared to go to war for you. All of them. Amazing. I don't know what you did, but whatever it was, you did it well." He leaned back in his chair and smiled slightly, letting the compliment he'd just fed me sink in. Truthfully, I was relieved more than anything else. I appreciated his kind words, but all I could feel at that moment was relief.

A merger is never an easy proposition. People are uprooted from all that is familiar to them and dropped suddenly into an entirely new system, and they are expected to be grateful for the opportunity. What's more, they're expected to fit into the new corporate environment almost immediately. I sensed that this sort of attitude was especially prevalent at JPMorgan, where we Bear people were seen as interlopers who were stealing jobs, simply because we'd been rescued by big, bad JPMorgan. It seemed to me that resentments ran deep with some of our counterparts at JP, which was understandable to a degree. But the fact of the matter is that we were truly innocent in this whole deal. We were the victims more than anything else. But that was our side of the story.

If you flipped that coin over, you got a good look at a whole new side. We were Bear Stearns, the Wall Street mavericks who didn't care about anyone but ourselves. We did things our own way, and the rest of the world could just get out of our way. And to top it all off, we'd only been around for 85 years. I say "only" because when we stood our history next to that of JPMorgan, we were infants to JP's status as immortal Wall Street institution. So basically we were incorrigible children in the minds of a lot of older Wall Street firms.

▲ ▲ ▲

It's difficult to pinpoint a specific historical date to serve as the founding date of JPMorgan, simply because its history is muddled with various mergers and spin-offs. The company that had bought us was actually Chase Bank, which owned JPMorgan. JPMorgan, in turn, served as the investment banking arm of Chase, and operated in that capacity with a sort of quasi-independence, thus the name JPMorgan Chase. So it's a two-pronged story that brings together JPMorgan and Chase into the single firm that would be the future conqueror of Bear Stearns. And what a complicated story it.

JPMorgan, for all intents and purposes, began its history in 1799 with the formation of the Manhattan Company by Aaron Burr. The supposed purpose of the Manhattan Company was to supply New York City with clean water during the yellow fever epidemic that was ravaging the city at the time. Underneath that façade of public service, though, was another purpose, namely the formation of a new bank. Burr had managed to insert a clause into the company's charter that allowed him to use leftover capital in whatever other business he might wish to engage in. And, lo and behold, the water supply business didn't drain the Manhattan Company's capital reserves. So Burr founded the Manhattan Bank in 1799, locating it at 40 Wall Street, just down from where the New York Stock Exchange building would rise at the dawn of the 20th century. And, incidentally, the location was also about a block west of the old City Bank, the same one that our good friend Edward Smith visited that Saturday morning en route to his extended stay at Sing Sing Prison in 1831.

By 1808, the Manhattan Company had sold its water business to the City of New York, and then began to focus its energy entirely on the banking industry. The Bank of Manhattan, as it was now known, served as an example for others to follow, especially in the way the bank obtained its charter. The water supply business had been, in a manner of thinking, an early example of what Wall Street people call a special purpose vehicle (SPV). SPVs got a bad reputation during the Enron scandal that captivated the nation's attention during the first few years of the 21st century, when it was disclosed that Enron accountants were using SPVs as a way of hiding debts from the public. But in its most basic sense, an SPV is a company or a subsidiary that is created in order to serve as a counterparty. In today's business world, you see SPVs being used as a way for a large corporation to finance a project without putting the corporation itself at risk. In the case of the Manhattan Company, though, there was no risk involved. It's just that the larger, more public project—the water supply business— was being used as a way to finance another project—the creation of the bank. And plenty of people caught on to the idea, and pretty quickly, too. Suddenly everybody in town was wanting to build a railroad or a canal, and use the same concept as Burr had used. In other words, everybody wanted to be in the banking business because of the lucrative potential the industry offered, and they were willing to bend the rules in order to get themselves established in it.

Banking certainly was a good business to be in at that time, due to things like westward expansion. Given the growing country and its accompanying growing economy, banks had no shortage of people seeking loans to start new enterprises. By the end of the 19th century, the Bank of Manhattan had grown into one of the largest banks in the country in terms of the overall number of individual depositors. Around that same time, the Chase National Bank was established and named for Abraham Lincoln's Secretary of the Treasury, Salmon P. Chase. And while Chase National started out the 20th Century as a fledgling bank, it soon grew into a Wall Street powerhouse under the guidance of Albert Hank Wiggin, who actively sought out corporate accounts. Hand-in-hand with that activity went the establishment of a variety of trust services.

Trust services are offerings by which a third party (a trustee), in this case the bank itself, serves as the intermediary between two other parties, the trustor and the beneficiary. For example, if an elderly person wants to finance his grandchild's education, he can set up an account (a trust fund) for that purpose. The grandparent is the trustor, the grandchild is the beneficiary. The third party overseeing the disbursement of the funds—be it a bank or an accountant or whoever—is the trustee. And the applications for trust services go far beyond merely paying tuition for a grandchild; the range of applications is limited only by the imagination of people with money to give. Of course, the services don't come free; there's a bank fee attached, which was why they were such a profitable service for Chase National.

Running parallel to Chase National's trust work was the organization of the Chase Securities Corporation in 1917, which is yet another sort of trustee corporation. Chase Securities served to distribute and underwrite stocks and bonds. When a bank chooses to underwrite a stock, it means that the bank is buying the entirety of a company's initial public offering. So let's say that company X decides they want to go public. They issue a certain number of shares of stock in order to raise money; that money comes from the investment bank. The investment bank in turn sells the shares of stock to the public for, it hopes, a higher price than they paid to the company. That difference in the two prices is known as the underwriting spread. In some cases, multiple investment banks will team together to underwrite a single company's stock, thus creating an underwriting syndicate. And while the underwriting process is not the typical trust service, it is along the same lines, in the sense that the bank is serving as a third-party and acting as the liaison between two other parties, the company and the public.

The two banks—the Bank of Manhattan and Chase National—were going along separately until 1932, when Chase National was suddenly thrust into the ugly spotlight of financial impropriety and crisis. Wiggins was forced to resign as chairman of the bank due to charges of using bank funds to engage in stock speculation. And as an interesting aside to the that scandal, during the course of the investigation it was discovered that Mr. Wiggins had profited quite handsomely during the Stock Market crash of 1929. He'd apparently shorted his own bank's stock and made a staggering $4 million as a result of some timely sales. And just to add insult to insider trading, he'd used some of the bank's operating funds to finance his personal trades. But that scandal, as financial scandals are prone to do, eventually disappeared from the public's radar screen and the bank went on with the business of banking. After the dust settled and World War II had finally ended, Chase had expanded it reach to several international venues, but was still lacking a major presence domestically at home in the United States, a financial market that was growing exponentially in postwar America. The Bank of Manhattan, however, had 67 separate branches within the confines of the city of Manhattan alone. The merger of the two banks brought together Chase's international reach and Bank of Manhattan's sprawling domestic customer base; it was a match made in banking heaven. When the firms' merger was complete in 1955, Chase Manhattan was born.

Then came the 1980's, a time of greed like the world had never seen before. It was going to be a bad decade for Chase Manhattan. The bank's problems, like so many problems over the course of history, arose from the same source from which the bank derived its very existence: money. Money, money, money. In the 80's, everybody wanted money and everybody had money. Everyone, it seemed, except for Drysdale Government Securities. DGS was a spin-off of Drysdale Securities, which was an established Wall Street brokerage house. But DGS was built on a foundation of misinformation, starting with their claims of over $20 million in operating capital. The truth wouldn't come out until it was too late; the company actually began life $190 million in debt. As news about DGS emerged, it was discovered that the officers of the firm were engaging in what can best be labeled a Ponzi scheme, and that scheme was perpetuated at the financial expense of Chase Manhattan.

Charles Ponzi was a European immigrant who is credited with starting one of the first pyramid schemes designed to defraud investors in 1918.

At the time, many immigrants were using the international postal reply coupons (IRC) to correspond with loved ones overseas. IRCs were created in 1906 as a way of simplifying international mailing rates for customers in the days before airmail. Due to varying postal rates, it was oftentimes challenging for people to determine the correct postage to apply to a piece of mail bound for an international destination. The IRCs allowed postal customers to use a single coupon to cover postage to any county. The coupons were sold worldwide; the difference was that coupons cost different amounts in different locations.

Ponzi figured out that he could turn a profit if he purchased IRCs in a location with lower postal rates and then converted them to individual postage stamps in an area with higher rates. He sold the idea to investors after creating his own "company," which he named the Securities Exchange Company. After securing upwards of $1 million from unsuspecting victims, Ponzi used some of the money to pay early investors, keeping most of it for himself. The huge sums the early investors saw as their returns led them to invest more, which Ponzi used in part to pay off later investors. He continued to run the scheme—and made quite a lot of money doing so—until 1920, when the whole thing collapsed and Ponzi pleaded guilty to mail fraud.

The officers of Drysdale Government Securities were doing much the same thing, though in a much more complex fashion. Basically they were selling bonds they had bought, and then using the money generated by the sales to cover their own expenses and to pay themselves rather than paying interest obligations. It didn't take long for things to spin out of control for DGS, but not before they defaulted on $160 million to Chase Manhattan. The bank ended up losing a total of $270 million in trading expenses as a result of the fraudulent pyramid scheme. In the end, Drysdale Government Securities' two top officers, Joseph Ossorio and David Heuwetter, ended up pleading guilty to a host of felony charges in 1984.

But that massive loss was just the start of a bad decade for Chase Manhattan, and unfortunately for the bank, there were no convenient targets to point at as the cause for the losses. It was simply good old fashioned bad luck at this point. The bank took a beating in the oil crisis during the decade, getting hit for another $161 million in unsecured loans for oil and gas interests in Oklahoma. Later, in 1987, the country of Brazil announced that it would no longer be paying its foreign debt, at least for the time being. Chase was a major creditor of Brazil's, so that announcement was especially painful for the bank. Chase ended 1987 with a loss of $894.5 million, the worst financial performance for a bank since the Great Depression. The bank responded by laying off 10% of its workforce in hopes of trimming costs. At the end of the decade, the commercial real estate market bubble burst, and Chase lost even more money on loan defaults. In a moment of prescient and ironic foresight of things to come, the *New York Times* reported that Chase Manhattan was a prime target for takeover.

It was clearly time for a shake-up. The board of directors suggested that

NEW YORK—JULY 10, 2003: Stockbroker John H. Slade, 95, answers questions during an interview on July 10, 2003 at Bear Stearns headquarters in New York. The Holocaust escapee and Wall Street veteran is still in good shape and has no plans to hang up his trader's jacket. "I'm happy to go to work every morning," said the securities mogul, who works as senior managing director at Bear Stearns' international department and honorary chairman of the firm's executive committee. *(Photo by Don Emmert/AFP/Getty Images)*

the current CEO, Willard Butcher, take early retirement, which Butcher opted to do. He was soon after replaced with Thomas Labrecque. Labrecque circled the wagons, so to speak, and cut the bank's fat. International operations were scaled back, employees were laid off, expenses were cut wherever possible. It was a bare-bones sort of operation designed to return Chase to profitability. In 1996, Chase was acquired by Chemical Bank, though the latter opted to keep Chase's name attached to the new bank, which was, at the time, the largest in the country.

At this point in time, the financial world was one of seemingly constant mergers and acquisitions, with major firms joining together to create single, unified and monstrously large firms. For example, this was when Citigroup was formed via the merger of Citicorp and Travelers Group, the same Travelers Group that owned the investment bank Salomon Smith Barney (which was itself a firm born of the merger of Salomon Brothers and Smith Barney). It was suddenly very much the "in thing" to merge with an investment bank; Chase Manhattan was out of the loop because they were, to this point, investment bank-less. The bank had acquired a few small investment outfits, but nothing like Salomon Smith Barney. They'd have to wait their turn to get a shot at one of the big players in Wall Street's burgeoning investment banking world. They'd have to wait for JPMorgan to come along in 2000.

Just like every other firm in this convoluted story, JPMorgan started out life with a different name. And, in this case, a different country. George Peabody founded a merchant banking firm in London in 1838, and soon after named Junius S. Morgan as his business partner. Junius took over the business in 1864 and renamed it J.S. Morgan & Co. Junius's son John Pierpont Morgan—JP to his friends—had established a New York office and, when his father died in 1890, combined J.S. Morgan & Co. and his own company into one firm, JPMorgan. The new firm thrived until the crash of 1929. After the enactment of the Glass-Steagall Act in 1933 and the ensuing separation of commercial and investment banking, JP spun-off the investment banking portion of the firm, which became the august institution today known as Morgan Stanley & Co. But the officers of JPMorgan never lost interest in investment banking and through the 60's and 70's, the firm dabbled in international investment banking, where Glass-Steagall wasn't enforceable. By the 1980's, the Federal Reserve had loosened the regulations associated with Glass-Steagall, and by 1990 JPMorgan had been granted permission to handle corporate debt securities and equities. They were now officially part of the investment banking game.

In 2000, Chase Manhattan merged with JPMorgan in a deal that was valued at approximately $32 billion. The new financial megalith was the third largest banking firm in the country, behind only mammoths Citigroup and Bank of America. Like most other mergers, this one wasn't without its pitfalls. Yes, it created a huge new firm. Yes, it generated hundreds of millions of dollars in income. But all that came at the expense of lost jobs and other cost-cutting measures that always seem to arise when two major corporations join forces. And turf wars. You've always got turf wars when two big business join together. *The Brady Bunch* was a fantasy; mixed families never get along anywhere near that well. And remember what I said about investment bankers being a bunch of overgrown and whiney seventh graders. Long story short, it's not a pleasant marriage when the two groups get suddenly yoked together. It's more like a bunch of angry dogs all thrown into a ring together at the same time. Place your bets and get out of the way, because things are going to get ugly fast. And that's what I was afraid was going to happen with the JPMorgan takeover of Bear Stearns.

▲ ▲ ▲

It was that fear of turf wars and hostile behavior that hung in the recesses of my brain like a cloud on that last day of Bear's existence, Friday, May 30, 2008. It was the end of an era, and not in some clichéd way of speaking. It was the end of an 85-year run for Bear Stearns, and it was the end of our professional lives as we knew them. The following Monday, those who had job offers in hand, would report to a different supervisor in a different office with a different name and a different title. And most importantly, those with job offers would suddenly have places on an organizational chart. And it's just like the first day of seventh grade when you're suddenly in a new classroom with a new bunch of classmates and everyone has to establish their place in the classroom pecking order. When you get a new office with a new supervisor with a new title within your new place on a new organizational chart, you have to fight to establish your reputation. And when you're kicking somebody else out so that seat you yourself can take their place, you're going to have to fight twice as hard. It's just the nature of the game.

But when I woke up that morning, those thoughts were, at least momentarily, far from my mind. I went through my regular morning routine. *Just another day,* I kept thinking. *Just another day.* But on the way downtown, though, it hit me that this was not just another day. Far from it. This was it. This was the last day for the venerable Bear Stearns. After today, the firm would be a footnote in Wall Street's lengthy history, something people would one day talk about in the same way they speak today of classic cars or lost ways of life. One of those do-you-remember-when subjects. That was, I think, the most difficult element to wrap my mind around. I was okay with the fact that I was no longer working for Bear specifically. In this business, there were no guarantees. You did the best you could and hoped that you would be rewarded for your efforts. But you never really knew if you'd be at the same firm the next year or not.

No, it wasn't the change so much that bothered me as it was the finality of the whole thing. Gone was the Bear Stearns that had so attracted me in my earlier days. Gone. Never more to return. Adios to the vibrant, living, breathing organism that defied Wall Street standards.

I thought of how much history had passed through those offices. People like John Slade, the German immigrant who had worked for Bear for seven full decades, starting as a $15 a week runner in 1936 and who continued to work until near his death at age 97, still putting in four days a week as a stock trader. Or people like Alan Greenberg—"Ace" to those of us who knew him—who had served the company so loyally. Ace was the literal heart and soul of Bear, never asking anyone to do anything that he himself didn't do himself, including the establishment of the policy that we all had to contribute 4% of income to charity. I loved these people like they were my own family, and the house that they had built was now crumbling. I felt sadness for those men today. What must they have been thinking, wherever they were, as they watched Bear slide slowly down, nothing to stop its descent, until it ceased to exist?

Mixed with that sadness was a sense of my own involvement with such a historic moment. I felt privileged to have been a part of this firm and to be a part of this exact moment in the firm's history. I reflected on my childhood and how far I'd come from my small-town upbringing. My parents had hoped I'd join the local fire department or pursue a career in a similar civic profession in that rural outpost where I'd grown up. I had to laugh at the recollection. To them, it was no doubt a wildly lucrative career choice, becoming a fireman. It was mind-boggling for me to think of myself here, now, standing on the precipice of history, at the epicenter of one of the most important financial events of our time. I'd come a long way from aspirations of being a fireman.

But this whole situation—the craziness, the ups and the downs, the adrenaline rushes, the lulls—it was what I had wanted from day one, and I wouldn't have changed a thing even if I could. I've been blessed to this point with an amazing life full of adventures and successes. Working for Bear was everything I'd imagined and dreamed about as a kid, listening to that walkman, dreaming about the big world somewhere out there. In a place where they made deals and sold bonds and traded stocks. In a place where people handled millions—even billions—of dollars. Incomprehensible amounts of money. And the responsibility that goes with those amounts. My young mind at the time could never have conjured up the fantasy that was my reality that morning.

I managed to work myself into a mindset of optimism and excitement. And truth be told, it wasn't a false optimism, either. Like I said, my life had been rewarding past my wildest expectations, and I knew how lucky I'd been to have gotten the opportunities I'd had. And those opportunities had built a foundation upon which I was now firmly planted, ready to take whatever the world had to throw at me. Bring on the future. I'd take it with a smile, no matter what.

When I arrived at the office, I relied on that optimism I'd built up within myself for what I anticipated would greet my arrival. I felt like a father to the traders assigned to my desk, and I wanted to set the tone for the day. I was afraid that they'd be emotional, worried, anxious. I wanted to be the leader and set the tone of positive optimism, riding the wave of excitement I'd already created within my brain. As I walked in the door, I had barely a second to take in my surroundings before I was handed a piece of paper that took only a few lines to make its declaration. The Bear had officially been pronounced dead.

The press release had come from the JP communications department, and it announced the finalization of the merger in that mundane manner that only well-written press releases can achieve. It was just the facts, plain and simple and sterile: "JPMorgan Chase & Co. (NYSE: JPM) announced today that it has completed its acquisition of The Bear Stearns Companies, Inc., effective 11:59 p.m. EDT on May 30, 2008." No way to deny it now; the takeover was official and complete, down to the minute of when it had happened. The final sale dictated that each single share of Bear stock had been converted into 0.21573 shares of JPMorgan stock. Again the attention to detail was almost painful to note. They had the share value in rela-tion to JP's stock down to the hundred-thousandths of a dollar. It was almost scientific in its exactness. For a moment, my optimism faltered.

But once on the trading floor, it returned in a flood. I was pleasantly surprised to discover that the mood wasn't as gloomy as I'd anticipated. Bitter-sweet is an apt description, as folks were torn between sadness at what they knew was the end of an historic era culminating in the destruc-tion of the firm they'd grown to love and excitement about the prospects of what their future lives held for them in different companies or even dif-ferent careers. I clearly wasn't alone in my optimistic outlook. Ironically enough, though, I think that the people headed to careers with JPMorgan were the least happy of all; they were being absorbed into the organiza-tional charts and grey suits of the conqueror.

And while some might find it difficult to find any sort of sympathy for people making six figures-plus on Wall Street, you have to understand that all of us were drawn to Bear not because of the money. We were drawn to Bear because of the lack of structure, the free-and-loose attitude that pre-vailed throughout the firm. And the loss of that attitude was depressing.

But most of all, we were sad because it felt a lot like a divorce in that building on that morning. Bear was a family. A big, crazy, sometimes dys-functional one, but a family nonetheless. Bear Stearns had the lowest turnover rate of any major firm on Wall Street, a statistic that was due in massive part to the family atmosphere that was created and fostered throughout the entire firm. When I'd started at Bear on that March morn-ing in 2002, I'd been scared down to the bone of what I was about to embark on. I was terrified that I wasn't strong enough, energetic enough, tough enough, savvy enough, whatever enough to survive at Bear. But I'd been absorbed into the family and I'd thrived under the family's tutelage. And as I looked around me at my band of traders and the others on the trading floor, I saw a mass of people, all of whom were just like me. They'd no doubt been just as scared on their first days. And they'd all thrived right along with me, wrapped in the safe embrace of the Bear Stearns family.

In the end, 45% of the roughly 14,000 Bear Stearns employees were retained by JPMorgan, which means that 55% were sent packing. That's approximately 7,700 people who lost jobs as a result of the merger, and that's just on the Bear side of things. In order for JP to make room for the 6,300-odd Bear employees they decided to keep, a few JP folks were going to lose their jobs, too. The company managed to keep from publicizing any concrete numbers, but most estimates hovered around the 4,000 mark. Those cuts in jobs at both Bear and JP contributed to the over 22,000 Wall Street employees who lost their jobs in the 12-month period from June 1, 2007–June 1, 2008. With that backdrop, the carnage and destruction were complete. A firm 85 years in the creation had been destroyed, completely taken over by invading forces, and it had really only taken a matter of several days to effectively decimate the company. Over 11,000 individuals had lost their jobs in the ensuing reorganization. Not all of those individuals were necessarily upset about the fact that they wouldn't be part of the JP family, but the number itself was still a staggering figure.

Nobody without an offer from JPMorgan who worked on the trading floor was worried about their respective futures. We all realized that the short-term opportunities on Wall Street weren't the best, given the current economic climate gripping the country, so those who hadn't taken jobs with JP weren't anticipating immediate openings in other firms. But we'd all been involved with the market long enough to have the faith that bad times, no matter how dark they might seem, would end. You just had to fasten your seatbelt and hang on for the ride. And we'd worked for Bear Stearns, which immediately set us apart from the rest of the pool of would-be applicants when that time came and brighter financial days were upon us. But most of all, self-confidence that was so apparent was an example of the sort of people who work on trading floors, regardless of the firm. By definition, people who make their living as traders are driven people. They're not the type to boast for too long about success and they're also not the type to grow too morose about losses. Either way it's just a new chapter, so it's time to move along. Nobody need shed a tear for the traders; they'd be just fine, financially and otherwise.

It was the administrative staff that we all felt for. The secretaries, the mail guys, the people who did the real grunt work in the trenches at the office. The people who worked so hard every day to make our own work days that much easier. Due to the very nature of their work, there's an over-abundance of people to fill a limited number of places in the business world. These were the people for whom we all felt the deepest sympathy. They'd been more innocent of any wrong in this whole thing than anyone, but yet they were the ones who would end up paying the highest price. Every time I saw one of the administrative staff in the office that day, I felt a pang of guilt, a twinge of sorrow because there wasn't something more I could do to make their lives easier; they'd certainly done their fair share for all of us. In the end, we took up a collection for our floor's mail guy. It wasn't a vast sum of money that we managed to raise, but it would hopefully send the message that he'd been appreciated and that he wasn't forgotten. And what's more, it was hopefully going to be enough to help him get through until he was able to get back on his feet with a new job.

The guilt that I was feeling was reflected in the face and words of a couple of guys from the prime brokerage division, who were experiencing what could best be called survivor's guilt. JPMorgan had been wanting for years to get into the prime brokerage side of things, but had never gotten around to it. To buy a prime brokerage outfit is very costly, and to build one from the ground-up is incredibly time consuming. So the Bear prime brokerage division had been an absolute Godsend for JP. In addition to getting the division they'd been coveting all these years, they were getting some of the best people in the business to run it. Most, if not all, of the Bear prime brokerage folks took jobs with JP, and we'd all known early on that they'd be getting those offers. We didn't resent them for it; a few of us had joked that we wished we'd had the foresight to go into prime brokerage ourselves, but none of us held a grudge. It was just the luck of the draw. One guy from prime brokerage who had a pretty serious case of survivor's guilt was telling me how he felt so badly for all the other Bear employees who now faced uncertain futures. I tried my best to soothe his emotions by pointing out that most of the equities derivatives department had also gotten jobs; the high retention rate was a reflection of how good the people were who had worked for Bear. And that fact meant that everybody would land on their feet in the end. There was nothing for him or anyone else to feel guilty about.

I took the time on that afternoon to reflect on what had happened over the last few months, and the only metaphor that really worked in my mind was that of a war. We'd been to war and seen the carnage and destruction that only a war can cause. The new firm, the one that had been born out of the absorption of Bear Stearns by JPMorgan, had been created from that carnage and destruction. Those of us who lived through it are fortunate to have had the experience. We learned a lot about ourselves and we learned a lot about others. We learned about the evils that men are capable of in the quest for the almighty dollar. We'd seen peoples' dreams shattered and our lives turned inside-out and upside-down. We'd seen people turn on one another at the drop of a hat. But we all banded together and survived, just like the family that we considered ourselves to be. We managed to support one another and helped to keep each others' spirits up. And now it was time to reenter the world, the world after the war.

At the end of the day on that Friday, there weren't any tears or painful goodbyes. We'd already done all of that by now. Tonight it was just numbness, knowing that there was literally no tomorrow for Bear. And as I left the Bear Stearns building at 383 Madison Avenue that night, I, too, thought of literature. But it wasn't Holden Caulfield that crossed my mind. It was, rather, the young protagonist from William Golding's *Lord of the Flies,* a book that I remembered from my earliest high school days.

The part of the story that came to me was at the end of the book, when the British Naval officer has arrived to rescue the boys from the island on which they'd been stranded, and the ferocious child-warriors are once again cast as just children. At that point, young Ralph, who was forced into an adult-like leadership role early on in the novel, has been relieved of his duties and he no longer has to maintain an adult-like façade. He is, finally, able to resort to being a child again, for the first time in a long time, and he cries like the child that he is: "Ralph wept for the end of innocence, the darkness of man's heart, and the fall through the air of the true, wise friend called Piggy."

The revolving door spun slowly behind me as I left the building. I looked back over my shoulder, briefly, taking in the firm's name in silver lettering above the entrance. Nothing would ever be the same again, not for the firm and not for any of its former employees. We'd all grown calloused from the beating we'd taken over the course of the last couple of months. We were now faced with the same dilemma as the kids at the end of Golding's masterpiece. We had to assimilate into a world where we were no longer Bear employees. Now we were just normal people who'd happened to work for one of the greatest investment banks the world had ever known. We'd get through this, of that much I was sure. Things would change, of course, and we'd have different jobs in different environments, but we'd all survive in the long run.

But like Ralph, we first needed to weep for all that we'd lost.

CHAPTER FOURTEEN

Survival of the Fittest

"Those things which are precious
are saved only by sacrifice."
—David Kenyon Webster

On November 20, 1820, the whaleship *Essex* was stove-in by a whale and sank in the South Pacific, over 2000 miles from the nearest port. Twenty men—the entire crew of the ship—crammed into three small boats and attempted to sail to South America. The crews on those boats were eventually forced to resort to cannibalism, eating the flesh of the already dead to sustain those that were still living. As discussed by Nathaniel Philbrick in his seminal work on the tragedy *In the Heart of the Sea: The Tragedy of the Whaleship Essex,* on February 6, 1821, one of the boats had shrunk in number to four occupants, and those four had run out of food. The youngest person on that particular boat, a sixteen-year old named Charles Ramsdell, suggested something that, although no doubt on the minds of the other three men, was so taboo that none of them dared talk about it. Ramsdell suggested the men draw lots to determine who would be killed in order for the others to have a supply of food.

At first resistant to it, Captain George Pollard, who was in charge of the men on that boat, finally relented and allowed the crew members to go forward with it. It was no doubt a terrible decision to make, but the result of the drawing would make that terrible decision even worse. The lot fell to a young man named Owen Coffin, the cousin of Captain Pollard himself. Not one to fight his destiny, Coffin said of his fate, "I like it as well as any other." The sailors then drew lots again to see who would be the executioner. Charles Ramsdell, the person who had suggested the idea in the first place, drew the paper that assigned the recipient the grisly task of killing his friend. Young Owen put his head on the side of the boat and

Ramsdell shot him. When they were pulled from the water, they had been afloat in a 30-foot boat for 95 days; the levels of human endurance have rarely been tested as strenuously. Of the three in that boat who lived after Coffin's assassination, two would survive long enough to be rescued, kept alive, in part, by the food source provided by the sacrifice of Owen Coffin.

The story of the killing of Owen Coffin for food is an appropriate parallel for the destruction of Bear Stearns in that both of us were sacrificed for the betterment of those around us. I have no doubt that Bear was allowed to implode while those with the power to prevent its happening stood by and watched. It is vitally important to understand that all Bear needed was an injection of capital from an outside investor, somebody willing to show a little faith in the firm's ability to recover. One person to cast the rumors aside, to prove that they were nothing more than rumors. Had that happened, I am certain that I would still be working for Bear. But it didn't happen. We didn't get the sudden infusion of cash we so desperately needed, and the firm became completely insolvent.

I don't for a second fault Jamie Dimon for taking advantage of the deal that was offered him, regardless of what some of my colleagues had to say about him and his firm in the wake of our takeover. I'm a capitalist at heart, and I think that Jamie pulled off the deal of the century. Dimon himself said that he expected the deal to pull in $1 billion in after-tax profit for JPMorgan by 2009. That's not a bad return on an investment. And more power to the guy who was able to put it together and get it approved by everyone who had to sign off on it. And don't kid yourself; there was a hell of a lot of risk involved in this little transaction, risk he took upon himself. He recognized what was there and, shotgun or no, he found himself a pretty nice little bride.

It often comes as a surprise to the average American investor when he discovers that he is invested in companies he has never heard of and has no idea of what they do. But such is the world where mutual funds have opened the doors of investing to just about anyone. Mutual funds are funds that an investor buys a share of, much like shares of stock. The funds themselves are managed by an investment advisor who picks stocks (or bonds or currency exchanges or whatever it is that the fund is invested in), and the fund's value reflects the changes in those stock prices. A vast majority of investors today have positions in mutual funds, due in large part to the fact that the funds allow investors to rely on someone else's wisdom to go after the market. And the explosion of the Individual Retirement

Account (IRA) market has also helped to fuel the growth in mutual funds' popularity.

IRAs allow people to contribute a certain amount annually to a fund that is designed to assist with income at retirement. It's a pretty simple concept. You put your money in, it grows over time, you take your money out when you retire. It's that middle part that is a little tricky for some people, though, because growing money is a tricky business. After all, our parents weren't kidding when they said that money doesn't grow on trees. Due to the non-existence of that mythical money-bearing tree, investors are forced to link an IRA to some kind of investment strategy that will reap returns on their investment. For millions of people, mutual funds are the strategy of choice.

As an example, let's take a middle-aged gentleman—let's say he's 50, just for argument's sake—he wants to retire at the age of 65 and he's been contributing to his IRA for the last 20 years. He's got a pretty good nest egg going there, assuming he's been contributing the maximum allowed every year to a mutual fund that he's attached to his IRA. Maximum allowable amounts vary by year; let's say it's a $5,000 cap, just to make things easy. For twenty years, he's been contributing $5,000 annually, which means he's got $100,000, excluding the money he's made on returns from his mutual fund investment. Again, just for argument's sake, let's say that he's had an average return on his investment over the last 20 years, and his total IRA value to date is $400,000.

But he looks up one day and all of a sudden his IRA is worth less. A lot less. He reads in the business section of the paper that some company called Bear Stearns collapsed, and that defaults on mortgages have caused a credit crisis on Wall Street and that credit crisis is linked in some way to Bear Stearns. The paper manages to use enough MBA jargon to make the whole issue so incomprehensible to the average reader that it's almost not even worth printing the story. So he goes to his computer and pulls up the information on his IRA. He looks at the prospectus. There's nothing about Bear Stearns as one of the stocks in the fund. There's nothing about mortgage lenders in the fund. He's been paying his own mortgage on time; never been late on a payment once in his life, in fact. He doesn't own any personal stock in Bear and can find absolutely no connection to either the company or the mortgage industry sector whatsoever anywhere within his IRA information provided by his broker. So why is he now faced with the prospect of delaying retirement because of this whole mess?

The simple answer is that there is no simple answer. In order to really understand what happened, the first thing our investor has to understand is that the components of the world's economy are all intrinsically linked in more ways than he can possibly imagine. The simplest way to understand it is to consider what is called the butterfly effect, which is a layman's way of explaining chaos theory. The butterfly effect suggests that the tiniest of disturbances—like the one created in the airspace around a butterfly when it flaps its wings—is enough to modify weather patterns. The most common invoked to illustrate the concept is one that uses a mythical butterfly flying around somewhere in equatorial Africa. The butterfly flaps its wings at a specific moment in time, and thereby creates a disturbance in the air around it. That disturbance combines with other disturbances in the area, and eventually those disturbances all build into a single disturbance that is becomes a hurricane. If that butterfly hadn't flapped its wings at that exact moment, then, the theory suggests, the hurricane itself wouldn't have formed. The message is that every action and event that takes place in the world, no matter how seemingly insignificant, can have a powerful affect on actions and events throughout the world.

The world's economy is similarly interrelated. A disturbance in one sector of the economy can have far-reaching effects on other sectors of the economy, sectors that may or may not appear to be readily linked to the sector in question. A spike in the price of oil, for example, will most certainly have an effect on oil stocks. That connection is pretty obvious. But the trickle-down theory comes into play. When the price of oil goes up, so, too, does the price of gasoline, and because gasoline gets more expensive, perhaps people aren't buying cars like they used to, which hits automotive stocks. Again, we're still in the ballpark of direct links. But consider the fact that higher gas prices mean higher transportation costs for things like food and other consumer goods. And when people have to start paying more for everyday necessities, things can get ugly in a hurry. Because people are paying so much for things they have to have in order to survive, maybe mortgage payments are suddenly later and later and interest starts to rack up on credit card balances. If things get really bad, people end up being forced to declare bankruptcy and houses end up in foreclosure. When all of that starts happening, as so many of us on Wall Street can attest, investment banks get hit hard, due to their deep investments in things like mortgage bonds.

All of that because the price of gas went up.

SURVIVAL OF THE FITTEST

The message here is that the world's economy is like a chain in that it is only as strong as its weakest link. When everything is clicking along the way we all hope it will, we have an economic boom. But when something major happens to throw that smooth ride off its course, there's a domino effect, just like with the butterfly. In the case of Bear, the housing market became seriously devalued, which made CDOs like mortgage bonds a much riskier investment. As the economy began to slow down, people began to default on their mortgages. Suddenly those mortgage bonds were ticking time bombs, due to the fact that the collateral wasn't worth as much as the loan itself; so there was nothing to back up the bonds if the loan went into default. Throw in a few rumors about liquidity to make things sound even worse than they already are, and Bear Stearns goes under in the space of a week. The world's economy is that interconnected. And, horrifyingly enough, it's also that fragile.

One thing that this interconnected nature of the economy points to is the incredible importance of a diversified economic base. In other words, monopolies are incredibly dangerous in this economy. In an ideal world, things like antitrust laws exist to prevent any single company from becoming so large that it will have the potential to destroy the economy through its downfall. Using the investment banking industry as an example, if there were a single investment bank in the United States and that investment bank met with the same fate as Bear Stearns, the world's economy would find itself in an economic depression that would make 1929 look like a minor stock market correction. And it wouldn't be just the US; that depression would rack the entire world with financial ravages that are best reserved for nightmares. As it is, there are several major investment banks, plus scores of lesser-known banks, that are all in competition for clients. That competition serves as a form of safety net for the economy, at least in theory, because if one fails, there are plenty of others to come in and take their place. This safety net, though, assumes that each bank is independent and that one bank's actions don't have any affect on another's.

The reality is, though, if the Federal Reserve Bank had not taken the actions they did, the theory of the butterfly effect would have taken root on Wall Street and Bear would have been just the first in a rapid succession of investment banks to plummet into the depths of insolvency. Consider the words of Ben Bernanke, Chairman of the Federal Reserve. Bernanke, speaking to the Joint Economic Committee in the US Congress on April 2, 2008, said, "With financial conditions fragile, the sudden failure of Bear Stearns likely would have led to a chaotic unwinding of positions in those markets and could have severely shaken confidence. The damage caused by a default by Bear Stearns could have been severe and extremely difficult to contain."

Bernanke was trying to explain to Congress why he'd done what he'd done when he opened the discount window to investment banks. But self-defense motives aside, when the Chairman of the Fed uses words like "chaotic unwinding" and "damage could have been severe and extremely difficult to contain," you have to understand that the man is talking fire-and-brimstone. The Fed Chairman, regardless of who he is, is charged with keeping the nation's economy on a smooth course. The job is a miserable one, with the Chairman living life under the most powerful of microscopes. A colleague once joked that he'd been at a cocktail party with then-Chairman Alan Greenspan, and Greenspan had sneezed. Seven men simultaneously called their brokers, because they were nervous about the message Greenspan's nasal expulsion might have foretold. So Bernanke couldn't have used words like "absolute disaster," because that would have set off a financial avalanche. "Chaotic unwinding," however, is Fed-speak for the same thing.

So what we saw in the Bear Stearns collapse was a kind of tough love lesson, but one with all the requisite safety nets in place to ensure that the punishment wouldn't lead to any kind of worldwide financial disaster. In my view of things the Federal Reserve Bank of New York and the United States Treasury had declared that it was time for investment banks to pay for their sins, to pay for the stress and heartache they'd caused to those people who went to work every morning and did their jobs and contributed to their IRAs every year, only to see their investments drop in value because a few guys on Wall Street made some bad bets. The day of reckoning was upon us, and when Bear started to slide, he let it go. I doubt he cast the figure of the melodramatic villain with a sly smile on his face, but he let it happen. It needed to happen. It was the only way to send a message strong enough. And I think his message got the attention of the rest of Wall Street, to say the least.

Investing is as close to legalized gambling as you might hope to come. The whole process is fraught with risk; it's the nature of the game. What makes it more palatable to general human sensibilities, though, is the fact that the risk is a calculated one. Whereas a blackjack dealer has the odds in his favor, an investor is able to research an investment and then make his decision based on the results of that research and thereby even the odds a little bit. But what happens if the investor in question isn't getting the full story on his investment? What if the person to whom he is entrusting his financial well being is misleading him or withholding information? That situation is what we call a moral hazard.

Moral hazard can be more than just lying to an investor, though. The term also encompasses those situations when an investment manager takes unusual or undo risks in order to make a profit for himself, regardless of what happens to the eventual return on the investment. Oftentimes in cases of moral hazard, an investment manager will make a profit prior to the settling of a contract, and his client will end up losing a great deal of money despite the manager's profit-taking. And investors, too, can be

NEW YORK—MARCH 24: The JP Morgan Chase building is seen March 24, 2008 in New York City. A new agreement will give Bear Stearns shareholders ten dollars per share, five times the payout outlined in a JPMorgan Chase & Co. buyout deal last week. *(Photo by Chris Hondros/Getty Images)*

guilty of moral hazard in a related way. For example, if an investor willingly takes a huge risk and he loses everything, we all shake our heads at him and say he was just foolish with his money. However, if that same investor takes the same huge risk because he's found a way to minimize the loss—in the event he loses at all—and maximize his return, then he's also enmeshed in moral hazard. The mortgage market is a prime example.

The potential returns on levering up CDO within a fund and other securitization businesses can be very lucrative for any investment bank. The downside is two-fold. At the front end, there are mortgages that are being created and sold, mortgages that should never have been originated in the first place. And on the other side, the fund's investors will end up getting stuck with the tab when the potential risks associated with an over-leveraged fund become reality.

A mortgage is a risk for the mortgage holder. There's no two ways about that equation. Any time you loan money to somebody for any purpose, there's a chance you'll never see your money again. But with mortgage lenders, there's a transfer of that risk that passes the loan around like a hot potato until it's finally been farmed out as an investment opportunity and the risk is so far diluted that an individual default here or there typically isn't a major issue. But what we've seen in the mortgage lending business in recent years is nothing short of predatory behavior. For example, a young couple walks into their local mortgage broker in Middle America, USA. They're newly married, looking at buying their first home. They've pinched and saved and scraped together the down payment. They've begged and borrowed. They've got just enough. And then they meet their new best friend, the guy who's "going to make it happen for them." You see, this guy needs to make one more loan of about $200,000 to make the million-dollar-a-month club at his office. And that means he and the wife get a vacation to Hawaii, compliments of the boss. And he's got to get it all done by today. Lucky for him, this pair of suckers just walked into his office.

So they start talking, and it turns out the couple needs $150,000; that puts our broker $50,000 short of his goal. Not to be deterred, he starts doing some calculations, over the protestations of the couple that they don't need that much. He assures him that he'll "make the numbers work" in order "to bring their ratios in line." This is their first time through this ringer, so they don't know what to expect. They are forced to trust their new best friend in the world; they don't have a choice in the matter. They're like hikers wandering around the woods with no map and no compass who suddenly stumble upon a local who offers to guide them home. He fudges a few numbers and adds a little to each of their salaries. After all, they're friends, and this is what friends do for one another. The couple leaves with a $200,000 loan that they didn't need in the first place and which they probably can't afford when it comes time to start making the payments. But the mortgage broker doesn't care. By the time these people start paying that mortgage, he'll be in Hawaii and the mortgage will have been transferred from his office to another bank to yet another financial institution to an investment bank to a group of investors. In other words, he no longer has any responsibility. So rampant had this sort of behavior become that in 2008, during the month of May in the United States, one home in every 483 received at least one communication of foreclosure intentions. That means that better than 2% of American homeowners had defaulted on their mortgage payments by May 2008, due in part to predatory lending tactics.

Moral hazard is a way of explaining the ridiculously low share price that JPMorgan offered for Bear. It was a way of punishing the stockholders, most of whom were innocent of anything resembling blame in this game. But remember, too, that Bear Stearns was one-third employee-owned. We were unique in that respect. And we were, at least ostensibly, guilty of perpetuating this massive moral hazard by being a party to the selling of mortgage-backed securities. The theory holds that if we hadn't created the market, the brokers wouldn't have had the incentives to oversell the mortgages. The establishment wanted to teach all of us—the institutions themselves, those of us who staffed those institutions and those who made their money off the expertise of those of us who staffed those institutions—a lesson once and for all about responsibility. And there was no better way to teach that lesson than by offering up a sacrifice.

Bear really was the perfect sacrifice for this teaching moment. On the one hand, Bear was only the fifth-largest investment bank in the US, so we weren't so huge that it was impossible for us to fail. But at the same time, we were big enough to be major, big enough to send a message that everyone else at the table better pay attention because a major investment bank was going under. And underlying those opposing sentiments—we were too big to fail but we weren't too big to fail—was the potential for other banks to meet the same fate. Paulson had to do something drastic to stop that from happening. Which is exactly what he did. His opening of the discount window was as drastic a measure as he could have taken in his position. But he waited for Bear to go under before he finally decided to pull out that drastic measure. In other words, Paulson wanted to send a message to Wall Street, and Bear was the messenger. As soon as he'd made his point, though, he wanted to reassure nervous investors that it wouldn't—couldn't—happen again. It didn't need to happen again; he'd made his point.

What still upsets me today, even after all the time that has passed since the actual collapse, is that the Treasury waited until we'd gone past the point of no return financially before opening the discount window to investment banks. When it was too late to save Bear, the Treasury threw out life jackets for everyone else, everyone else who wasn't even in the water yet. Meanwhile, Bear drowned.

Were this a murder trial, the prosecution would have no burden to prove motive. Prosecutors are under no obligation to explain to a jury why a defendant may or may not have committed the crime of which they are accused; to do so merely provides the prosecutor with further evidence that can be used against the accused in order to sway the minds of the jurors. And though this is not a typical murder trial, I appreciate the idea that I'm not responsible for reading minds and providing motives. That said, though, I would suggest that Paulson had the motive—going back to his days at Goldie—because Bear had refused to assist in the LTCM buy-out. Yes it sounds like a petty grudge to hold. But the fact of the matter is that it's exactly the sort of mindset that investment bankers have, being the overgrown seventh graders that they are. We are blessed—or cursed, depending on your perspective—with incredibly powerful memories. We can remember dates, times, people, places. We can remember stock prices and their various fluctuations going back for months. We can remember it all. And we always remember wrongs done to us. We never forget those. And what's more, we never let an opportunity to revenge a wrong done to us pass by unheeded. We're good like that.

▲ ▲ ▲

A relatively unpublicized element of the universe contained within the Financial District of Manhattan is the fact that foreign investments are a huge driving force behind the United States economy and, I would suggest to you, were also a huge reason for the Fed's anxiousness to secure an American investment bank as the purchaser and to do so quickly, so as to prevent a foreign investor from swooping in scooping up Bear. And that anxiousness to keep Bear in the United States and the desire for a swift settlement, I'd further suggest, is why the purchase price was so bargain-basement low. In what can only be called the final ironic twist of this whole too-ridiculous-to-be-believed sequence of ironic events, the Fed basically circumvented the entire premise of the free market economy on which the capitalistic system—the same one that has built the investment banking industry and the American economy itself—by refusing to allow for competition within the market. In essence, the deal was brokered privately, without the benefit of competing offers, so a bastion to capitalism was sold off in what would one might say was quite possibly the diametric opposite of capitalism itself.

In *The Wealth of Nations,* the veritable blueprint for a capitalistic system of economics, Adam Smith discusses the concept of an invisible hand that guides the economy, the idea of a *laissez-faire* system, French for "let do." That invisible hand is controlled by competition within the market place. In the most basic sense, when two or more entities are selling the same thing, they must compete with each other in order to offer the best product at the lowest price. The theory holds that the consumers will demand lower prices and higher quality, given that they are the ones paying the price. And sellers will be forced to conform to their buying public's wishes.

Herein lies the problem with monopolies, from a capitalist's perspective. If a single entity controls all of the production for a particular commodity, then there is no incentive for that company to offer more competitive pricing or higher quality. We can fall back on the example of blue jeans that we used to discuss advertising. Let's say that blue jeans are suddenly a required piece of clothing for a particular profession, like some sort of uniform. Now, if you're the only person in the world making blue jeans, you can charge whatever you want for them. So since you can pick your price, you go with $200. If people want blue jeans, they'll pay it. They have no choice, because you're the only game in town; and since they're required to wear them, they're stuck paying your price. However, if somebody else comes along and starts making blue jeans and only charges $20, you can bet you're going to see a vast number of your clients heading to the competition. You're going to be forced to either lower your prices or raise your quality to justify the higher price (or perhaps even both), or face going out of business. Capitalism and its invisible hand at work.

And while the sale of Bear Stearns to JPMorgan involved a little more complexity than that example suggests, the same tenets hold true for both scenarios. The deal as it was initially brokered by the Fed involved JPMorgan buying Bear for $2 a share. Nothing new there. But $2 a share is about as close to $0 as you can get, $0 as in bankruptcy. And you have to remember that the share price is the value of the company; a $0 share price does in fact mean that the company is bankrupt for all intents and purposes. But you also have to remember that Bear was too critical to the United States financial system to be allowed to fail, due to, among other things, the interconnected nature of the economic system as a whole. And what's more, while we were only the fifth largest investment bank in the country, we were one of the leading clearing brokers and prime brokers in the United States. So no matter what way you chose to look at the situation, we could not be allowed to fail completely.

So in the interest of worldwide financial peace, Bear was allowed to become quasi-bankrupt, at $2 a share. Like I said, it's the next best thing to complete insolvency. At that price, we should have had bidders going absolutely nuts trying to buy us. Especially international bidders. But nothing. No calls, no interest, no offers. This despite the fact that foreign investments are huge driving forces on Wall Street; sovereign wealth funds are big business in the FiDi.

A sovereign wealth fund (SWF) is an investment fund owned wholly by a foreign entity and which serves as a sort of dedicated pension fund for a particular country. Part of the rationale behind the funds, from the foreign country's perspective, is that they offer the country a relatively low-risk way of offsetting some of the risk of that country's own economy. Because they are trying to minimize risk, sovereign wealth fund managers tend to be more passive in their approach to investing, preferring to invest with a long-term outlook. So they're not the meddling sort of investor who is constantly shifting money from one sector to another.

Sovereign wealth funds face a host of domestic regulations in the United States, most of which are focused on national security. The Committee on Foreign Investment in the United States (CFIUS) is the group charged with making sure that foreign investors aren't allowed access to sectors of the American economy that would expose sensitive elements of the nation's defense. While that might sound somewhat anti-American in the sense that they're prohibiting a specific group of people from engaging in investment activities in certain sectors of the economy, CFIUS does perform a vital safety role. The committee is made up of members of various US agencies, including the Department of Defense, the Department of Homeland Security, the Department of State and the like. And it just so happens to be chaired by the Secretary of the Treasury, our good friend Hank Paulson.

One of the most publicized cases faced by CFIUS was the proposed investment in the Peninsular and Oriental Steam Navigation Company (P&O) by a sovereign fund from Dubai called Dubai Ports World (DP). With an innocuous sounding name like Peninsular and Oriental Steam Navigation Company, it seems like P&O would be far from the world of national security-related issues. However, P&O was the leaseholder for harbors in New York City, in addition to several others on the east coast of the United States. The public outcry that resulted from the possibility of an Arab country literally owning New York Harbor—especially in the post-September 11 world—was enough to cause DP to transfer ownership to a US-based entity rather than become engulfed in the political firestorm that was brewing if they chose to pursue the ownership deal.

In recent months, many sovereign wealth fund managers have been reluctant to pursue major deals in America, because they feel that they are getting reputations for being easy money offered by fools. But that doesn't mean there's not a competition among investment banks to woo the sovereign wealth funds, even after the P&O issues that rankled so many members of Congress and the American public. In fact, the whole P&O mess makes it all the more interesting that Hank Paulson himself spent a great deal of time in the Middle East courting sovereign wealth fund managers in the months following the Bear meltdown.

In addition to foreign investments and the issues and pitfalls associated with them, the United States economy is also just one part of the worldwide global economy. Despite many Americans' belief that the US is somehow the center of the financial universe, the fact of the matter is that we're just one cog in the machine. Because the world's different economies are so interconnected, in fact, trading in foreign currencies is a major facet of the investing world with a lot of people making—and losing—a lot of money on investments in the foreign exchange. The foreign exchange (ForEx) is the exchange that handles currency trading; the ForEx sees an average turnover of $3.2 trillion every day. Like I said, currency trading is a major business.

Many people find it strange that money can be bought and sold like stocks or bonds or boxes of cereal, but currency itself is just another commodity. And just like any other commodity, it boils down to the simple laws of supply and demand. If more people want a particular currency in relation to another, then its value will go up. Alternatively, if fewer people want the currency, it's value will decline in relation to another. Take the United States dollar (USD) versus the Euro. If more people want Euros than want dollars, you'll see the value of the USD decline in comparison to the Euro. For the average American, this relationship really isn't an issue until they want to go to Europe and find that they only get a fraction of a Euro for each of their USDs. However, for currency investors, individual currencies are just like stocks. As we've seen, stock prices fluctuate based on demand for the stock, a demand influenced by how well a company performs; that's pretty easy to grasp. But then what drives the demand for a currency that is, seemingly, static in its value? I mean, a dollar is a dollar, right?

Well, yes and no. Let's say that you're just one more time buying blue jeans (who knew you could get so much mileage out of a pair of jeans?) and the only manufacturer of blue jeans is in London. Yes, it's a monopoly, but it's easier if we examine it from that perspective. You buy your jeans at your favorite store, paying in US dollars. Those dollars are sent to the jeans distributor who then sends them to the jeans maker in London, where they are converted into English pounds (GBP). The more jeans people buy, the more money goes to England and the more dollars that are converted to pounds. Because you then have a surplus of GBP, it creates a trading surplus. In this example, because the only currency being used for the procurement of jeans is GBP, that surplus in turn drives up the value of the pound in relation to the dollar. The same sort of model holds true for any foreign product, be it cars, clothing, jewelry, whatever. So investors can bet on the fluctuations of a currency's value in the same way that they can with a stock's value. If they guess right, there's a fortune to be made, just as there is in the stock market. It's that whole picking-the-right-side of the betting part that trips up a lot of would-be Warren Buffetts.

Now let's return to the United States, where our country is carrying a relatively large trade deficit. It's important to understand that a trade deficit is not a debt per se. Rather, it means that the US is making less money off of exports than it is spending on imports. Of course, that can lead to a monetary debt, but for our purposes here, I want to keep it in the context of the trade deficit alone. What is called the net exports (NX) is the value of the difference. If the value of the NX is positive, meaning you're selling more than you're buying, then you've got what is called a trade surplus; if the opposite is the case and you're buying more than you're selling, it's called a trade deficit. Think of the whole thing the same way as you would your personal bank account. If you've got less money coming in than you do going out, it's going to create a problematic situation. You've managed to get yourself into the equivalent of a trade deficit.

As a result of that trade deficit, the demand for the USD has gone down relative to other major world currencies. And what that means is that American investments are a bargain for holders of foreign currency, because for each unit of their currency, be it a pound or a euro or a yen or whatever, they can get more USDs. More buck for their yen, if you will.

Combine that devaluation of the USD with the explosion of wealth we've seen across the world, especially in places in the Middle East and Asia, and you have created the perfect setting for the emergence of a foreign investor—be it an individual or a fund—to come in as a white knight and save Bear. Or at least buy the firm. It's a bargain for the foreign investor, due to the fact that the firm is going for way below market value (in USD, no less, which is even more to the foreign investor's benefit). And what's more, Bear's presence internationally was comparatively small, something that would have been especially attractive to overseas banks. Because of our huge presence domestically, we could have complemented a foreign bank's overseas presence without the addition of an overlap of services. It was the perfect situation, from a foreign investor's standpoint. But still, there were no takers.

And from a more American way of looking at things economically speaking, the introduction of a white knight—foreign or domestic— would have driven the sale price up; it would have been capitalism at work in its purest form. The competition would have been great for the situation at hand. Bear could have been kept alive. Jobs would have been saved—somewhere in the neighborhood of 11,000 jobs—and the shareholders would have not seen the massive losses in their portfolios that they ended up with. But the deal was done before any foreign capital could have gotten involved.

Interestingly enough, though, some executives from Bear had actually approached a foreign investor on their own on Friday, March 14. They weren't seeking to sell the company so much as they were seeking a capital infusion from a foreign investor. When all was said and done, though,

I really think this wasn't so much of an attempt to save the firm as it was an attempt to artificially raise the then-$2 share price with a make-believe bidding war. If we could at least spark an interest in a foreign investor, it might just force JPMorgan into bidding up the price.

Temesek Holdings, which is a Singapore-based sovereign fund, was contacted late in the day on Friday, March 14, in Singapore (twelve hours ahead of New York time) with a request for an undisclosed amount of money, according to various news accounts. If we could have gotten that money, if Temesek would have taken the chance, it would have saved the day. But by that time, the JPMorgan sale was all but finalized, which leads me to believe that whoever it was that sent the request wasn't putting any real faith in it; this was the ultimate Hail Mary pass from our quarterback. It was the sort of thing you do just so nobody can ever say you didn't try everything. It was almost a legacy-preserving action for a few of our execs at that point. The major hang-up with the deal ended up being that Temesek was given about forty-eight hours to decide, which made it impossible for them to do any kind of meaningful due diligence. Additionally, Bear was seen by many in the international community as a very "American" firm, due in no small part to our limited overseas exposure. So for an Asian firm to inject a massive amount of cash into our firm, it would be a difficult thing to explain, politically, to the rest of the country. But in the end, regardless of the rationale, officials at Temesek refused to take the bait. They cited both political and practical issues as the concerns which led them to make the decision to pass on the chance to invest in Bear.

So we come back to the idea that the Treasury and the Fed set out to exclude the possibility of any other firm bidding against JP for the rights to buy Bear Stearns. As I've discussed, foreign investors would have been at something of an unfair bidding advantage, given that the USD was so devalued compared to other currencies. For example, given the relative strength of the GBP compared to the USD at the time, it would have been an easy buy for an English group like HSBC or Barclays. And that's exactly the problem. It would have been so easy for a foreign bank to gobble up Bear Stearns because of their unfair advantage in terms of the currency valuation that US banks would have had no real fighting chance. And the United States government couldn't risk sending the fifth largest investment bank in the US off to join forces with a foreign entity. It would have done nothing but further devalue the USD and other key American financial assets that need to be protected in order to keep the nation's and the world's economies both on an even keel.

So that helps to explain why there was a need to pass Bear off to an American bank, as well as why the deal was done so quickly and without any semblance of the capitalistic spirit that built the industry as a whole. But it doesn't explain why JPMorgan specifically was the winner of the Bear Stearns lottery. Yes, they're an American firm, but so are countless other investment banks. Why JP? The answer that makes the most sense is the fact that the deal had to be put together on such an immediate time-line that JP was the only logical choice.

Truth be told, there weren't a lot of American investment banks who were in the financial position to be buying Bear. Citigroup, the largest investment bank in the country, was reeling from write-downs and losses suffered during the mortgage bond market meltdown and ensuing credit crisis; at last count, they'd gotten hit with over $40 billion in losses. So the last thing Citi was looking for was yet another way to throw money away. Goldman Sachs? Not likely. They already had a world-class prime brokerage department, and to add Bear to the mix would have been an unneeded and unwanted distraction, not to mention an overlap of services. Plus, Goldie owns J. Aron, the single largest commodities broker in the world. So neither Citi or Goldie needed or wanted Bear. Merrill and Lehman were both planning on bankruptcy proceedings themselves if Bear went down, so clearly they were in no shape to pony up the funds needed to take over the firm. And then there was one.

So then the pointer on the investment bank wheel of fortune landed squarely on JPMorgan and Jamie Dimon. Dimon has a reputation as a risk taker, and, as he himself put it in an interview with *New York Magazine,* any time you put together a deal in 36 hours, that deal is inevitably going to include "uncertainties we don't even know about." But Jamie spent his early days after graduation from Harvard Business School doing what were, in essence, LBOs with financial wizard Sandy Weill while the two were together at Citicorp. So he knew about taking over a company and running it efficiently, and he certainly wasn't afraid to make cuts in order to make the money part of the deal work. JPMorgan, though not necessarily looking for an opportunity to expand their prime brokerage department, wasn't going to turn down the chance at taking on some of the best minds in the business to add to their stable either, an idea supported by the fact that 100% of Bear's prime brokerage folks were offered jobs after the merger. And most importantly in the whole equation, JPMorgan, for whatever reason, had remained relatively unscathed through the entire credit crisis, especially compared to the other potential players.

So Dimon it would be. He was willing and able to do a deal in a day-and-a-half—a deal that involved quite a lot of risk that was both known and unknown—and he was capable of having it signed and delivered prior to the opening of the Asian markets on the morning of March 17. JPMorgan would take over the firm and the financial world would be safe once again, though a little bit wiser for the experience.

In hindsight, it's obvious to everyone that Bear should have heeded the warning flags being sent up by the rampant rumors, the warning flags saying that we needed to raise capital. Financial markets follow cycles, up and down, and most of us knew that we were heading into a down cycle at the time. And truthfully, the collapse of Bear could have been avoided if we'd managed to find a firm to take us over. But no search for such a savior was ever launched in earnest. But why not? The question still haunts us today, and there are no absolute answers.

Part of the answer lies in the culture of the firm. We were mavericks, fighters, survivors. We'd been through fights before and managed to survive. That bravado, though, wasn't doing us any favors. If anything, that survivor mentality was making us more vulnerable because we managed to convince ourselves that there really was no fight we couldn't survive, no crisis we couldn't sneak through. It was arrogance and it was our downfall.

Another part of the answer lies in the fact that people inside the Bear offices were clinging to the hopes that a deal done the previous October would save the firm. Citic Securities, a Chinese-based securities firm, had agreed to purchase 9.9% of Bear Stearns. The hope was that it would give Bear a much larger presence in Asian markets and the investment potentials contained therein. But the problem with the deal in general is that it didn't involve the huge influx of capital we needed. It was a quid-pro-quo relationship, where the Chinese would invest $1 billion in Bear, and Bear would invest the same amount in Citic. One analyst said of the deal, "It's a bunt. It's not a grand slam." Most importantly, the Citic deal would have made it very difficult for another firm to come in and take Bear over completely.

And a third part of the answer lies in the fact that Bear prided itself on the fact that the firm was one-third employee owned. We were unique among Wall Street investment banks in that respect, and our executives didn't want to make a deal that would be a dilutive transaction. A dilutive transaction is one that dilutes, or lowers, the Earnings Per Share (EPS) of the firm. In the case of Bear, if we had been acquired by outright by another firm, it would have been dilutive for us. Bear employees would have seen less return on their shares, and that wasn't the Bear Stearns way. And thought it was what ended up happening anyway, it wasn't the desired outcome, so it wasn't sought out as a solution in the beginning.

A colleague of mine, speaking months after the fact, made the comment that he thought that the federal government's actions might best be described as those of the antithesis of the American capitalistic system. I had to disagree. His logic was that Paulson, cast in the role of dictator, had made what might be called unilateral decisions about the takeover of Bear, putting the interests of the financial world above the spirit of capitalism that built that world. And in so doing, he managed to keep opposition— or competition—out of the equation.

I had to point out for him that because of Paulson's actions—and Dimon's willingness to play along with his ideas—the entire United States financial system was saved from complete destruction. And there is truly no way to stress that fact enough. The team of Paulson and Dimon literally saved the American financial system from a tsunami the likes of which would have wiped out the entire economy. Had Bear gone under, only to be followed in short order by Lehman and Merrill, panic like the world has never known would have engulfed financiers from New York to New Delhi, and the world's economy would have literally collapsed. It would have taken years to recover. At the risk of making them out to be the collective second coming of the Messiah, there are no words capable of adequately explaining the disaster that was prevented by Jamie Dimon and Hank Paulson. Regardless of what you think of corporate CEOs or Treasury Secretaries or whatever else, these two were instrumental in avoiding a worldwide financial collapse. So after considering it carefully, I'd call Hank Paulson someone who made a life-saving decision when that decision most needed to be made.

This is not to say that I don't feel like Hank Paulson betrayed Bear in that he allowed the firm to go under. I sincerely feel that way more often than not, even with my time removed from the immediacy of the event itself. But he also ended up doing exactly what needed to be done in order to prevent the same thing from ever happening again. And for that, all of us who make our living in the financial sector should be forever grateful to him. In the end, Bear was sacrificed so that every other bank might learn exactly how lucky they were not to be in similar circumstances. And once Paulson had made that point clear, he made sure it would never happen again. Like a good democratically elected leader, he knew the mantra about power corrupting and absolute power corrupting absolutely. He allowed himself, perhaps, to play a little crooked pool But when the rubber hit the road, he made sure nobody else suffered. Yes, I'll stand by my original opinion.

CHAPTER FIFTEEN

So What?

*"Tut, tut, child! Everything's got a moral,
if only you can find it."*
—THE DUCHESS, *ALICE IN WONDERLAND*

Darrell Royal, one of college football's legendary coaches, once said that he thought that everyone who graduated from the University of Texas, in addition to their selected course of study, must have also received a degree in football coaching. His reasoning was pretty simple: "Every one of them sits up there in the stands and tells you how they would have done it and why their way would have been better than what you did," he said of his days as a coach directing the team for the Longhorn faithful. It's a phenomenon that sports networks have taken to calling "Monday morning quarterbacking," this practice fans have adopted of using hindsight to analyze and critique a given situation from the previous weekend's game. But as I was to discover after the collapse of Bear Stearns, it wasn't a practice confined to the realm of sports. Plenty of analysts offered up their own opinions and pet theories on what had happened with Bear, how the collapse could have been avoided or who was to blame for the whole thing. And most importantly, an immense amount of time and brainpower was dedicated to figuring out what it all meant for the rest of Wall Street and the larger financial world as a whole. That seemed to be the most important goal for so many of those Monday morning quarterbacks. They wouldn't rest until they'd succeeded in divining a moral from this tragedy. And that's what this whole unfortunate sequence of events really was. A tragedy in every sense of the word.

In the *Poetics,* Aristotle says by way of a definition of tragedy that the genre is, "An imitation of an action that is serious, complete, and of a certain magnitude [...] in the form of action, not of narrative; with incidents arousing pity and fear, wherewith to accomplish its [catharsis] of such emotions." Additionally, a tragedy is actually a relatively standardized form of storytelling according to Aristotle, with several necessary components contained within the framework. The story must feature a tragic hero, a character who has some sort of inherent tragic flaw, a characteristic that works in such a way within the context of the story so as to precipitate the hero's demise during some kind of epic battle. That demise must bring forth from the audience feelings of pity for the hero and a fear of the same thing happening to themselves.

Aristotle said of the tragic hero, "A man cannot become a hero until he can see the root of his own downfall." However, in order for the hero to operate on such a plane that he is able to elicit the requisite pity for his eventual destruction, he must begin the story at a non-elevated status, unaware of the existence of his tragic flaw and unaware that he is on course to bring on his own downfall. This lack of status can be demonstrated in one of several ways. One such way is to explain the hero's humble beginnings—perhaps it's the king who rose to his position after years of loyal service to the people whom he now serves as ruler. Or, in a setting more apropos to this discussion, perhaps it's the kid who worked his way up from the mailroom to become CEO of the firm. The purpose here is to create a hero the audience can identify with, a character in whom they can see elements of themselves.

In addition to being able to relate to the hero on a human level, the audience must also see in the hero some sort of imperfection, but not so much so that he is deemed to be evil. If the hero is perfect and he is destroyed anyway, there is clearly no justice in the world and, although tragic, there is no moral lesson to be learned; if he is evil and is destroyed, he simply got what he deserves.

And perhaps the most talked-about characteristic of a tragic hero is that of hubris, or personal pride. It is the hero's pride that prevents him from seeing what is happening around him and which prevents him from saving himself from the destruction he brings on by his own deeds. Because he is blinded by his hubris, he cannot alter his actions to avoid his destiny.

The story that composes the tragedy itself, Aristotle tells us, must have a beginning, a middle and an end, and the story must not be presented as a narrative. In other words, for the story to truly be tragic, we must see it acted out before our very eyes as opposed to having someone relate a tragic tale to us. There must be some climax in the action, followed by a dénouement, also known as the resolution. The climax is most often the death or destruction of the tragic hero, an event which is, as I've said, brought on by his own hubris and precipitated by his tragic flaw. The resolution of the story following the hero's downfall is the part of the story that should result in a cathartic moment for the audience, that part of the performance where the audience experiences a purging of emotions consisting of pity for the tragic hero and fear that they could one day find themselves in the position of tragic hero. The hope in the end is that the audience will learn a moral lesson from the catharsis, and change their own ways so as to avoid facing a similar tragic outcome in their own lives.

The tragedy that was the story of Bear Stearns rivaled *Oedipus Rex* for following the standard set down in the *Poetics* in 350 B.C. Our play, if we can call it that, was put on for the benefit of an audience of investment bankers, primarily, with a few hundred million other audience members looking on with keen interest. It was they who were to divine the moral lesson presented within the play and, in turn, to apply that moral lesson to their own modes of existence. Whatever that moral lesson may have been.

Following the outline set down by Aristotle, we can check off the specifics of this story as they are manifested in the genre of tragedy. Clearly the story involves a subject matter of a serious nature and with a level of measurable magnitude—there's nothing quite so serious as the prospect of complete and utter financial destruction of the world's economy to qualify as a subject with some semblance of gravitas. And the action portrayed in the story is certainly complete; the dissolution of Bear Stearns was the final step in that equation. Cessation of existence is probably the most complete action one can hope to encounter. The story itself was certainly not narrative; I and thousands of others can vouch for the fact that this really happened. We lived it; our wildest dreams come true would have been to wake up one morning to discover it had all been some fantastically horrible story dreamed up in a Hollywood movie studio.

As for a tragic hero, take your pick; our story is littered with them. Perhaps we should focus on Jimmy Cayne, our bridge playing former CEO. He was the one responsible for Bear's refusal to participate in the Long Term Capital Management bailout in 1998, and he was also at the helm when the Bear hedge funds collapsed in 2007. Both events were potentially instrumental in the outcome of this tragedy, and perhaps fanned the flames of Hank Paulson's allowing Bear to slip away. His failure to participate in the LTCM bailout and his failure to be present during the hedge fund crisis might both be said to have resulted from excessive pride. But Jimmy was no longer really part of the Bear executive structure at the end, so he can claim to have washed his hands of the whole mess long before the collapse.

So maybe we should assign the all-important label to our CEO at the end, Alan Schwartz. Alan is a tragic hero of a different sort. I am of the absolutely unwavering belief that Alan was in no way responsible for what happened; he just inherited a sinking ship and was asked to steer it. It was as if the captain of the *Titanic* had handed off the wheel to someone else after the ship had struck the iceberg. Would that person then be to blame for the ship's sinking? He was, in that scenario, the last one on the helm. But regardless of who had the wheel when the ship sank, there was a long sequence of events that led up to that final horrific moment.

Maybe, then, we should call a host of others involved in the collapse the tragic hero. Perhaps the title should go to all of the investment managers who failed to heed Ace Greenberg's advice to get out of the mortgage bond business. Or maybe we should bestow it upon the investors themselves, the people who blindly gave their money to the managers at Bear. There's certainly no shortage of possible actors able to play the part. In short, it's nearly impossible to decide on just one, simply because everyone's individual interpretations of the events differ, and in each case you've got a different villain and a different hero. The difficulty inherent in finding a specific person to call the tragic hero in this drama points to a major difficulty arising from the whole situation, a difficulty that has plagued just about every investigation that has sought to explain more fully what exactly happened. There are no easy answers to this crisis, and it's impossible to wrap the event up neatly and put it in a box, regardless of how neatly it might seem to fit at first glance.

But we labor on, trying to do it anyway. Seeking that moral lesson that all good tragedies have, that nugget of wisdom we're supposed to glean from this crisis. There's got to be a reason for this. There's got to be a reason that Bear went down. There's got to be a lesson for us to learn from this tragedy, or else it's just a story of destruction. And it's hard for us to fathom that much senseless destruction just for the sake of destruction. If we can divine some greater truth from it, then it makes it easier to take.

Or at least psychiatrists tell us that it does.

SO WHAT?

▲ ▲ ▲

In a *Wall Street Journal* piece about the collapse that appeared a month or so after the event itself, Alan Schwartz was quoted as having told a group of Bear execs, "This is a whole lot of noise," a statement he made in reference to the rumors of Bear's cash shortage that began circulating early on that fateful week in March. But he could just as easily have been saying it about the Monday morning quarterbacking that was going on all around us. One pundit referred to Bear as having had an "addiction to leverage," the implication being that we were in over our heads with leveraged debts and we thus got exactly what we deserved. Yes we had our fair share of leverage. That was no secret to anybody who'd been paying even the remotest bit of attention. But the leverage wasn't the root cause. It simply created an environment that facilitated the collapse once the first domino had fallen. And it didn't really help with that oh-so-important moral lesson. After all, every investment bank on Wall Street is just as leveraged as Bear. Why, then, didn't they have to pay with their lives? If that's the case, then we'll have to revert to the idea that there is a discernible lack of any justice in the universe, which does not a moral lesson create.

I read another gem in *Bloomberg Markets,* an article that spouted off the fact that there were people in certain governmental circles who had ascribed the fault to a lack of oversight. Barney Frank, the chairman of the House Financial Services Committee, said, "We now see a situation where more damage was done by inadequate regulation. What we have is a systemic problem, and that's what we want to address." Frank was subscribing to the viewpoint that overgrown seventh graders run amok on Wall Street had gotten themselves into a little bit of trouble, and now they needed to be scolded. What we really needed, apparently, was an adult to show us how to do it. With all due respect to Mr. Frank, he'd fail as a critic of tragedy. This explanation of his, just like the one offered up by the would-be substance abuse counselor who was commenting on the firm's addiction to leverage, doesn't explain why Bear fell. If this lack of regulation was "systemic," then the entire industry, God help us, should have collapsed en masse. So we need another explanation.

And there were a host of other explanations. As the weeks and months passed, we were treated to a smorgasbord of explanations. And opinions. Everybody who was anybody had an opinion. And all of the explanations and all of the opinions were trying to show us why it was that Bear had collapsed and what moral lesson other firms could learn. If it wasn't because of our leveraged stakes or the lack of regulation, then it was just something we all should have seen coming. Between the weakening economy and the subprime mortgage issues, it was bound to happen. Of course, none of the people with this opinion were able to explain why it was that Bear was the investment bank singled out to pay the ultimate price for the weakening economy and the subprime mortgage crisis, thus negating any potential moral to the story. In my experience, when these people were pressed, they usually fell back on either the fact that we were over-leveraged or that we were out of control with the lack of regulation. At least you couldn't accuse them of not having read up on the disaster. One noncommittal soul that I spoke with about the collapse, when pressed for the exact reason that Bear was singled out came up with, "Just because."

And as much as I hate to contradict the experts and the financial gurus and the Congressional leaders, what was to become known as one of the most electrifying financial disasters in Wall Street's esteemed history wasn't the by-product of greedy men in expensive suits thinking they were above the laws of nature. Nor was it the inevitable result of a lack of regulatory oversight. And it wasn't just because.

Nassim Taleb, author of *The Black Swan,* put it best. He posed the following question to me at a financial conference: "If ten guys are playing Russian roulette, and one of them blows his brains out, is he any more stupid than the other nine guys he's playing with?"

The answer to that macabre rhetorical question is a resounding no. The dead man just happened to be the one who was unlucky enough to pull the trigger at the wrong time. And in a manner of thinking, that death is a sort of Darwinism. Not in the sense that it's survival of the fittest, but rather in the way that modifications may come from an event that will allow others to survive. In the case of the Russian roulette game, the nine guys who didn't kill themselves may rethink the whole idea of participating in this suicidal game, thereby prolonging their own lives. The death of one educates the rest, and in turn saves them from a similar fate.

The Bear Stearns collapse was much the same sort of situation. Investment banks all over the world were playing a variation of Russian roulette, spinning the chamber of economic risk and pulling the trigger. When the hammer fell and there was no report of a bullet firing, that bank passed the revolver to the next bank in line. Bear Stearns just happened to be the bank who pulled the trigger on a loaded chamber. But where is the moral lesson to be found in bad luck? Just as the example of Russian roulette can be looked at as a sort of social Darwinism, the collapse of Bear was its own sort of Darwinism, what I like to call Darwinian Capitalism. There is really no better way to describe what happened to Bear Stearns than to call it a Darwinian fight for life. We didn't go down peacefully and gently. We went down kicking and clawing the whole way. But we weren't strong enough to survive. Our death was to serve as a catalyst for a change in behavior in the stronger amongst us, a change that would prolong their own existences.

The problem with so many of the theories about what happened and why is that they are looking for a single root cause, and I think that stems from the fact that so many of those opinions come from people who weren't living it day-by-day, but instead came to the game when it was already over and then tried to offer color commentary for a newspaper article.

The people subscribing so heartily to these theories want to hang their hats on one issue, one problem that can be rectified. They're treating the economy as a whole as a cancer patient, and Bear as an individual organ. The organ in question developed cancer and was removed from the body; but the surgeon wanted to ensure that there was no spread of the disease. Thus by declaring the cause—and it's important to keep it to a single cause, because we don't want to confuse people—identified and fixed, we ensure this never happens again. It doesn't matter so much if the cause that is singled out is the right cause. What matters is that people feel safer because something—anything, really—has been done to make sure this never happens again. And while certain actions by the Fed have more or less guaranteed that no future investment banks will suffer the same fate as Bear, there is no single factor that brought on the collapse. For better or worse, this was the result of a conflation of widely varied events that seemed to have no relation to one another until they all met in a single, hideous aggregate that served to destroy Bear Stearns almost overnight.

That said, the collapse of Bear Stearns was not an inevitability; far from it, in fact. Just like I don't think I can stress too much the severity of the real and present danger that was present within this catastrophe, I don't think I can stress too much, either, the fact that if the firm had just gotten an injection of capital, then all would have ended up being well. I don't doubt that the firm would have been battered and abused by the various economic downturns in the market, but it would have lived to fight another day and thousands of people would still have jobs. It's easy to suggest that, of course, from this vantage point. The injection didn't materialize and the firm went under. Therefore my postulate is correct due to a sort of negative reasoning. I will go to my grave with the regret that we didn't at least get the chance to try it.

What is most distressing about this event is that Bear actually had the money to keep itself afloat; when the whole thing started, we didn't actually need an outside investor. But rumors are a powerful force, something way beyond the control of us mere mortals, especially rumors about money. The bigger the dollar signs, the more powerful the rumors. We were the victim of rumors about a lot of money; thus they were incredibly powerful. So powerful, in fact, that they took on a life of their own. They became reality. And suddenly the revolver was loaded with a single bullet and passed to us. We spun the chamber. We weren't alone in this game; all the investment banks in town were playing Russian roulette with us. Bear just happened to pull the trigger when the chamber was loaded. And as unsatisfying an explanation as that is for many people, it's the only accurate explanation. But I come back to my search for a moral, and as accurate as this explanation may be, it still leaves me without the satisfaction or peace of mind that a final lesson might provide.

Darwin's theory of evolution is predicated on the idea that members of a species will move towards a higher state of existence based on their genetic and behavior modifications. If we look at Bear's demise as economic Darwinism, then it stands to reason that those not brought asunder—those who didn't blow their brains out in the game of Russian roulette—have acquired some sort of positive mutation, some kind of beneficial alteration that will bring them to a more advanced state of existence. In other words, those other investment banks learned a lesson from the story.

At last, a moral shines through.

▲ ▲ ▲

As I discussed earlier, at its most basic level, the stock market is a battle of two opposing forces, forces that have come to be represented by bears and bulls. The bulls, representing the rising stock prices, are locked in a constant fight with their nemesis, the bears, representing falling stock prices. On the surface, it's a pretty simple concept; you look for the bulls and avoid the bears. But savvy investors know that there is plenty of money to be made in a bear market; it's just a question of knowing how to play the forces to your own financial advantage. One such method of making money in a bear market is shorting stocks. But as history has shown time and again, it's a risky game that investors play when they short stocks. In a bear market, there are few better ways to make a lot of money as an investor. By the same token, there are also few better ways to lose an equal amount of money. One way it's easy to lose is by judging the timing of the market incorrectly.

For example, let's say you're reading the market reports, and you find that a stock that you've been following for some time now is showing signs of turning bearish. Maybe its price has exceeded even the most generous of estimates and it has been dipping in recent days. Maybe the stock's sector is showing outward signs of weakness. Maybe you just have a gut feeling that the stock price is about to drop. Whatever your rationale, let's say you decide to short the stock in question. But then something unexpected, at least to your way of thinking, happens, and the stock price continues on its upward climb, defying the suggestion that it was turning bearish. You guessed wrong. And now you're stuck. Because you shorted the stock and its price went up, now you've got to cover your position at a higher cost. You just got caught in a situation where investors who are trying to capitalize on a bear market get trapped in a snare of their own making.

You just got caught in what investors call a bear trap.

It's just like the game of Russian roulette with ten guys, one of whom blows his brains out. None of the other nine are any more or less intelligent; they just got lucky this time. Using the same logic, if ten guys all short the same stock and only one gets caught in a bear trap, is he any more stupid than the rest? Not necessarily; he just had the misfortune of getting caught. But the other nine better grow smarter as a result of seeing what happened to their buddy. A lot of wisdom comes from experience and a lot of experience comes from bad decisions. And that means you have to pay attention to not only the bad decisions you yourself make, but also the ones people around you make.

We can only hope that other investment banks learned a lesson from the demise of Bear Stearns. We just have to hope they were all paying enough attention to grasp the educational message our destruction offered. But only time will tell if they got that message. The lesson to be learned from Bear's demise is clear. It's up to the other banks to go forward, to achieve that state of a more refined and perfected existence in the world of investment banking, to work to make sure that this never happens again. That's the moral of the story here.

It's up to them to avoid the same trap that killed the Bear.

Epilogue

"Well, Stu, I'll tell you. Surfing's not a sport.
It's a way of life. It's no hobby.
It's a way of looking at that wave and saying,
'Hey bud, let's party!'"

—JEFF SPICOLI, FAST TIMES AT RIDGEMONT HIGH

The original settlers of the country of New Zealand were thought to be Polynesians who came to the island nation some time between 950 and 1130 AD. From there, the first Europeans arrived in 1642 when Abel Janszoon Tasman arrived from Holland; Tasman never actually set foot on the island, however. It was not until 1769, when both James Cook and Jean Francois Marie de Surville arrived—neither actually knowing that the other was there at the same time—that Europeans would officially "discover" the island. From that point on, New Zealand became a port of call for whaling ships, traders and religious missionaries. When they arrived on the coast of New Zealand, the Europeans found a group of indigenous people that came to be called the Māori, a name that means "the original people" in their language. The name, as is often the case in colonized societies, only came into existence as a term used to describe the people after the Europeans arrived; the arrival itself created the need for such a descriptor, as before the Europeans, there was only one group in residence.

The Māori language is one of the three official languages of New Zealand. Linguists classify it as a Polynesian language, and place it in the subgroup of Tahitic languages. Close linguistic relatives of Māori include the language spoken on the Hawaiian Islands and that spoken on Easter Island, as well as that spoken in the Marquesas Islands. Māori has two distinctly different dialects; the country of New Zealand is, in actuality, a pair of islands, and each of the pair of islands has its own individual dialect. Regardless of which dialect it is that is being spoken at a given moment, it is, to my ear, a beautifully musical language.

The first time I experienced the Māori language was on a surfing trip to Gisborne, New Zealand, the sort of trip that surfers call a "surfari." During my time there, I befriended a fisherman who was a few years older than I. As we talked over beers in the late afternoons after a day of surfing, he taught me a few words of his native language, and after my departure, he and I corresponded via monthly letters. He closed every letter with the phrase, "Hai konā rā," which he explained to me meant, "I will end my letter here. Farewell to you, with love." It was a traditional concluding phrase, he said. But of all the Māori words that my sea-going friend taught me, one of my favorite is "hāhā," which means "to go and seek."

Many of my colleagues find it odd that I, a Wall Street investment banker, can just as easily talk about point breaks and what a pain in the ass those little beach grommets can be as I can about LBOs and derivatives. But it's true and I freely admit it. I love to surf. In fact, I acquired so much of a reputation for being a surfer during graduate school that during my final semester of business school, my fellow MBA candidates voted me the most likely to retire from a career in finance and go surfing. And at the risk of making my classmates look like prophets, I have, true to their predictions, become something of an avid surfer.

My love of surfing first took root in my early twenties, and has since bloomed into something more. It's hard to put it into words. Obsession sends the wrong message, but surfing for me is more than a hobby, just like Jeff Spicoli explained in *Fast Times at Ridgemont High.* That said, though, I don't want to cover myself with the mantle of "surfer bum" who feels that surfing is, to quote Spicoli, a way of life. Regardless of how I choose to classify the sport as it pertains to my life, I've found that much of what guides me in surfing also guides me in my professional life. And no, this isn't the part that I talk about ditching work in order to surf. Rather, I think that both surfing and investment banking require the participant to incorporate similar techniques in their approach in order to ensure success in both fields of endeavor.

When you're surfing somewhere you've never been before, it's not a good idea to just hop in the water and go. You need to analyze the conditions first, to see where the waves are breaking and what direction they're breaking in. You have to pay attention to things like the time between waves, as well as the time between sets of waves. You've got to determine the locations of underwater reefs and other obstructions, because they'll certainly affect how the waves will break and, if you're not careful, how your arm will break, too. In some cases, you've got to make sure you're not going to piss off any of the locals by jumping in where you, as a tourist, aren't necessarily welcome until you've proven your abilities. Once you've determined where you think you best fit in to this whole scene, you suit up and paddle your way out to the lineup.

Waiting on the right wave is one part experience and one part patience. To the untrained eye, it is sometimes difficult to figure out why a surfer will choose to allow a particular wave to pass him by as he sits atop his board, floating aimlessly, eyes trained on the horizon, whereas he'll immediately go after another one that is seemingly identical. To those same untrained eyes, waves look more-or-less identical to one another. But such couldn't be further from the truth.

Choosing a wave, for a surfer, is not just a random selection from a group of identical offerings. You position yourself outside the break and wait for a swell that builds within the take-off zone, that wave that is just right. You know it when you see it by the open wave face growing gradually larger in front of you. When you start to paddle for it, you've got a few seconds to find a clear take-off spot where you're not going to run in to anyone or drop in on top of someone who caught the wave before you. Assuming you've got room, then you need to figure out whether or not the wave is going to build gradually or close on you. If it's the latter, you want to bail out immediately, because it's not going to be a pleasant ride. If you think it's going to build gradually, though, you then have to decide if it's breaking to the right or the left, meaning which side of the wave the whitewater is forming on. If it's forming to your left as you look at the beach, it's a right handed break; if it's on your right, it's a left handed break. Typically breaks are consistent, so if you've been paying attention, you'll know which direction the wave is breaking, and you aim your board in that direction.

Once you catch the wave and stand up on your board, you've got to be constantly monitoring everything going on around you. That wave is more than just a patch of ocean; it's a living energy that is as unpredictable as anything can be, and if you lose your concentration for just a second, it'll eat you alive. You need to cut back in order to keep yourself moving, building speed as you slide down the face of the wave, working to keep your balance. It's an utterly complete exercise that challenges you mentally and physically, all the while stimulating your senses with an indescribable adrenaline rush. And though it might sound a little clichéd, there really is no word quite like "intense" to describe the experience of catching the perfect wave and, with a tip of the hat to the quintessential surfer boys themselves, finding yourself sitting on top of the world. And for those of us fortunate enough to get to that pinnacle, we suddenly find what it is that has eluded us to this point, that shapeless mystical state of existence. We find that which we were seeking.

It is the end of our hāhā.

In other words, it's the same experience as working for a major investment bank. On Wall Street, just as in surfing, you've got to analyze the environment, figure out where the rises and falls are going to be coming, when the dips are likely to turn into jumps. Most of all, you have to decide when to jump in and when to bail out. And right now, for me, it's time to bail out; I'll jump back in soon enough, though. But for now, it's time to bail out and relax on the beach for just a minute or two.

▲ ▲ ▲

I read recently that Ashley Dupre, she of Emperor's Club VIP fame, moved on from her role of distracting the world from news of impending financial meltdowns. After discovering that she had appeared briefly topless in a "Girls Gone Wild" video, Internet bloggers and gossip sites buzzed with pirated photos and clips of the young prostitute-turned-minor celebrity. She sued the Girls Gone Wild company and its founder Joe Francis for $10 million, citing the fact that she'd been manipulated into exposing herself for the camera after producers got her drunk while she was just a seventeen-year-old on spring break. Her singing career, though, showed signs of promise; she signed a management contract with Jerry Blair, who counts among his clients such pop music stars as Mariah Carey and Mika. Meanwhile, three of Dupre's bosses at the Emperor's Club VIP, two women named Temeka Rachelle Lewis and Cecil Suwal and an older gentleman named Mark Brener, all pleaded guilty to a host of criminal charges and face a couple of years in prison as a result of their actions.

After resigning as governor on March 17, Eliot Spitzer all but disappeared from the public spotlight. Whereas I used to see him occasionally on my morning runs, after resigning the governorship, he chose to take his exercise elsewhere. He was replaced in the governor's office by David

EPILOGUE

A. Paterson, the former lieutenant governor of New York under Spitzer. With Paterson's appointment, New York had its first African American governor in the state's history. Within a few days, it became public knowledge that New York's first African-American governor was also a philanderer, as he admitted to having affairs with "multiple women," including at least one state employee. All was fair in love and war, though, as his wife countered his admission with one of her own: She, too, had been unfaithful to her husband. The new governor then assured his constituency that he and his wife "have a marriage like many Americans, maybe even many of you."

And life in America picked up right where it had left off.

The rest of the players in this drama have gone their separate ways. Jimmy Cayne is safely ensconced in his apartment in the Plaza overlooking Central Park, no doubt contemplating his next bridge tournament. Alan Schwartz, the CEO who went down with the ship, was offered the position of non-executive vice chairman at JPMorgan. True to the person that he is and will always be in my mind, Alan declined the offer; he felt it wouldn't be fair to the several thousand former Bear employees who hadn't been offered jobs with JP. They don't make them like that anymore.

And me, well, I'm just keeping on keeping on.

This story, like all stories, has a beginning and an end, and this moment in time is neither. It just happens to be yet another moment in a life lived, to this point, with great gusto and drive. I consider myself to be among the most fortunate people anywhere on the planet. I had the opportunity to work for one of the greatest firms in the history of Wall Street, and I had a front row seat to history. As for what's next, I have no idea what my future holds for me. But I am not in the least bit concerned. For now, I'll go surfing. Perhaps somewhere in New Zealand. Some remote village on the western coast of the North Island, some place that has never seen a cellular tower or a fax machine.

I do know that I love adventure; that love is the passion that drove me to Africa to work as a young man, and it is the passion which continues to drive me to look for new opportunities in new emerging markets. I seek out experiences in the furthest-flung corners of the globe, and I think adventure is in the air for me again. So let's roll the dice and let fate determine where we end up. Let 'er rip. I'm off to live through yet another adventure. It's what the Māori call hāhā.

Hai konā rā.

Index

INDEX

INDEX

INDEX

INDEX

For sales, editorial information, subsidiary rights information
or a catalog, please write or phone or e-mail
Brick Tower Press
1230 Park Avenue
New York, NY 10128, US
Sales: 1-800-68-BRICK
Tel: 212-427-7139 Fax: 212-860-8852
www.BrickTowerPress.com
email: bricktower@aol.com.

For sales in the United States, please contact
National Book Network
nbnbooks.com
Orders: 800-462-6420
Fax: 800-338-4550
custserv@nbnbooks.com

For sales in the UK and Europe please contact our distributor,
Gazelle Book Services
Falcon House, Queens Square
Lancaster, LA1 1RN, UK
Tel: (01524) 68765 Fax: (01524) 63232
email: gazelle4go@aol.com.

For Australian and New Zealand sales please contact
Bookwise International
174 Cormack Road, Wingfield, 5013, South Australia
Tel: 61 (0) 419 340056 Fax: 61 (0)8 8268 1010
email: karen.emmerson@bookwise.com.au